Contemporary France

Contemporary States and Societies

This series provides lively and accessible introductions to key countries and regions of the world, conceived and designed to meet the needs of today's students. The authors are all experts with specialist knowledge of the country or region concerned and have been chosen also for their ability to communicate clearly to a non-specialist readership. Each text has been specially commissioned for the series and is structured according to a common format.

Published

Contemporary India
Katharine Adeney
and Andrew Wyatt

Contemporary Russia (2ed)
Edwin Bacon with
Matthew Wyman

Contemporary South Africa (2ed)
Anthony Butler

Contemporary France
Helen Drake

Contemporary America (3ed)
Russell Duncan
and Joseph Goddard

Contemporary China
Alan Hunter and John Sexton

Contemporary Japan (2ed)
Duncan McCargo

Contemporary Britain (2ed)
John McCormick

Contemporary Latin America (2ed)
Ronaldo Munck

Forthcoming

Contemporary Spain
Paul Kennedy

Contemporary Asia
John McKay

Contemporary Ireland
Eoin O'Malley

Also planned

Contemporary Africa
Contemporary Europe
Contemporary Germany

Contemporary States and Societies
Series Standing Order
ISBN 978–0–333–75402–3 hardcover
ISBN 978–0–333–80319–6 paperback
(*outside North America only*)

You can receive future titles in this series as they are published by placing a standing order. Please contact your bookseller or, in the case of difficulty, write to us at the address below with your name and address, the title of the series and the ISBN quoted above.

Customer Services Department, Palgrave Ltd
Houndmills, Basingstoke, Hampshire RG21 6XS, England, UK.

Contemporary France

Helen Drake

palgrave
macmillan

2011

First published 2011 by
PALGRAVE MACMILLAN

Palgrave Macmillan in the UK is an imprint of Macmillan Publishers Limited, registered in England, company number 785998, of Houndmills, Basingstoke, Hampshire RG21 6XS.

Palgrave Macmillan in the US is a division of St Martin's Press LLC, 175 Fifth Avenue, New York, NY 10010.

Palgrave Macmillan is the global academic imprint of the above companies and has companies and representatives throughout the world.

Palgrave® and Macmillan® are registered trademarks in the United States, the United Kingdom, Europe and other countries

ISBN 978–0–333–79243–8 hardback
ISBN 978–0–333–79244–5 paperback

This book is printed on paper suitable for recycling and made from fully managed and sustained forest sources. Logging, pulping and manufacturing processes are expected to conform to the environmental regulations of the country of origin.

A catalogue record for this book is available from the British Library.

A catalog record for this book is available from the Library of Congress.

10   9   8   7   6   5   4   3   2   1
20   19   18   17   16   15   14   13   12   11

Printed in China

In memory of my Dad, Albert Francis Drake (1913–2002),
and with fond thoughts of Pamela Allen (1923–2006),
a firm believer in the 'real France'

Contents

List of Illustrations, Figures, Maps, Tables and Boxes

Illustrations

Figures

Maps

Tables

Boxes

Acknowledgements

This has been a long haul. I would like to thank Steven Kennedy for commissioning the book, and then waiting for it to materialize. My thanks also to the British Academy for material support in the form of Small Grant SG35607, and to those colleagues at Loughborough and beyond who generously believed in the project throughout. My friends have kindly kept the faith as well. Finally, without the Drakes and the Allens, especially Dave, I can't imagine how I would have ever finished: thank you.

HELEN DRAKE

List of Abbreviations

ATTAC	Association pour la taxation financière et l'aide aux citoyens
BSE	Bovine spongiform encephalopathy
CAC-40	Cotisation assistée en continu
CAP	Common Agricultural Policy
CCTV	Closed circuit television
CNC	Centre national du cinéma et de l'image animée
CNN	Cable news network
CNPT	Chasse, Nature, Pêche, Tradition
CSA	Conseil supérieur de l'audiovisuel
CSG	Contribution sociale géneralisée
D-ROM	Département-région d'Outre-Mer
EC	European Community
ECB	European Central Bank
ECSC	European Coal and Steel Community
EEC	European Economic Community
EMU	Economic and Monetary Union
ENA	École nationale d'administration
EU	European Union
EURATOM	European Atomic Energy Community
FDI	Foreign direct investment
FLN	Front de Libération Nationale
FN	Front national
G-20	Group of 20 Finance Ministers and Central Bank Governors
G8	Group of 8
GATT	General Agreement on Tariffs and Trade
GDF	Gaz de France
GDP	Gross domestic product
GMO	Genetically modified organism
IMF	International Monetary Fund
LCR	Ligue Communiste Revolutionnaire

MNR	Mouvement national républicain
MoDem	Mouvement démocrate
MRP	Mouvement des républicains populaires
NATO	North Atlantic Treaty Organization
OECD	Organisation for Economic Cooperation and Development
OIF	l'Organisation internationale de la Francophonie
OSCE	Organization for Security and Co-operation in Europe
PBS	Public broadcasting service
PCF	Parti communiste français
PS	Parti socialiste
RECAMP	Reinforcement of African Peace-keeping Capacities
RESF	Reseau éducation sans frontières
RPR	Rassemblement pour la République
RTT	Réduction du temps de travail
SEM	Single European Market
TGV	Train à grande vitesse
TOM	Territoire d'outre mer
UDF	Union pour la démocratie française
UMP	Union pour un mouvement populaire
UN	United Nations
UNESCO	United Nations Educational, Scientific and Cultural Organization
USA	United States of America
VR	Fifth Republic
WTO	World Trade Organization

Map of France

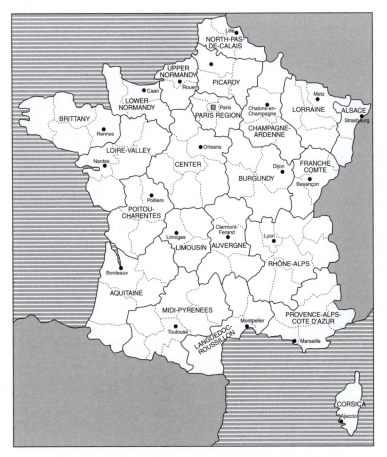

Introduction

Contemporary France projects iconic images onto the world on an industrial scale. Anyone can conjure up a mind's eye cliché of France, everyone has their favourite stereotype of French national character, Francophobia and Francophilia are flourishing. All these pictures and all these emotions have played a vital part in the construction of French national identity. They foster feelings of familiarity with France, as well the sense that the French consider themselves to be uniquely different from any other nation on earth, and quite possibly superior. They promote a unified and proud French nation with a shared and lasting sense of history and its traditions. In reality, France is as disparate, disjointed and changeable as any other Western democratic country.

In nineteenth-century France, local identities, customs, tastes and languages mattered far more to the French people than notions of nationhood. The wars, conscription, transportation and educational reforms of the turn of the twentieth century went some way to 'turning peasants into Frenchmen', in Eugen Weber's famous terms (1976) but, by the outbreak of World War II, France remained a profoundly rural society with distinct regional loyalties. In today's France, some regional identities and cultures remain strong (especially for Basques, Bretons, and Corsicans), but their political significance is patchy. In the second half of the twentieth century, following a traumatic war experience, France transformed itself almost beyond recognition in terms of its political, economic, social and even cultural identity. The modernization agenda of the thirty years following the end of the War, based on economic growth, industrialization and internationalization, was so successful in its own terms that these years were dubbed the 'glorious' decades. By contrast, the student riots and general strikes of May 1968 in France signalled that material comforts were insufficient to quell the quest for social and intellectual renewal that typified this icy period in the Cold War, and France was not alone in this respect. In the present

1

day, France continues to be a country as rich, technologically advanced and economically open as most of its neighbours and allies, challenged as they all are by the dramatic global changes of the late twentieth and early twenty-first centuries.

Dealing with the impact of over half a century of change on national identity is a challenge that defines contemporary France and inspires this book. In the course of the following chapters, we see how often France seeks to solve its contemporary problems in partnership with others, especially within the European Union, and we assess the impact of this for the credibility of a political culture built on the credo of national sovereignty. We probe the divide between France and the 'Anglo-Saxons' – Britain and the USA – that still looms large in France, where every new French president is scrutinized for signs of excessive pro-Americanism, where McDonald's has its largest European market, and where Euro Disney shores up France's status as the world's number one tourist destination. We ask whether the philosophy of French republicanism, as summed up in the revolutionary slogan of *liberté, égalité et fraternité*, is an adequate guideline for public policy in the face of fast-moving social norms, and costly expectations of the state. We see that, in France, an open, cosmopolitan and permeable society coexists with rigid and hierarchical codes of behaviour and the lingering social privileges of class and wealth.

In Chapter 1 (History and Legacies), we begin by acknowledging the significance of history to contemporary French life. It is physically prominent, educationally cherished, but politically problematic, and France is definitely still coming to terms with the living past. Memories of the injustices of France's colonial role and its subsequent battles of decolonization are vividly recalled in the disquiet, today, amongst young French citizens of immigrant origin, many of whom experience discrimination on a daily basis. Meanwhile, revisionism and even negationism – Holocaust denial – are not unheard of in contemporary France, even after the high-profile war crimes trials of the 1980s and 1990s; and the political instrumentalization of history remains a concern.

In Chapter 2 (France and the French) we see that, in any case, notions of *French* – meaning *national* – history were largely anachronistic before the late nineteenth century and the 'discovery of France' by the French themselves, to use Graham Robb's evocative term (2007). France was tribal and local for far longer than it has been a unified and 'indivisible' nation, as the 1958 Constitution has it.

Diversity defines France in the twenty-first century and, in this chapter, we review the variety of its physical geography and the cosmopolitanism of its population, and assess the significance of these attributes for present-day policy. We probe the importance of rural notions such as *terroire* and *territoire* to the French, and to the profitability of their tourist attractions and their products, and we find our way through the complexities of French nationality and immigration legislation to consider the problems of 'integration' both for newcomers to the French nation, and for those who have resided long-term in the country, without ever feeling fully French.

Yet, diverse social identities are supposed to be trumped by Frenchness, and the quest for this elusive state of affairs is an important aspect of French politics, as we see in Chapter 3 (Politics and Political Culture). French republicanism in today's Fifth French Republic constitutes a political culture and a variant of democracy that leans towards the abstract, and looks back to the past. It has bred the notion that French politics is somehow exceptional, and thus incomparable to other liberal democracies. The root of this claim to exceptionalism lies in the 1789 French Revolution, which has certainly bred a style of politics in which direct democracy and flowery rhetoric have their rightful place. Yet, it is now nearly a quarter of a century since France celebrated the bicentenary of its 1789 French Revolution, and today's political parties define themselves in terms of today's problems and issues, and with reference to their counterparts elsewhere in Europe and beyond. Thus, women have found themselves legislated into a more representative presence in political life than at any other time in this traditionally patriarchal society. However, in this chapter, we see that the match between political supply and demand in France is far from perfect, and its opportunities still limited to a relatively small and exclusive elite. Even in France, democracy is imperfect and incomplete. These facts of French political life have created space for movements such as the far right National Front, who are nevertheless kept out of power by electoral systems specifically designed to protect the French from themselves.

In a similar fashion, the structures of French government derive from a set of circumstances which, in 1958, at the beginning of today's Fifth French Republic, threatened the country's very existence. The system that emerged was designed for 'great men' such as the Republic's founder, Charles de Gaulle, who trusted themselves with control of the levers of political power. We see in Chapter 4

(Government, Policy-Making and the Republican State) that, over time and in the hands of mere mortals, this 'semi-presidential' system of power-sharing between a directly-elected President and his hand-picked Prime Minister, in a regime where powers are concentrated into the executive, has allowed for a certain degree of political irre-sponsibility at the very top of the state. We see too that the French 'state' has a historical and symbolic importance that outstrips its actual functions, but which ensures its survival in the face of chal-lenges to the size of its bureaucracy, the reach of its influence down into the smallest French village, or the elitism of its public servants.

In Chapter 5 (A Social French Republic) we consider how well-equipped France really is, in terms of its politics, state and govern-ment, to deliver public policy that upholds the cohesion of the nation. In theory, contemporary French society is organized along the strict lines of its republican ideals; namely the provision, protection and promotion of individual freedom (*liberté*), equality (*égalité*) and soli-darity (*fraternité*). Achieving this balance is in reality, and inevitably, a tall order in France, whose population is numerous, ageing and diverse; where Catholic morality lives on; where scepticism and suspicion of the Anglo-American-style embrace of difference – not to mention 'political correctness' – taints official discourse and policy; and where 'civil society' is an alien concept based on a 'repugnance' for British and American liberal, pluralistic societies, as Hayward (2007) has it. We investigate the welfare state in France, which incor-porates the world-renowned and staggeringly costly health system; we explore the realities of the secular state and, in particular, the rele-vance of the notion of *laïcité* – secularism *à la française* – as its philosophical underpinning; and we enquire into the scope and limi-tations of an education system purposely designed both to train an elite and to achieve more democratic goals, as befits a country that regards itself as one of the most civilized on earth.

Culturally speaking, France has an extensive past of elitist and grandiose activity, overshadowing the very value of the 'lesser' arts. For at least 400 years, French leaders have spent heavily on cultural policies designed to project images of national splendour, in its chateaux, art and, latterly, technologies. Culture in France is definitely political, and it is also commercially beneficial; last, but not least, it is a matter of national identity. At the start of the twentieth century, at precisely the time when nation-building and defence was seen as a matter of life and death, French regional languages suffered from repression, and the populations of France's colonial 'possessions' were bludgeoned with French culture in the form of the French language, not to mention the Catholic religion. In Chapter 6 (Culture and Identity), we see that culture and leisure have become accessible to virtually all in France, increasingly inside the home, and increasingly permeated by influences that lie well beyond the control of the state: culture as practised by people in their daily lives is an international, and often virtual, affair. This does not stop the state from making efforts, some successful and others less so, to protect the French language and to promote European culture by means of legislation that curbs market forces at the national and international levels.

In Chapter 7 (Economy and Business), we find much to bewilder the France-watcher. France is neither a liberal market economy, nor a social market economy in the German style. It is sceptical and highly critical of *laissez-faire*, 'Anglo-Saxon' style political economy, but the French state is in retreat from market forces. Perhaps it is here that France is genuinely in a class of its own, having crafted a unique model of socio-economic development, despite the openness of its economy and its presence in all the important world economic forums. At the level of political language, a struggle with the very morality of money for money's sake is played out, and we observe expressions of genuine horror at the consequences for mind, body and soul of excessive, consumerist consumption of material goods. France is no stranger to big business, and Paris is the world capital of luxury. Yet, President Sarkozy was mocked for openly embracing such values in his so-called 'bling-bling' months after entering the Elysée palace in 2007. In the economy, above all other areas of policy, France has tethered its fortunes to the European Union and its single currency Euro zone. Europe is France's biggest export market and, at present, its only hope for weathering the storm of competition from newly developing economies.

But the European Union is also the biggest form of constraint on state power, and this theme characterizes our final Chapter 8 (France in the World). France, as is the case for many other EU countries, finds that the state alone, in one country – even France – is powerless – or, at best, insufficient – to tackle, let alone resolve, the pressing and potentially most threatening of its problems: the mass migrations of people towards Europe; the security and sustainability of energy supplies, and their safety; minimizing the impact of climate change and so on. Here, the security of the nation and the integrity of the French territory are potentially at threat, and it is the President's job

Box I.1   France: key facts, figures and indicators

Capital city	Paris
Size (area)	550, 000 sq km (largest country in Western Europe); farms and forests account for 80% of area of mainland France
Population (2009, estimate)	64.3 million inhabitants (including overseas territories)
Net migration (2009, estimate)	76,000
Population density	98.1 inhabitants per sq km
GDP (2007)	US$2.8 trillion
GDP per capita (2007)	US$46,000
GDP (% of total)	Services 76%; industry 20%; agriculture 3%
Public debt (2010, estimate % of GDP)	80%
Trade balance (2007)	– €52 billion
Unemployment rate (2007)	8%
Unemployment rate 18–24 years (2007)	19.3%
Life expectancy	84.3 years (women); 77.5 years (men)
Religions	Roman Catholic, Protestant, Muslim, Jewish.
Languages	French; regional dialects and languages exist, but use is minimal
Government type	Semi-presidential regime (directly-elected president and appointed Prime Minister)
Administrative organization	Unitary Mainland (metropolitan) France: 22 regions, 96 departments and c. 36 000 communes Overseas: 5 Department-Regions (D-Roms); other overseas territories
Executive	Dual: directly-elected President and appointed Prime Minister
Legislature	Bicameral: National Assembly (lower, elected in two-round elections), Senate (upper, elected by Electoral college)
Head of State	President Nicolas Sarkozy (2007 – present)
Head of Government	Prime Minister François Fillon (2007 – present)

to counter this. As a former imperial and colonial power, France has experienced some angst in adjusting to its modest size and limited influence in the present day in a world seemingly populated by hyper powers, rogue states and terrorists with nuclear weapons almost in their grasp. Paris accordingly works hard to influence peoples across the world using both soft and hard forms of power, both of which are increasingly placed at the disposal of multi-national and joint efforts to secure global peace and prosperity.

We conclude that if France is to prosper as a unique form of republican democracy – whether or not it transmutes into a Sixth French Republic, as advocated by President Sarkozy's political opponents in 2007 – then it has no alternative but to pursue the ongoing process of converting its abstract philosophy of society into a practical republicanism for everyday use. Younger generations are doing this for themselves, some leaving France behind while they make their lives elsewhere; others rebelling against a life of not quite belonging in France. But we do find, overall, that France is still France, to paraphrase R.F. Kuisel (in Flynn, 1995: 31–2), no more or less likely to implode, or fall victim to natural or man-made disaster, and no more or less equipped to face those prospects than its European neighbours or North American cousins.

1

History and Legacies

Introduction

History looms large in contemporary France. The teaching of history is central to French school curricula, and the writing of history by French scholars is renowned worldwide. Local councils and the central state invest in elaborate displays of the past to attract tourist revenues, and the passion for heritage (*le patrimoine*) is widespread in France. History and remembrance are physically everywhere in France, from the poignant war memorials in the tiniest French village and the vast Allied cemeteries of northern France, to the huge, enigmatic brown signs beckoning motorists to exit France's motorways and explore local history and tradition. In imagining the past, we conjure up regimes toppling in chaotic crisis; larger-than-life monarchs, emperors, dictators and presidents; centuries-long, bloody wars, preferably waged against the 'English', or between religions; and we are invited to shudder at the sights and smells of the 1789 French Revolution and 'the figure of the sharp female called La Guillotine' (Dickens, 2000: 283).

French history is, indeed, characterized by much conflict and violence, and disagreements over the record colour contemporary French politics: legislation is passed and repealed as leaders attempt to forge and commemorate collective memories of painful past episodes such as the German occupation of 1940–44, or the Algerian war of independence (1954–62). Historians still tussle over the causes of the French Revolution of 1789, and some protest at what they believe is the instrumentalization of history by contemporary politicians. Many historical divisions have nevertheless been overcome, and the recurrent civil wars of the eighteenth, nineteenth and even twentieth centuries do now seem to be a thing of the past. Contemporary France is firmly wedded to a republican political regime, with royalism limited to a passion for the late British Princess Diana and the playboys and girls of the Monaco dynasty, and support for a strong, personalized presidency. The Catholic Church coexists with republicanism but has no role in political life in a formally secular state; support for Communism has declined to, probably, the point of no return; a legislative edifice is in place to pacify intra-French tensions between the sexes, genders, generations and races; and relations are peaceful with those allies with whom ties have been most troubled in the past – namely, the 'Anglo-Saxons' (the USA and the UK) and Germany.

Thus, the goal of a France secure in its twenty-first-century identity is tantalizingly close: France today is effectively one state, one territory, one people and one nation: a single, 'indivisible' entity, as the 1958 Constitution proclaims. Politics is still framed and debated in terms of grand ideas and principles passed down from centuries of history. But rhetoric is one thing, and reality another. From the outside, France might look turbulent and agitated, as it has on many occasions in its past. On the inside, arguments are less about the past, and more about the immediate future. Twenty-first-century France can, perhaps, finally take its history for granted.

In this chapter, we review the emergence of the modern French nation-state from the Roman Empire. We track its evolution into the *ancien régime* – the old order – of the medieval and Renaissance monarchy which laid the foundations for the strong, centralized state for which France is still known today, and on which aspects of its identity are shaped. We consider the eruption of patriotic nationalism associated with the 1789 French Revolution, and the sense of exceptionalism that it has bequeathed to contemporary France: an idealized belief in the universal and exportable values of democracy, human rights and egalitarianism.

On this basis, our chapter then focuses on the exceptional transformations undergone by the French society, economy, markets and politics from the mid–late twentieth century to today's post-Cold War era. We emphasize the reconstruction of French identity undertaken by Charles de Gaulle in the 1960s, and the twenty-first-century challenges to the French sense of national self. The twentieth century in so many ways challenged the very identity and existence of France, and existential angst is a problem that current politicians have not fully banished from their mindsets. We balance images of political chaos with a sense of the conservative and continuous forces that are just as much part of the legacy of France's past.

Table 1.1   Key dates and milestones in French history

10,000 BC	Cave paintings at Lascaux, south-west France
58–49 BC	Julius Caesar conquers Gaul
496	Baptism of Clovis, King of the Franks
786–814	Charlemagne's Empire
1066	The Norman Conquest
1096–1270	The Crusades
1337–1453	The Hundred Years' War with England
1431	Joan of Arc burned at the stake in Rouen
1598	Edict of Nantes (revoked 1685)
1643–1715	Reign of Louis XIV at Versailles
1789	Beginning of the French Revolution on 14 July
1804	Napoleon I crowned Emperor
1805–1815	Napoleonic battles including Trafalgar, Austerlitz and Waterloo
1830–1848	France conquers Algeria
1848	Universal male suffrage
1871	France loses Franco-Prussian War
1880	National Day (14 July) established
1882	Jules Ferry laws establishing free, secular and compulsory primary school education
1901	Law providing for the freedom of association
1904	Entente cordiale between France and Britain
1905	Law separating Church and State
1914–18	World War I
1919	The Versailles Treaty
1936	Popular Front government and the Matignon agreements providing workers' rights including paid holidays
1939	World War II begins
1940	Armistice with Germany de Gaulle calls for French resistance
1944	Allied Normandy landings in June begin the liberation of France. Women get the vote
1950	Schuman Declaration (9 May) begins *la construction européenne*: European integration
1951	Signature of Treaty of Paris creating the European Coal and Steel Community: France one of the six founder members (France, Germany, Italy, Belgium, Netherlands, Luxemburg)
1954	Loss of French colonies in Indochina Algerian war begins
1958	Algerian war triggers return of Charles de Gaulle and founding of Fifth French Republic
1962	Constitutional amendment providing for direct election of President of the Republic by universal suffrage
1968	Student uprisings, general strike

Table 1.1   *continued*

1975	Legalisation of abortion and divorce by consent
	Programme of nuclear power generation
1981	Abolition of death penalty
	Liberalization of television and radio
1984	National Front breakthrough in European Parliament elections
1990–91	France takes part in first Gulf War
1992	Approval of the Maastricht Treaty paving the road to European Economic and Monetary Union
1994	Inauguration of the Channel Tunnel linking France and England
1998	'Rainbow' French football team wins World Cup
1989–90	Fall of the Berlin Wall and the reunification of Germany
2001	End of military conscription
2002	France starts using the Euro – the European single currency
2003	France refuses to join the US-led coalition in Iraq in the second Gulf War
2004	Law banning Islamic headscarves and other 'conspicuous' religious signs in state schools
2010	Parliamentary debate on banning clothing that 'hides the face' – notably the Islamic *burqa* and *niqab* – anywhere in public
	French football team returns in disgrace after losing in the first round of the World Cup in South Africa: President Sarkozy launches an enquiry

Sources: Data from Baycroft (2008); Crook (2002); Davidson (1971); Evans and Godin (2004); Ledésert, D.M. (1976).

The Making of the French Nation-State

From Roman Gaul to Renaissance France

When discussing prehistoric, ancient and medieval France, contemporary notions of *national* identity – let alone national *consciousness* – are anachronistic, since these periods all established the diversity – regional, cultural, tribal – that, to this day, challenges aspirations to French national unity. The Romans conquered the native Celts in 1BC, assimilated them, then left them to successive waves of invading barbarian (foreign) tribes. Prehistoric man had already left traces of social organization, the evidence of which is best known in the shape of the cave paintings at Lascaux in the Dordogne region of south-west France (on public show in replica form), and the eerie standing stones of Brittany.

Under Roman rule, France was known as Gaul and, of the tribal invaders, the fifth-century Germanic Franks lent their name to what is now France. The Romans left their physical marks on Gaul, many of which still stand today (of which the *Pont du Gard*; and the *Maison Carrée* in Nîmes). Significantly, Julius Caesar's *pax romana* brought stability and shape to Gaul, by means of what we would today call centralized language and communications policies, and a unitary legal system. These were all enforceable by legions of Roman soldiers, as immortalized in Goscinny's cartoon illustrations of the plucky and comic Astérix facing down the intruder.

The Catholic Church slowly took over from the Roman Empire as a source of minimal cohesion between disparate peoples. Clovis, King of the Salian (northern) Franks, converted to the Christian faith in the late fifth century, and many followed his example, giving them something in common, although hardly a nationality as we now understand it. The combination of Clovis and Church was significant in shaping medieval France, where Paris and its region, the Île de France, were already emerging as the epicentre of power; today, the area is France's biggest and richest region. Clovis's descendants were the Merovingians, by all accounts long-haired and loutish, and with the time and energy to extend the kingdom to Burgundy and Provence. But their lax rule allowed aristocratic rivals to emerge, and from these emerged the Carolingian line, via the well-known historical figures of Martel and Pepin. The best-known son of the Carolingians was Charlemagne. Crowned Holy Roman Emperor in AD800, his legendary influence was a civilizing force in the 'Dark Ages' (the ninth and tenth centuries), even naturalizing Viking invaders. His immediate legacy was the territory of West Francia, the physical template for contemporary France but, after his death, his Empire disintegrated, shrinking by the tenth century to an area little bigger than today's Île de France region.

Anglo-French rivalry marked this period in France, and cross-Channel competition exists today, albeit within a stable and friendly partnership: war is unthinkable between the two formerly and frequently warring neighbours. William the Conqueror's victory in England in 1066 rebounded against the stability and territorial ambitions of French royal authority insofar as his successors mounted repeated challenges to French monarchs over a lengthy period, which included the Hundred Years' War (1337–1453) and the burning of Joan of Arc by the English. But, by the end of the War, the French had made considerable territorial gains from the English contenders, including the large and rich province of Aquitaine in the south-west, thus consolidating the royal domains. The quest by the British to colonize this region nevertheless continues to this day in the far more peaceful shape of second homes and British exiles seeking the 'good life' in rural France.

In other respects, too, these were centuries of consolidation the impact of which is still felt today. King Philippe Augustus (1180–1223) paved Paris, and the foundations of the spectacular gothic cathedral of Notre Dame de Paris were laid in these years. The Sorbonne university was established in 1257 and, with it, the roots of Paris's contemporary reputation as a seat of learning and knowledge, as well as the growing role of the French language (alongside Latin) in these fields. By the fourteenth century, French royal prestige was high and, by the early fifteenth century, the territory of France had expanded to resemble its contemporary shape. Papal authority had, for a while (1309–1377), been established in France, in Avignon, and a sense of national identity was emerging around these develop-ments. The Renaissance of the sixteenth century strengthened this feeling, and many of today's extrovert symbols of utter Frenchness – the chateaux of the Loire, the Louvre, French literature, the French language (the King's *langue d'oil*, or language of the north) – date from these days.

The 'Ancien Régime': The Emergence of the Modern French State

The France of the *ancien régime* – the old, or 'former', pre-revolu-tionary order of the seventeenth and eighteenth centuries – was ravaged by religious strife and wars. The Wars of Religion (1562–98) brought bloodshed and a waste of human talent; the Saint Bartholemew's massacre of six thousand French Protestants on 24 August 1572 stands out as a particularly bloody historical date. Under the reign of Louis XIV (1643–1715), the French Huguenot Protestants were eventually exiled, taking much creative and intel-lectual know-how with them. But these earlier years and these battles also gave France its first Bourbon King, Henry IV. Having converted to Catholicism and offered limited tolerance to the Huguenots in the form of the 1598 Edict of Nantes, he ushered in the 1600s. That epoch was known as *le grand siècle* ('splendid century'), and it marked a revival in the standards of the French monarchy measured in terms of ruthlessness, authoritarianism, images of greatness and expense, all in the name of French nation and state-building.

Henry IV's immediate successors, Louis XIII and Louis XIV, established the most sumptious period of French royal history ever, and their names and those of their ministers (Richelieu, Mazarin, Colbert) are engraved on the French psyche as symbols of when France was great, however troubled. Their 'absolutist' systems of authority (kings were deemed to answer to no one but God) ensured new levels of administrative efficiency, as did Richelieu's *intendants*, precursors of today's departmental *préfets* (see Chapter 4). This was also a time of ostentatious greatness, ranging from works of archicture (Versailles, near Paris); art and culture (the creation of the Academy by Richelieu in 1635; the royal patronage of manufacture and science); and imperialism (1648 saw the Treaty of Westphalia sealing victory over the Hapsburgs). Despite serious popular uprisings against royal authority – which, in retrospect, were a dress rehearsal for the French Revolution – France was strong, and the monarch powerful. But aggressive foreign policies were ruinously expensive, and taxation systems required the cooperation of potential challengers to royal authority in the shape of the regional *parlements* (courts), and the aristocratic lawyers that peopled them.

By the time of the outbreak of the French Revolution in 1789, 'France' and the 'French' had, thus, neither been created by any continuous, strategic action on the part of a single dynastic leadership, nor by a spontaneous, popular process of unification at a given point in time. Instead, the French state and nation had emerged from centuries of war (foreign, civil, religious), waged by leaders of varying abilities and desires, but sharing a quest for power, and whose authority was always and inevitably vulnerable to challenge, and luck. 'Society' was highly disparate, composed of groups – the noble aristocrats, the bourgeoisie, the clergy, the peasants, the workers – enjoying vastly different sets of privileges and opportunities, which created permanently combustible mixtures of resentments. A form of centralizing authority did appear over time, although in a punctuated, often chaotic manner, in the shape of authoritarian – royal and clerical – structures intended to save costs and consolidate power by the imposition of norms of language, religion, justice and taxation. These met with varying success.

1789–1799: A Decade of Revolution

The French Revolution of 1789 was a decisive episode in French history. Its impact is still felt in contemporary French political culture, even though the process by which democratic, republican politics subsequently took root in France was long, tortuous and frequently deadly. The French Revolution was, in all respects, dramatic. It produced a set of apocryphal characters, amply represented ever since in literature, film and art, and it engaged a series of battles at home and abroad that still resonate in France today, however faintly. It lent a patriotic dimension to the formation of French identity, gave root to the modern-day concepts of nation and nationalism, and is at the heart of the notion of French 'exceptionalism' that bolsters France in its global ambitions in the present day. The French Revolution was not a sudden event, neither did it change France overnight, but its best-known effects were momentous, particularly for its losers and their interests. The *ancien régime* was definitively repudiated by the physical elimination, by guillotine, of its leading figures, including the King and Queen; and by the abolition of noble and feudal privilege through destroying the 'orders' of the old system – the clergy, nobility, lawyers, crafts and guildsmen.

The Revolution had no initial blueprint, and the line between the Revolution and the stable Republicanism of present-day France is over two hundred years long, broken and rejoined in several places (see Chapter 3). The ideals of the revolutionaries, as expressed in the 1789 Declaration of the Rights of Man and the Citizen, spawned the vocabulary of contemporary French politics: popular sovereignty, the rule of law, equality before the law, free speech, and political representation. Today's Constitution, moreover, begins with explicit reference to the 1789 text (see Box 1.1). But two centuries were needed for these notions to become embedded as standard political practice, and they are still being revised in line with contemporary social norms.

The Napoleonic Empire, 1799–1815

By 1799 army officer Napoleon Bonaparte was sufficiently admired for his victories in the Revolutionary wars that he was able to exploit the confusion of the revolutionary decade and take power by a *coup d'état* on 18–19 Brumaire (9 November) 1799. He was appointed

Box 1.1   A founding text of French democracy

From the 1789 Declaration of the Rights of Man and the Citizen:

Article 1
'Men are born and remain free and equal in rights. Social distinctions may be based only on considerations of the common good.'

Article 2
'The aim of every political association is the preservation of the natural and imprescriptible rights of man. These rights are Liberty, Property, Safety and Resistance to Oppression.'

Article 3
'The aim of all sovereignty lies essentially in the Nation. No corporate body, no individual may exercise any authority that does not expressly emanate from it.'

From the 1958 (current) French Constitution:

Preamble
'The French people solemnly proclaim their attachment to the Rights of Man and the principles of national sovereignty as defined by the Declaration of 1789.'

Source: Data from Elysée (2010a).

First Consul for ten years but, after only five, on 18 May 1804 he had himself crowned the first Emperor of his new hereditary Empire. Napoleon's regime maintained the revolutionary ideal of popular sovereignty, but perverted it into the shape of a presumed bond between the people and the great leader himself. Within this bond, and under his charismatic – authoritarian – guidance, the people could express their will in carefully-manufactured plebiscites, but not in free elections; neither did they enjoy free speech or a free press, which were curtailed and censured in these years. Echoes of this style of personalized leadership have persisted into contemporary France and its provisions for a powerful president, as we elaborate in Chapters 3 and 4: when President Nicolas Sarkozy was elected in May 2007, comparisons with Napoleon Bonaparte, comic and serious, were common media currency.

The backbone of the French state in the Napoleonic era, also still recognizable today, was a professional, elitist bureaucracy, trained up in the new *lycées* – senior schools – established during this time, and on which state senior schools are modelled in France today. Napoleon also controlled the Church in the form of a Concordat signed with Rome in 1802. Finally, and significantly for contemporary France, he governed the whole of the French territory by means of a uniform legal system – the Napoleonic codes – and an administrative machine answerable to the Emperor, and which rewarded its faithful servants with the newly-created *Légion d'honneur*. Napoleon's domestic reforms could not guarantee the success of his wars and he abdicated in April 1814, after his military retreat from Russia and before making his '100 days' comeback, which ended in 1815 in further military defeat at the famous battle of Waterloo at the hands of Britain's Duke of Wellington.

Nineteenth-Century Restorations: Monarchy, Empire and Republic

Which regime would secure both national reconciliation (internal stability) and military success (external prestige), and in what circumstances? The default setting of the nineteenth century was a restored, constitutional monarchy, trapped between the historical pulls of authoritarianism and, on occasions, revolutionary republicanism. The context was burgeoning industrialization, mass literacy, the rise and rise of the property-owning bourgeoisie; the Romanticism of nineteenth century art, literature and philosophy; and new signs of the French propensity for glamour and glory. These were the years when Baron Haussmann drove the wide *grands boulevards* into Paris, bearing their characteristically well-proportioned buildings that are so distinctive of today's French capital city; the Arc de Triomphe was completed; colonies and territory were won (Algeria, Nice and Savoy); and Emperor Louis-Napoleon Bonaparte (1851–1870) and the Emperess Princess Eugénie indulged in a socially liberal lifestyle. More significant, universal male suffrage and the abolition of slavery in the colonies were also legacies of the nineteenth century.

But the popular uprisings of 1830 and the workers' revolution of 1848 drove the monarchy (Bourbon King Louis XVIII and the Orleanist 'citizen-king' Louis-Philippe, respectively) into exile in England. The Paris Commune of 1870, following France's military defeat by Prussia, brought about the painful loss of Alsace and Lorraine, and the end of the Second Empire. These were all versions of a civil war that the 1789 Revolution had not definitively resolved.

Politically speaking, France in the nineteenth century oscillated between popular claims for more freedom, equality and fraternity (electoral reform, better working conditions) and brutally repressive responses by a variety of authoritarian regimes.

1870–1940: The Third Republic

Following the defeat of 1870, the Third French Republic (1870–1940) lasted nearly ten times longer than its predecessors combined. French republicanism had matured, spurred on by the raised consciousness acquired through free and lay education, free expression, free association, and gains in workers' rights, most visibly the 40-hour week and the 12 working days holiday entitlement, which brought leisure into working peoples' lives, and into the economy. By 1905, Church and State had been definitively separated, as they are to this day in the French, secular state, closing power struggles between the Catholic Church and the State. It was no coincidence that, in this climate, it was deemed safe to reinstate the symbols of 1789: the *Marseillaise* as national anthem, 14 July as a public holiday, and the revolutionary rally-cry *liberté, égalité et fraternité* etched onto public buildings. The blooming of French arts in this *belle époque* was matched by advances in science and engineering, regularly showcased to the world in Exhibition form: the Eiffel Tower stands today to remind us of this period.

Free and compulsory education was also a conduit for the imposition of the French language, and for prescribed children's stories of how France became France. These were all vehicles for raising the consciousness of the existence of a *nation*, France. Patriotism was, indeed, tangible – its dark side a spirit of revenge (*la revanche*) towards Germany following the 1870 defeat, and the ugly xenophobic nationalism encapsulated in the writing of racialist Maurice Barrès. The fear of the outsider was especially targeted against the notional Jew – as symbolized by the Dreyfus affair at the turn of the century – and at Bolshevik Russia. Narrow definitions of French identity based on concepts of race, territory and roots offered fertile ground for what was to follow a generation later. The horrors and vast human losses of the World War I battlefields (most memorably, the Somme and Verdun) united the French more than they divided them; and the Republicans maintained France's status as a world presence, and cultural pole of attraction. But population growth was low, swathes of the economy were weak and inefficient, and centuries of French hegemony on the European continent were evidently at an end.

The Third Republic did not withstand the German invasion of France in June 1940. Germany's intentions were overwhelmingly aggressive, and the reasons for French capitulation, appeasment and collaboration with the occupier are to be found in the appeal, for some, of a French place in a Germanic, Aryan Europe; and in Germany's reaction to the ruinous reparations imposed by the World War I settlement. Yet, the collapse of the Third Republic into the authoritarian Vichy regime resonated with the introverted, virulent nationalism that had shadowed the successes of the Third Republic and to which Bolshevik Russia was more alien and hateful than Nazi Germany.

The Postwar Transformations of France

It is no exaggeration to speak of a transformation to describe the decades in France that followed the shocks and aftershocks of World War II. Domestic politics, France's place in the international system, its relations with the USA, its economy, its society, its self-image: all these found themselves challenged. If a nation-state can experience existential angst, then this was the condition of postwar France. Beyond physical reconstruction and the settling of scores, the priority for France's postwar leaders was to rebuild the identity of France to deal, somehow, with the trauma of the war years and its repercussions, including the rapid loss of the French Empire, and the latent civil war between supporters of Vichy and de Gaulle's Free French. This was done through appeals to myth, nostalgia and selective memory, and by a series of history-making decisions around goals that would characterize France for at least the next fifty years: modernization, Europeanization, decolonization and the quest for international greatness – *la grandeur*.

France's World War II: Tales of Occupation, Resistance and Liberation

In the confusion of the rout of the French military by the invading German army in June 1940, the government of the Third Republic simply fled, abdicating responsibility to the hero of the World War I battle of Verdun, Marshal Pétain, by now well into his eighties, for extracting the best treatment possible from Germany, via an armistice. Marshal Pétain and Prime Minister Pierre Laval (respectively exiled and executed for their roles at the end of the War) seized the opportunity of this dramatic change in France's fortunes to instigate a domestic revolution of their own. This was their *révolution nationale*, based on a crude design to turn back the clock to an imagined pre-Republican, halcyon, era of national purity. Executive authority in the new regime, based at Vichy in the – initially – unoccupied zone, was concentrated in Pétain's role; the mantra *travail, famille, patrie* (work, family, country) replaced the revolutionary *liberté, égalité, fraternité*, and the French Catholic Church was co-opted into the adventure. Traditional values, as the Vichyites saw them, had returned, and would restore the French nation to its former greatness – despite the awkward fact that it was under German occupation.

Vichy had its winners and enthusiasts beyond the regime's leaders. Collaboration with the German occupier was a spectrum of behaviours and activities, with active resistance at one end of the scale, and enthusiastic cooperation at the other, and most French people fell somewhere in between. There was one obvious exception: Charles de Gaulle. General de Gaulle, military officer under Pétain's command in World War I, was drafted into the first of the Vichy governments as junior defence minister, but fled to London at the time of the June 1940 armistice to raise British support for the French resistance; the rest is history.

The story of de Gaulle's war is fascinating because it reveals the fragility of his enterprise; namely, to organize the 'Free French' – those military and civilians, from mainland France and France's African colonies who, like him, rejected the Vichy settlement – into a fighting force and a homeland, guerilla-type resistance movement (see Box 1.2). De Gaulle was repudiated on many occasions by the wartime leaders of the USA and the UK, President F.D. Roosevelt and Prime Minister Winston Churchill, who made repeated efforts to persuade Vichy France – legitimate France, as the allies saw it – to join the war. The resistance movement itself was internally split; yet, it was from within the resistance movement that the skeletal structures and policies – and, importantly, the legitimacy of the first postwar government – took shape, and loyalties and reputations formed. The French Communist Party gained public acceptance, for example, for its role in the resistance; and it was also from within the resistance that the most mythical and symbolic aspects of de Gaulle's leadership qualities derived.

Box 1.2   Charles de Gaulle's call to arms, 18 June 1940

'The leaders who have been at the head of the French armies for many years have formed a government.

This government, alleging the defeat of our armies, has entered into communication with the enemy to stop the fighting.

To be sure, we have been submerged, we are submerged, by the enemy's mechanised forces, on land and in the air.

It is the Germans' tanks, planes and tactics that have made us fall back, infinitely more than their numbers. It is the Germans' tanks, planes and tactics that have so taken our leaders by surprise as to bring them to the point that they have reached today.

But has the last word been said? Must hope vanish? Is the defeat final? No!

Believe me, for I know what I am talking about and I tell you that nothing is lost for France. The same means that beat us may one day bring us victory.

For France is not alone. She is not alone! She is not alone! She has an immense Empire behind her. She can unite with the British Empire, which commands the sea and which is carrying on with the struggle. Like England, she can make an unlimited use of the vast industries of the United States.

This war is not confined to the unhappy territory of our country. This war has not been decided by the Battle of France. This war is a world-wide war. All the faults, all the delays, all the sufferings do not do away with the fact that in the world there are all the means for one day crushing our enemies. Today we are struck down by the mechanised force; in the future we can conquer by greater mechanised force. The fate of the world lies there.

I, General de Gaulle, now in London, call upon the French officers and soldiers who are on British soil or who may be on it, with their arms or without them, I call upon the engineers and the specialised workers in the armaments industry who are or who may be on British soil, to get in contact with me.

Whatever happens, the flame of French resistance must not and shall not go out. Tomorrow, as I have done today, I shall speak again from London.'

Source: A. Corbett and D. Johnson (eds) (2000) *A Day in June. Britain and de Gaulle, 1940* (London, Franco-British Council, British Section), p.11: http://www. francobritishcouncil.org.uk/data/files/reports/A-day-in-June-whole-document 25May.pdf [accessed 5 October 2010].

This mythologizing of De Gaulle's actions in the Vichy period was fundamental, from de Gaulle's perspective, in allowing France and the French to emerge from the War with some sense of national unity around the idea that the French Republic had been maintained despite Vichy and thanks to the resistance movement of the 'non-guilty' French (BBC, 2001). The narrative extended to the glorification of the role of French forces in the Liberation of 1944–45, although today's memorials to the critical role played by the Allies in this drama tell another story (see Illustration 1.1). The *épuration* (purges) – the summary punishment or execution meted out in 1944–45 to tens of thousands of French people for their alleged wartime collaboration – was the most visible evidence of this black and white view of events. The ambiguities and grey areas of Vichy should have humbled the French, and subsequently did but, for as long as de Gaulle was in charge, humility was not in the French national interest.

Illustration 1.1   Omaha Beach, Normandy
Memorial to the Allied Forces of Operation Overlord.

Modernization, Europeanization and Decolonization

The confusion and ambiguities of the War years constituted yet another context ripe for a French civil war; instead, somehow, in the dangerous international climate of the Cold War, the turbulence was channeled into the creative chaos of the Fourth Republic (1946–58). This regime instigated a programme of domestic reconstruction on the one hand and, on the other, international rehabilitation through decolonization and the anchoring of France, however half-heartedly, to the Western camp in the Cold War. Two decades after the end of World War II, by the late 1960s, France was bigger demographically and wealthier, economically, than at any time in the previous 100 years. But it was still riven with divisions which, in 1958, exploded into near civil war surrounding the loss of France's most prized colony: Algeria.

By 1946, de Gaulle himself had already withdrawn from the provisional government that took power following the liberation of France in 1944, inter-party unity having proved elusive in the context of the emerging Cold War. In particular, the French Communist Party, buoyed in popularity and membership by its association with active resistance, could not reconcile itself to the dose of capitalist conservatism that would have made it a parliamentary ally of the socialists and centrists. The Catholic, centrist MRP (*mouvement des républicains populaires*) had limited appeal thanks to its confessional character; the Socialists were split on many issues; Pierre Poujade's nationalist movement challenged stability; and de Gaulle's supporters continually undermined the regime and its leaders.

This was not a good basis on which to rebuild the shattered French nation, reconstruct the economy, or assist the country to adjust to its postwar role in the world. Of these three objectives, most successful was socio-economic revival; international influence and a new external identity for France would come later, with de Gaulle's return as President of the Fifth Republic in 1958. Ambitions of social progress were enshrined in the 1946 Constitution; women now had the vote, and new systems were instituted for state-led, 'technocratic' economic planning. This indicative, five-year rolling 'plan' produced a startling reversal of fortunes, typified by economic growth and real changes to daily lives. The French population began to boom, in part through rising immigration, in part because of a postwar baby boom (the population grew by over 12 million over the thirty years from 1946). Thus were born French consumers, henceforth protected from the worst misfortunes by a burgeoning welfare state (*l'état-providence*). New towns and homes were built and equipped to far higher standards than many were accustomed to: new generations of French people became fans of the cars, refrigerators, washing machines, televisions and telephones and other home comforts that they saw their American counterparts enjoying in films, and even in their own neighbourhood (in the case of the US forces stationed at NATO's then HQ outside Paris). Urbanization, industrialization and tertiarization altered the image of a profoundly rural country, itself transformed by the tractor. New jobs – on production lines, in supermarkets – were created, altering socio-professional hierarchies accordingly; and France laid the foundations for its (now declining) successes as an exporting nation. These were modern times: the beginning of the *'trentes glorieuses'* – the thirty 'glorious' years of economic expansion from 1946–75.

The international context to such expansion was the emergence of a bipolar world order in which the Cold War between the USSR and the USA held their allies and satellites to ransom by various means. Thus, under pressure from the USA in the form of the European Recovery Program (the 'Marshall Plan' for economic reconstruction), innovative thinkers in postwar France got to work. Under the specific guidance of French international businessman-cum-political visionary Jean Monnet, they proposed a ground-breaking scheme for Franco-German reconciliation in the form of a potentially Europe-wide protected market for coal and steel: the 1951 European Coal and Steel Community (ECSC). This was a market opportunity for France that has shaped French economics to the present day (see Chapters 7 and 8) – specifically, but by no means exclusively, in the agricultural sector – and by 2000 had led to the adoption in France of the single European currency, the Euro. But this form of European unification was also a face-saving solution to forging a new friendship with Germany and, by 1958, French leaders had agreed to expand the experiment to the civilian use of nuclear technology and the entire market economy. These developments created EURATOM (the European Atomic Energy Community) and the EEC (the European Economic Community), respectively.

Despite further encouragement from the USA, leaders of the Fourth Republic could not agree to extend these new forms of European cooperation to the military and defence domains; and the ECSC and EEC emerged as precious successes during a period marked by foreign policy humiliations. These included the loss of French Indochina in 1954, the climb-down to the USA in the Suez crisis of 1956, and the growing unrest in Algeria – administratively a *part* of France – from the mid-1950s onwards. All of these developments drained the Fourth Republic of resources and legitimacy but, by 1958, it was Algeria's guerilla freedom-fighters, the FLN (*Front de libération nationale* – National Liberation Front) that brought the French army, losing lives and face, to the point of rebellion against the Paris politicians. Once again, *in extremis*, the French Republic seemed to need an injection of strong political leadership to contain revolution and maintain national unity. What better than another saviour figure? Charles de Gaulle's personal status, military credentials and political backing combined to make him irresistible to the army and government alike. In June 1958, the Fourth French Republic handed power to the General and, in September 1958, the French people, voting by referendum, agreed to his conditions for a new, Fifth French Republic. In 2008, this regime celebrated fifty years of existence.

Gaullist France in the Cold War Years

As first President of the Fifth Republic, between 1959 and 1969, de Gaulle set ambitious goals that guaranteed further transformations in the identity of France and, in particular, the face that it projected to the outside world. This world, as de Gaulle saw it, was characterized by an unstable and unfair distribution of power between the USSR and the USA which he set out to challenge; this was his 'Yalta complex', in reference to the February 1945 summit at which the borders of Europe and respective spheres of influence had been determined by the Allied powers, but to which France had not been invited. Thus, de Gaulle oversaw the development of a French nuclear deterrent, independent of American technology or strategy, and designed ostensibly to reach any target (the so-called *tous azimuts* doctrine), not just the Soviet threat. He also established a truly history-making friendship with the West German Chancellor Konrad Adenauer, which laid the foundations of the 'Franco-Saxon' (Haywood, 2007) European Communities of the 1970s and 1980s.

France, Europe and the USA

De Gaulle's intentions for the Franco-German relationship (in the absence of cooperation from the UK) were that it should constitute the bedrock of a third, European, military power in the world, a vision known in French as *l'Europe puissance*. This is an ambition and a terminology that still have currency in contemporary French political discourse, but which suffered from ambiguity from day one. How would this bloc relate to NATO, for example, whose aims are also the military protection of (then) Western Europe? De Gaulle's response in 1966 was shocking: he expelled NATO's HQ from France, and withdrew France from the organization, a posture not reversed until thirty years later, and then only partially (see Chapter 8). Simultaneously, de Gaulle's attempted to turn the EEC into a 'Union of States' with common policies in matters of defence, culture, education and the economy. But these efforts were unsuccessful, since the EEC's other members, notably Germany, were reluctant to take such steps towards destabilizing the European order in the dangerous Cold War years. De Gaulle's legacy in terms of European integration have, instead, been a strong French commitment to Europe's Common Agricultural Policy, and a highly structured form of Franco-German cooperation (see Chapters 7 and 8).

Domestically, de Gaulle's stand-off with the USA was reflected in his strident derision of American cultures and taste. This was a stance with firm roots in the Fourth Republic, when high-level protests against the import of Coca-Cola to France coexisted with generous but reluctant market access accorded to US-produced feature films. At stake in these battles was national identity, and the tussle between France and the USA for global influence through culture, market economics and military reach continues to this day (see Chapters 6 and 8).

Founding the Fifth French Republic

De Gaulle's identity wars extended to the nature of the regime itself in France. The Fifth French Republic was, in itself, a transformation, albeit with echos of previous – non-Republican – regimes. From 1958–62, de Gaulle, as President, overrode party and parliamentary politics to rule by a series of public referenda as he moved towards the difficult decision to accord Algeria its independence in 1962. This was a policy that almost cost him his life, courtesy of factions of the military and European settlers (known as *les pieds noirs*) for whom the expulsion from Algeria was a traumatic, impossible experience. De Gaulle was, despite appearances, a realist, and shedding Algeria was for him a price to be paid for France's international credibility and strength.

In 1962, such was his legitimacy at the time, de Gaulle unconstitutionally amended the Constitution itself in favour of a henceforth directly-elected president. Thus, even after his death, the Fifth Republic would have a strong executive president. Even this proposal he carried, again by referendum; we see in Chapter 4 that this provision for a popular, directly-elected president makes the French Head of State one of the most powerful leaders in the Western world within a unique regime. The instability of governments and the stranglehold of factional interests that had thwarted France's previous Republics were now replaced by a more stable political life which characterizes France still today.

Revolution? May 1968

The essence of Gaullism in de Gaulle's own day was his ability to reinvent French national identity as required by dramatic events, while simultaneously striving to shape the course of these events. De Gaulle probably did possess an extraordinary talent of insight into domestic and international realities, but this was coupled with an equally extraordinary determination to challenge certain of these, even at the expense of his personal credibility. Yet, de Gaulle was no magician, and the forces of change eventually escaped his control and cost him his grip over the country. His version of the French Republic had created an authoritarian – or, at least, patrician – framework of power, heavily reliant on his own personal legitimacy. He was an ageing and increasingly eccentric figure in the France of the late 1960s, in a context – Vietnam, the Beatles – typified by cultural and political consciousness-raising at home and abroad. His political style became an anachronism, and was fatally challenged – in full, televised view of the world – by what became known as the 'events' of May 1968. In Paris, a student-led youth revolt spread to workers who organized a general strike throughout the country. The police were a key figure in this drama, notorious for the brutality with which they suppressed the riots in Paris that was reminiscent of the repression of the nineteenth-century French revolutions. The events, indeed, took on a revolutionary aura, driven by angry, well-educated young men – and women! – new to political activism, in debates open to all, and subject to no apparent rules. They deployed a new vocabulary of political slogans ('it is forbidden to forbid'; 'under the pavement, the beach') and extolled personal freedom from social or cultural taboo.

But de Gaulle lost neither his head nor, intially, his presidential position and, in the immediate aftermath of May–June 1968, even saw his parliamentary majority reinforced, as conservative forces in French society once again rejected a revolutionary future. But by then, de Gaulle perhaps saw himself as the new *ancien régime*, a barrier to the next necessary phase in France's modernization. Within a year, he had resigned as President, after losing the fifth referendum of his presidency, and less than six months later he was dead. The immediate legacy of 1968 was a raft of reforming legislation (in the education sector, for example, to respond to the students whose protests had ignited the events; and further moves towards workers' rights), albeit of limited impact. The more lasting legacy was political: the parties of the Left had, in May 1968, failed to unite sufficiently to channel the events towards a peaceful overthrow of the Fifth Republic, which they claimed to detest; yet the events of 1968, in removing de Gaulle from the scene, opened a decade in which the Right became weakened by its own divisions, thus easing the Left's passage to power in 1981, after 23 years of opposition.

The 'glorious' years of fast economic growth and social transformation that had characterized the previous postwar decades were severely curtailed by the economic turbulence of the 1970s. The breakdown of the Bretton Woods financial system at the start of the decade, and the intense pressure on the price of crude oil at the end, exposed underlying weaknesses in the French economy (see Chapter 8), such as the heavy hand of the state in micro-economic decision-making, significant trade deficits, and a weak currency. French leaders turned the screws: President Valéry Giscard d'Estaing (1974–81; see Table 1.2), a political figure independent and distanced by a generation from de Gaulle's close circle, tried to call a halt to

Table 1.2   Presidents of the Fifth French Republic

Charles de Gaulle	1959–1969	Re-elected 1965 by direct election
Georges Pompidou	1969–1974	Died in office
Valéry Giscard d'Estaing	1974–1981	
François Mitterrand	1981–1995	Two seven-year terms
Jacques Chirac	1995–2007	One seven-year term and one five-year term
Nicolas Sarkozy	2007–present	

unskilled immigration in the mid-1970s, and persuade migrant workers to return home; and to seek currency protection within a European monetary system, with very limited results; and his final Prime Minister, Raymond Barre, turned to austerity measures to stem rising inflation and unemployment, again with little success.

The power of the French presidency as interpreted by de Gaulle was still evident in the form of world-renowned feats and achievements in many fields: the civil nuclear energy programme, the laying down of the high-speed train (the TGV – *train à grande vitesse*) network, the Pompidou centre and Montparnasse Tower constructions in Paris, the Anglo-French *Concorde* supersonic airplane were all intended as symbols of French *grandeur* for international, as much as domestic, consumption. France was more socially liberal under Giscard, with new rights for women, for example; and Giscard worked for détente in the Franco-American relationship. But he was undermined by would-be heirs to Gaullism from within his majority, rallied by future president Jacques Chirac; and the Communist Left allowed itself to be lured into electoral alliances with the reinvigorated Socialist Party under the leadership of François Mitterrand.

Change and Continuity: François Mitterrand's France

Mitterrand had once memorably described de Gaulle's leadership as a permanent *coup d'état*; yet, once he himself was elected to the powerful presidency in 1981, he reported back from the sumptuous Elysée Palace that the function, in fact, suited him rather well, and he went on to consolidate, not overturn, the Fifth French Republic. Mitterrand's 14-year presidency (1981–95) was the longest to date and, in many respects, he and his Socialist governments set France on the tracks to the twenty-first century, overturning 'traditions' such as the death penalty; encouraging the tolerance of difference – between genders, races and ethnicities; modernizing industrial structures; embracing new technologies and, more reluctantly, the market; making France a powerful leading member of the European Union. But when the twenty-first century came a decade early in 1989, in the form of the collapse of the Soviet Empire, Mitterrand suddenly aged, both literally and in contrast with the challenges of the new times. His own past began to catch up with him, too, and France's 'work of memory' in relation to painful twentieth-century events began in earnest.

The Socialist Experiment?

Was François Mitterrand a Socialist? He brought the Left to power in the Fifth Republic by presenting himself, successfully, as the leader of the whole of the French left. In reality, the French left was deeply divided. In keeping with an electoral platform written by the Socialist Party for candidate Mitterrand, and replete with a handful of Communist party ministers, the Fifth Republic's first Socialist governments, from 1981–83, embarked on a large-scale programme of nationalization (of banks and industry), along with a raft of social reforms designed to improve the conditions of France's working classes. These included longer statutory holidays, a rise in the minimum wage, a wealth tax, a ceiling of 60 years on the retirement age, and other redistributory measures. This programme set France apart from its EEC neighbours in its doomed pursuit of socialism in one country – with drastic results. Capital fled from the country, France lost international credibility, Communist ministers were fired, and three currency devaluations followed in quick succession in 1982 and 1983 under the guidance of France's Finance Minister, Jacques Delors.

Delors went on to become a central figure in the aftermath of this failure. Appointed President of the European Commission by Mitterrand in 1984, Delors piloted, from Brussels, what became known as the single European market programme (the SEM – see Chapter 7). This comprised a swathe of European-level legislative measures designed to complete the provisions of the original 1957 Treaty of Rome in favour of the free movement, within the EC, of goods, capital, services and money, by means of the removal of existing barriers of all kinds. Delors would have been unsuccessful without the support of French President Mitterrand and his German and British counterparts, Chancellor Helmut Kohl and Prime Minister Margaret Thatcher. The programme that they all sanctioned was predominantly one of economic liberalization and deregulation, and its implementation in France set new targets for the economy designed to bring economic gains in the form of industrial competitiveness (see Chapter 7). As a French Socialist who had campaigned in 1981 to 'break with capitalism', however, Mitterrand's policy U-turn, as it came to be known, cast the Socialist Party into a confused state regarding the market economy, with no clear sign, still today, of a satisfactory resolution.

Taking European cover in order to implement domestic economic reforms set 1980s France on a course that thus far has proved irreversible. François Mitterrand went on to persuade his population in a referendum in 1992 that the Maastricht Treaty – designed to create a single European currency alongside new European-level powers in matters of security and defence – was the correct answer to the new circumstances of a reunified Germany and a spent Soviet Union, whatever the cost to independent policy-making; 'Europe', Mitterrand declared to the French when campaigning for re-election in 1988, is our future. There was continuity and logic to this European commitment and close partnership with Germany; already, in the early 1980s, Mitterrand had supported Chancellor Kohl in his decision to allow the installation of US short-range missiles targeted at the Soviet Union. In the final decade of the Cold War, Mitterrand had turned out to be a far more enthusiastic Atlanticist than most had predicted.

Mitterrand's domestic legacy is complex: he sponsored socially liberal measures, and he set in train a signicant programme of decentralization that is still ongoing (see Chapter 4). In addition, he sanctioned spending on populist cultural events (see Chapter 6), and tended to the national pride and the international face of France by means of an architectural legacy that has helped to maintain the status of the French capital as the most visited city in the world. He survived an unprecedented episode of power-sharing – known as *la cohabitation* – when he was forced to appoint his long-time opponent Jacques Chirac as Prime Minister following the defeat of the Left in the 1986 legislative elections; and he emerged from the experience as a sort of father figure who the nation was content to re-elect in 1988 for an equally unprecedented, and unsurpassed, second seven-year term.

Age, illness and the past eventually caught up with François Mitterrand. He did not fight the 1995 presidential election, and he died in January 1996. He had remained enigmatic to the end: the first the general public knew of his mistress and illegitimate daughter was when *Paris Match* published their photos, shortly before they gathered at his graveside next to his wife, Danielle. As for the secret of his long-standing prostate cancer, that emerged only after his death when his doctor, Claude Gubler, committed the memories to publication in a book (*The Big Secret*) that sold tens of thousands of copies before being withdrawn from the shelves, and pulped. Mitterrand had already subjected himself to questions about the exact nature of his involvement with the Vichy regime in World War II, and details of his interest in the 1930s in far-right activities were by then already known. Fourteen years in power was, also, just excessive by contemporary democratic standards, and the very existence of the left in power in the 1980s had lent strength and legitimacy to the far right National Front whose leader, Jean-Marie le Pen, scored 15% (nearly 4 million votes) in the first round of the 1995 presidential election (and who increased his share to nearly 20% in 2002; see Chapter 3). Domestically and internationally, French identity was challenged by the developments of the late twentieth century and, in 1995, France elected Jacques Chirac (on his third attempt) to assist France in the transition from one century to the next. This would involve a reckoning with the recent, twentieth-century past.

From Jacques Chirac to Nicolas Sarkozy: France Enters the Twenty-First Century

In 1989, France had celebrated the bicentenary of the storming of the Bastille prison in 1789, prompting some historians to conclude that, two hundred years later, France had finally embraced the present, and relegated its revolutionary past to distant memory. This was controversial, but less troubling for contemporary politics than the events of the mid–late twentieth century, still within living memory, that cast a shadow over the present time. The extent of the complicity of Vichy officials with the German occupiers in the deportation to concentration camps of French and foreign Jews, and the truths of French repression in its colonial territories, especially Algeria, were the objects of legal, media and political attention in the very first years of the twenty-first century.

War Trials

Jean-Marie Le Pen's attitudes during the 1980s had encouraged a small minority of intellectuals and academics to trivialize – to revise or even 'negate' – France's responsibility in the World War II deportation of French and foreign Jews from France to Nazi concentration camps; this, predictably, had led to outrage. At the same time, the painstaking pursuit of war criminals had caught up with a number of French high-ranking collaborators, and the 1990s saw the high-profile trials of two of these. Paul Touvier, in 1994, was found guilty of crimes against humanity and sentenced to life imprisonment for his role as leader of Vichy's Militia police. In 1998, Maurice Papon, a regional official (general-secretary of the *préfecture* of Bordeaux) at the time of his orders for the deportation of French Jews, was found guilty of complicity in such crimes and sentenced to ten years in prison (he was released after three years on the grounds of ill health, and died in 2007).

Most noteworthy was that both men had gone on to exercise political influence in the decades after Vichy. Papon, as head of Paris Police in 1961, had failed to prevent or stop the bloody repression and murder of Algerians demonstrating in Paris to support the cause of Algerian independence. This continuity was an important aspect of the trials because it demonstrated the complicity not just of individuals such as Touvier and Papon, but of the machinery of the French state itself, in some of the darkest moments of French history. Similarly, the revelations in the 1990s, by victims and perpetrators alike, of the French army torture of Algerian nationalists (FLN) during the Algerian war reminded the French that such atrocities had occurred within the framework of the Republic, and effectively with its blessing. Not all were shamed by these revelations in comparison with their shame in losing Algeria itself, but President Chirac's response to these developments was to decree symbols of truth and reconciliation, including a day of national hommage to the victims of the Algerian conflict, the first of which took place in September 2001. In 1995, he also instigated the official recognition of the role of the French state in the crimes of the Vichy regime, and promised to pay in full, in accordance with a law of 1994, the retirement pensions of veteran colonial soldiers. However, it was not until a Council of State ruling in 2002 that action was taken in this respect. The Catholic Church, for its part, had issued an apology in 1997 for its complicity with the crimes of Vichy.

President Chirac's gestures to curtail the nostalgic perspective on twentieth-century French history were not without their opponents, or twists and turns. In 2005, he was forced to repeal legislation requiring teachers to ensure that the 'positive role' of France in its former colonies was part of the school curriculum; and his successor, Nicolas Sarkozy, on the very night of his election to the presidency on 6 May 2007, declared that France had no call to demean itself by 'repenting' for the past. Contemporary France has, thus, taken responsibility for the complicity of the French state in crimes against humanity, but has stopped short of *apologizing* for its history. Indeed, in his 2007 electoral campaign President Sarkozy had emphasized his intention to break with any number of taboos and traditions from the past. 'I was elected', he said in January 2008, 'because I promised fundamental change. I promised a clean break with old thinking, old behaviours and the ideas of the past, all of which have led our country into its present situation' (Sarkozy, 2008).

Ending the Past?

President Sarkozy's promise to break with the past was comprehensive; it was to apply to virtually all areas of French public policy-making and national life, starting with getting the French 'back to work' after a decade of the 35-hour working week. Yet, during Chirac's presidency many steps had already been taken towards embracing the twenty-first century. Domestically, the 1958 constitution had been amended to include the commitment to 'parity' in national elections in an attempt to increase the number of women in leading roles in French politics and parliament; but implementation of this provision would be slow. From 2002 onwards, the Constitution also included the mention of the Republic as being henceforth organized on a 'decentralized' basis, in recognition of the ongoing project to devolve power, resources and responsibility – and some, very limited autonomy – to France's regions and towns. The length of the presidential mandate was also reduced, during Chirac's presidency, from seven to five years, making cohabitation less likely, although not impossible, and bringing France closer into line with comparable democratic systems. Reforms to the market economy, instigated during the late 1980s, continued as public utilities were partially privatized and deregulated; and France upheld its performance as an exporting nation.

There were also domestic defeats and controversies for President Chirac. In 2004, he brought into law a toughening of the rules regarding *la laïcité* (secularism). The law banned the wearing by pupils in state schools of the 'conspicuous' signs of religion, especially the Muslim headscarf (*le voile*) and, although it won strong support in parliament and in public opinion, it projected a repressive image of France to the outside world, and was seen by its opponents as playing into the hands of the *Front national* in the fear it suggested of the power of Muslim culture in contemporary France. In May 2005, President Chirac lost an important referendum called to ratify the EU's 'Constitutional Treaty' (subsequently revised into the 'Lisbon

Treaty' and ratified by French parliament in February 2008). The loss was decisive (54% voted against) and demonstrated that, during his time in power, Jacques Chirac had failed to convince the French electorate that an enlarged European Union would bring benefits to the French. He himself described the Treaty text as too strongly 'Anglo-Saxon' in nature, underplaying the French role and interest in the EU's market economy. His successor, President Sarkozy, took more decisive action upon election in May 2007, chiding his EU counterparts into a debate on how the EU could be more 'protective' towards its citizens and workers.

At stake in this particular debate was a perennial French preoccupation with what Haywood (2007) has called France's 'Anglo-American counter-identity'. By this is meant a centuries-old rivalry with the USA and the UK, which we saw was revived by de Gaulle in the 1960s in the quest for French *grandeur*. Here too, President Chirac began the process of diminishing the false dichotomy between how the French and the 'Anglo-Americans' saw the twenty-first-century world order. In 1995, he ended nuclear testing, albeit with a final 'bang' in the South Pacific that outraged world – and French – public opinion. In 1998, Chirac, with Britain's Prime Minister Tony Blair, initiated closer European cooperation on matters of defence, security and foreign policy; and, upon election in 1995, he had already begun the process of professionalizing and rationalizing France's armed forces in keeping with this tack. He countenanced a closer relationship between France and NATO, and sought to install better working relations with the USA in general. He attempted to befriend and support the newly unified Germany, and intensify the high-level contacts between the two countries. But all of these initiatives were fraught with contradictions and, on occasions, frustrated by Chirac's own obstinacy to preserve a cherished room for manoeuvre for France in the international arena. De Gaulle's claims to offer the world a third way between the superpowers translated for Chirac into a determination to offer the emerging new world order an alternative to American-led military and strategic preferences (in the Middle East, in Africa and – most significantly – in Iraq in 2003), and French diplomatic history in the early 2000s was very much still in its early drafts, faced with the real and serious challenges of the global forces of terrorism, capitalism (of regulated and rogue forms), and fundamentalist religions in France and abroad.

Conclusions

At the close of the first decade of the twenty-first century, therefore, France had elected a president intent upon extricating France, as Nicolas Sarkozy saw it, from the straitjacket of history, and making France a country like any other. For President Sarkozy, literally nothing was off-limits – not the 1789 Revolution; not the 1968 cultural near-miss revolution so fondly remembered by France's baby-boom generation, in power during the 2000s; not the 'French social model', where workers' rights are carefully balanced against market imperatives. Sarkozy's revolution was to be moral as well as structural, and would instrumentalize history as necessary – and as politicians have always done.

Given the strength of history in France as a social science discipline, and the passions of living and selective memories, any presidential ambitions to rewrite France's past would inevitably be very limited in practice. Nevertheless, the hold of history – ancient, medieval, revolutionary, recent – over contemporary France was already loosening by 2007 in real terms and, in many ways, France does look a lot more like other countries than it did even only twenty years ago. It is definitely of its times; the most recent, big structural changes and upheavals were nearly half a century ago, and the Franco-French civil wars are a thing of the past. Today's divisions and challenges are matters of and for policy, not grand historical principles. Domestically and internationally, France faces problems that are common across Europe, if not the world – the role of Islam in society, the economic challenges of global markets, national security – and is increasingly turning to its neighbours and partners for ideas and assistance in resolving the most pressing of these.

2

France and the French

Introduction

Contemporary France is locked into an ongoing debate about French national identity in which the very notions of 'France' and 'the French' are under scrutiny. Today, fewer than 20% of the French population live in the country, only a tiny minority of them are farmers, and traditional-style small-scale farmers are literally dying out. Yet, the rurality that typified French life well into the twentieth century has put French agriculture and its produce on a political and cultural pedestal. 'French national identity', declared President Sarkozy in October 2009, 'is based on the special relationship between the French and "the land".' Similarly, the French Constitution declares the French territory to be 'indivisible', and the six-sided outline of mainland France – 'the Hexagon' – is synonymous with France itself. The country has not always been this shape, however, having traumatically lost its eastern provinces of Alsace and Lorraine to Germany between 1870 and 1919 (and, again, for the duration of World War II), and until the twentieth century, when transportation and education became widespread, the geometric shape of the country was not even familiar to many of its own citizens.

Today, *l'Hexagone* is symbolic of the unity of France (Flynn, 1995: 6). At the same time, French citizens in cyberspace challenge the French state's capacity to exercise sovereignty over this territory, as does France's membership of the European Union. The Hexagon, says Hayward (2007: 47), is a shrinking piece of an ever-expanding puzzle. French governments have willingly transferred powers to the institutions of the European Union over the past sixty years, and the physical borders between France and many of its neighbouring EU

countries have been rendered largely irrelevant by French membership of the EU's passport-free Schengen zone. The free movement of
EU nationals, moreover, and the EU's provisions for EU citizenship
more broadly, have introduced a new layer of resident to the already
complex challenge of 'naming and numbering' (Hargreaves, 2007:
10) who belongs to the nation, on what grounds, and who has the
right to be on French territory, and for what purposes.

Determining who belongs to the French nation, and under what
conditions, is at the heart of debates in France about national identity.
Demography itself is a serious subject in France, given the country's
history since the nineteenth century of low birth rates, and generations decimated by world war. France turned to its colonies for
supplies of human workers and fighters throughout much of the
twentieth century, and more philosophically likes to see itself as a
place of refuge (*une terre d'accueil*). Accordingly, France's population in the present day is cosmopolitan and multi-ethnic, shaped by
successive waves of immigration throughout much of the twentieth
century, as well as by the diversity of those who can trace their ances-
tors back to times before the territory was as unified as it is today.
France, declared President Sarkozy in 2009, is one of the most
diverse countries in the world, and always has been (2009b). Yet,
French policy today on race, immigration and ethnicity is fraught
with contradictions, and the endless quest for an *integrated* national
community saps the energy of policy-makers. Just as significant, it
also blights the daily lives of those who struggle to attain the
'Frenchness' that increasingly seems to trump more objective criteria
for accessing French citizenship, nationality, or even a life free from
discrimination. In Scott's terms (2007: 116), contemporary France is
characterized by a 'defensive nationalism' that is threatened by
change. Indeed, President Sarkozy followed his praise of French
diversity with the following message: being French means belonging
to a particular 'civilization', and respecting certain 'values' and
'customs' (2009b): not all values and behaviours are equal in France,
he declared. By way of example, said Sarkozy, France is a country
where there is no place for the *burqa*.

In this chapter, we address these key aspects of French national
identity associated with its territory and its population, and evaluate
the challenges that changes here are deemed to pose to contemporary
France. We first explore founding notions of contemporary French
identity, such as the matter of territory – the physical manifestation of
France – and challenges to its integrity, from transport technologies

and human mobility, amongst other factors. We look at *la terre* – the land, its resources, its management, and its mythical qualities; and at *le terroir* – the combination, in a specific area, of soil, climate and position that fuels claims of distinction and authenticity made for French food and wines, and for its tourist charms. Under these headings, we include an evaluation of how France is placed to withstand the challenges of climate change and energy insecurity, and explore the responses crafted by French leaders to date at national and, increasingly, international levels. In the second part of the chapter, we focus on the identity of the French – who are they, where are they from, and how do they identify themselves? In the words of the 'great debate' on French national identity launched by the government in 2009, 'what does it mean to be French' in twenty-first century France? This includes an overview of matters of race and ethnicity; policy on immigration, nationality and citizenship; and ongoing – but surely doomed – government attempts to define, conclusively, what is meant by 'French national identity'. In conclusion, we summarize and evaluate the key trends currently shaping France and the French within the bounds of their own country.

La Terre, Territory and *le Terroir*

Most of the boundaries of France are natural (principally, mountains, rivers and coasts), and France contains a great variety of physical features, as well as a range of climatic zones. These are factors that help explain why France remains the world's favourite tourist destination, with over 80 million tourist *sejourns* made in France every year, and why France's agricultural products range from beets in the north to olives and lemons in the south. Wine is produced in all four points of the French mainland, as well as in between, and accounts for almost one fifth of all French agricultural production.

France faces the English Channel (or *la Manche*, as it is called in France), and this coast offers high cliffs, fishing villages and the World War II landing beaches (see Illustration 2.1). The Atlantic coast is famed for its sands, its surf and, towards the far south-west, its huge sand dunes and views of the Pyrénées mountains and, beyond them, Spain. This is also the terrain of the Basque country, straddling the Franco-Spanish border and home to a distinctive language and culture. On the Mediterranean, the Côte d'Azur has been a favourite with tourists for several centuries, and is a rich

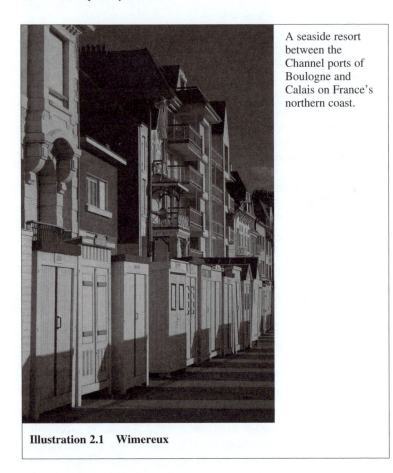

A seaside resort between the Channel ports of Boulogne and Calais on France's northern coast.

Illustration 2.1   Wimereux

region of the country. Inland, France is separated by the mountains of the Alps from Italy, the Pyrénées from Spain, the Vosges from Germany and the Jura from Switzerland, and by nearly 200 kilometres of the Rhine from Germany. The Alps and the Pyrénées are over 50 million years old, and Mont Blanc in the French Alps, at 4897 metres, is West Europe's highest peak.

The four major rivers of France (the Loire, the Garonne, the Seine and the Rhône), their tributaries and parallel canals offer spectacular limestone gorges, canyons, flat plains and beautiful navigable waterways, as well as their famous settlements: Paris on the Seine (the birthplace of modern France); Lyon on the Rhône where it meets the Saône river; and the chateaux that line the Loire, including former

Illustration 2.2   The Auvergne

The view from the Puy Mary in the Parc naturel régional des Volcans d'Auvergne (Regional Park of the Volcanos of the Auvergne), central France.

royal abodes. The *Massif Central* alone includes extinct volcanoes giving peaks of distinctive shape (see Illustration 2.2). East of Paris, by contrast, the land is flat but fertile, and in the north-east was traditionally home to important industrial centres (for coal and steel, for example).

These physical features are all accompanied by distinctive (but all temperate) climates, including an oceanic zone on France's western coast; continental weather patterns to the north-east; and the much sought-after Mediterranean and mountain climates. Together with the exotic locations of its overseas *départements*, the attractions of Paris and of its many vibrant regional cities, France is thus an extremely attractive European country.

France and its Overseas Territories

Mainland France, or *la France metropolitaine*, which includes the island of Corsica, accounts for over 95% of the country's population, and four fifths of its territory, with the rest spoken for by numerous overseas territories and communities, acquired when France was a colonial power. Four *départements* are in the tropics, have a combined population of 1.9 million, are politically integrated into France, and belong to the EU as part of France – the Euro is their currency too. A fifth department, Mayotte in the Indian Ocean, joined the others in 2009 after a popular vote by referendum. Administratively speaking, these territories are known as *D-ROMs*: overseas 'department-regions' (*départements-régions d'outre-mer*).

Three of the *départements* are mountainous islands: Martinique and Guadeloupe in the Caribbean, and Reunion in the Indian Ocean. The fourth, French Guyana in South America, is largely covered by rainforest. Both Guyana and Martinique voted by referendum, on 17 January 2010, against altering their status from *D-ROM to COM* – a single overseas authority or *collectivité d'outre-mer* (such as French Polynesia), which would have constituted a move (provided for under Article 74 of the French Constitution) towards greater autonomy from Paris (known as *autonomie encadrée*). Conversely, Mayotte chose to take the opposite route towards full *D-ROM* status.

France administers other distant overseas territories and communities that have more decision-making autonomy from Paris than the *D-ROMs*, as follows:

- in the Pacific Ocean: the 150 islands of French Polynesia (known administratively as a *pays d'outre-mer*: an overseas 'country'); and Wallis and Fortuna;
- in the Atlantic: Saint Pierre and Micquelon. These count administratively as *COMs* – overseas collectivities or *collectivités d'outre-mer*;
- in the Antarctic: the sparsely populated southern territories; governed administratively as *TOMs* (*territoires d'outre mer*: overseas territories);
- New Caledonia (capital Nouméa), is also in the Pacific Ocean and, administratively, is counted as a *pays d'outre-mer*, as in the case of French Polynesia. However, by the end of the 2000s, New Caledonia was undergoing a diplomatic process of public consultation by referenda as a route to gaining full independence from Paris by 2020; it is currently deemed therefore to have 'special status'.

France's overseas territories have been of particular strategic importance to the French space industry and, until the end of the twentieth century, as a testing ground for France's nuclear weapons; today, none but the Antarctic territories have autonomy in matters of defence. They are also part of France's tourist business; conversely, tourism is a vital source of income for these distant regions of France. Politically, moreover, they are minefields, since they lag significantly behind mainland France in terms of standards of living, with unemployment and the cost of living very high. They are, moreover, reminders of France's colonial past, as well as its involvement in the slave trade; and, in mainland France, French citizens from overseas can find themselves mistaken for 'foreigners' because of the colour of their skin. The riots that erupted in Guadeloupe in early 2009 were marked by serious violence, and subsequently spread to Reunion and French Guyana. At issue were the economic hardships caused by very high unemployment, low per capita income (half that of the mainland) and low salaries; peace was restored – for the time being – only after the promise of a hefty state aid package.

Habitats, Mobility and Transport

Visitors to mainland France itself, coming from more crowded European countries such as the UK or the Netherlands, are invariably struck by how spacious the country is. France may be smaller than the state of Texas, with a population nearly three times as big but, to a European visitor at least, France feels big in a North American way, with proper distances between urban sprawls. France is four times less crowded than England and the Netherlands, and half as densely populated as Germany. Of its surface area, 80% is rural, but only 20% of the population live there, and the vast majority of those are not farmers. Agricultural land has been lost over the decades to other uses, not only urbanization but also forestry: just over one quarter of France's land is covered by forest.

Despite these statistics, French land still constitutes a large share of the EU's agricultural land (approximately one fifth), and is used for meat and dairy herds, cheese and wine production, and the cultivation of sugars and cereals. This production makes France the world's second largest exporter of agricultural goods after the USA, and the main agricultural producer in the EU. Barely 5% of the working population actually works on the land, however, and agriculture accounts for little more than 2% of gross domestic product (GDP), even though agricultural production itself has grown (as has the average farm size), and the agro-business itself generates trade surpluses: France's main agricultural and food exports are wine, spirits, dairy and cereals. However, farmers in the dairy and beef industries struggle to maintain their incomes and competitiveness, particularly given the gradually decreasing support for agricultural production from the EU's Common Agricultural Policy as the EU expands its membership and resets its spending priorities (see Chapters 7 and 8).

Escaping to the country – if not necessarily to the farm – is as popular a pastime in France as it is in many other EU countries. The French countryside is highly sought after by jaded residents of French cities and other EU countries, in particular the UK and the Netherlands. Indeed, over half the French population itself lives in small towns and villages of no more than 20,000 inhabitants; and around 25,000 French villages have fewer than 700 inhabitants. The other half of the French population, on the other hand, lives in towns of 50,000 inhabitants or more. This is a departure from traditional France, when a 'rural' lifestyle implied working the land for agricultural output; in contrast, today's so-called 'neo-rurals' (or '*rurbains*' – urban folk aspiring to a rural lifestyle) practise a wide variety of activities in the countryside, linked principally to tourism (running bed-and-breakfast accommodation, for example) or the service industries; or they exercise professions where advanced communications technologies make location irrelevant. The lifestyles of urban and country dwellers are inexorably merging as a result, unlike the considerable differences in living standards and conditions that differentiated rural and urban dwelling in the postwar decades in France. Today's distinctions are between those living comfortably, whether urban or rural, and those living in less favourable surroundings, especially in France's outer-city suburbs – *la banlieue* (see Chapter 3). The number of second homes in France today, principally in the countryside, is estimated to be around 4 million and, in some parts of France, particularly in the centre and south-west, the 'invasion' of British and other European migrants have, in some cases, populated and revived otherwise dying rural communities (see Illustration 2.3).

French families themselves are moving away from the Paris region to live and work in more rural areas, and the populations of the west and south-west in particular have been growing – although not necessarily its *working* population. This movement towards the countryside, confirmed in the 1999 census, goes some way towards correcting the significant rural exodus that marked the *trente*

The sign reads 'For Sale', and gives as contact details 'England', followed by a UK telephone number. Dordogne has long been popular with British expatriates in France.

Illustration 2.3   France for sale? The Dordogne, south-west France

glorieuses – the modernization years – between the 1950s and the 1980s in France, when people moved to the cities en masse in search of work. That flight from the countryside had itself echoed earlier movements away from the rural France that are still, today, mythologized and presented (by politicians such as President Sarkozy, and by tourist boards) as the 'real France'; Graham Robb (2007: 330) expertly describes how, in the late nineteenth century, '[t]he rural population was flowing away to the cities, leaving the countryside exposed to the forces of Nature and foreign invasion. It was the patriotic duty of every French citizen to go on holiday to unpopular places.' Today, still, people – of course – continue to move to Paris and its rich region – the Île de France – in search of work and a different life; and the north-east of France has, in particular, lost people to this migratory trail. The picture is now more balanced, but contemporary France is still unmistakably urban, and has been since the 1960s; and the most notable aspect of this development has been the growth and popularity of France's medium-sized and large towns – its regional cities – such as Lille, Montpellier and Toulouse, Rennes, Bordeaux, Grenoble, Strasbourg and Nice. These come complete with modern transport systems, including trams, and a distinct and vibrant cultural life of their own. The number and variety of such cities is, indeed, one of France's many attractions: France has over 30 cities of 100,000 inhabitants or more, and more than 200 of over 30,000 people.

These patterns of human migration and habitation cannot be divorced from the development in contemporary France of efficient and fast long-distance travel networks, especially by rail and road. It is even possible to drive in a single day from France's Channel ports to its Mediterranean coast, thanks to France's network of toll motorways: the distance between the Channel port of Boulogne to the Mediterranean resort of Nice is just under 1200 kilometres, for which the 2007 Michelin road map of France gives an estimated driving time of just over 11 hours. Low-cost airlines offer a wide choice of options for travelling between regional airports in France and its European neighbours; and high-speed motorway and rail networks bring all major points of the country within reach of each other, as well as offering links between France and other European countries, both on the continent itself, and to its nearby island neighbours of the UK. The world-famous TGV (*train à grande vitesse*) high-speed trains run on a network that has seen a dramatic expansion since the early days in the 1980s. Travel times have been significantly cut, to the point where the Paris–Strasbourg journey (nearly 500 kilometres) takes a little over two hours, compared with the four hours of the past; by 2014, the journey between Paris and the regional capital of Brittany, Rennes (350 kilometres), will take less than one-and-a-half hours. Average TGV speeds are around 300 kilometres per hour.

France used to be notorious for a transport network where all lines radiated from Paris: times have changed. The Channel Tunnel, opened in 1996, now provides a fixed link between Britain and France. The rail journey by Eurostar takes a mere twenty minutes to get across the divide (out of a total journey time of two-and-a-half hours), and has brought the regional cities of France – as well as the cities beyond its borders, in Spain, Italy, Switzerland, and so on – within easy and comfortable reach of the UK, and especially London.

Also, passengers do not always have to change in Paris. Car ferries still link several French Channel ports (Calais and Bologne in the east; Dieppe, le Havre; Caen, St Malo and Roscoff towards the west) to the UK (and to Ireland), giving drivers a choice between these more sedate methods of breaching the Channel, and the high-speed 'Shuttle' link offered by the Channel Tunnel (car drivers and passengers, and also freight, are transported, in their vehicle, in metal coaches, along the Tunnel; it is not – yet – possible to drive oneself under the sea).

Thus, transport technology has added a new and further layer to the centuries-old relationship between France its neighbours. This very openness has compounded the sense of a 'loss' of France's traditional, agrarian identity that politicians can still, today, use to tap into veins of nostalgia for the 'real', or 'deep' France – the so-called *France profonde*.

'La France profonde'

Indeed, a key term in the lexicon of French rurality is '*la France profonde*', an expression that defies sensible translation, although Celia Brayfield's *Deep France* (2004) does justice to the ideas that it conveys; namely, positive connotations of tradition, authenticity and what is 'real' and 'true' – and their many ambiguities. For the French and their politicians, 'deep France' signifies progress, and the road travelled in half a century of modernization, for better or for worse. One aspect of this journey was the 'emptying' (*la désertification*) in the 1960s of the French countryside. This was the so-called 'rural exodus' of people to cities in search of work and careers, creating a 'French desert'; these expressions from social scientists have all passed into common parlance and signify the many transformations undergone by France in the second half of the twentieth century.

At the end of World War II, one third of the French population was living off, or otherwise connected to, the land. This was a population described as 'peasant' (*une population paysanne*); and the French term for peasant – *le paysan* – can still trigger nostalgic sentiments in contemporary France. The symbolic status of farmers, today, is encapsulated in the term *le paysan*, which does translate directly as 'peasant', but also conveys the positive meaning of guardian of the land as a way of life. Moreover, it relates to a significant (but not cohesive, or unified) social class in France that survived well into the mid-twentieth century (see Hayward, 2007: 119–20; and Baycroft,

2008: 85–92). The modern-day *agriculteur* is the business-like, entrepreneurial, usually educated, usually industrialized version of this traditional figure, with a consumer lifestyle that is very similar to that of city-dwellers; over one third of France's mayors, we note, are farmers of this type.

They are, moreover, emblematic of the productivist turn taken by French agriculture in the 1950s and 1960s (as seen in Chapter 1). Designed to generate growth and, ideally, even it out across the territory, this was a characteristic of the socio-economic boom of the *trente glorieuses*. These were the early days of the EU's Common Agricultural Policy and its support for the over-production of foodstuffs. It was also the heyday of the centralized planning of France's territory known as *l'aménagement du territoire*. In today's France, far more actors and interests are involved, alongside or instead of the central state, in planning out the use of the land, with small *communes* having considerable responsibility for planning permission, and regions closely associated with the handling of EU financial aid (see Chapter 4, for a discussion of the many and complex layers of local government in France). In rural France, today, agricultural production has to be balanced with economic development (especially job creation), the preservation and stewardship of the environment and, crucially, the promotion of the tourism that is so significant to France's economy (representing around 6% of France's GDP), and which sustains, in turn, rural life itself.

Tourism and Diversity

Indeed, the tourist to rural France will find themselves regaled with opportunities to sample what appears to be a wide diversity of produce, of *paysages*, and of physical beauty. Regions, *départements* and *pays* (groupings of areas with common cultural identities) all advertise their *terroir*, its distinctiveness, and its specialities. *Terroir*, we have said, is at the root of some of France's most famed and iconic produce, including its wine and cheeses. Steinberger (2009: 19) summarizes the idea of *terroir* as 'location, location, location' and as 'a central organizing principle of French viticulture'. Stephen Bayley, writing nearly a decade ago, hears the French explain *terroir* as 'the mystical union of landscape and weather and personality which gives specificity to a great wine' (Bayley, 2002). Clearly, the precise meaning of the notion of *terroir* varies according to the palate of the gastronome and the balance sheet of the producer. Thus, by way of example, when driving across small roads in central France, we may come across *la route des produits d'origine contrôlée transcorréziens* (the road of produce of certified origin from the Corrèze') in what is a deeply rural department of France.

Furthermore, rural France works hard to attract and to entertain its tourists, both national and international. Events and attractions are signed and signposted, and the smallest of villages stage art exhibitions open to all, usually free, often run by volunteers organized into special interest *associations*, and made possible courtesy of good amenities including the *salle des expositions* (exhibition space) or the tiny local tourist office. These frequently display a bewildering array of brochures and flyers for local accommodation, organized events, and advice on the many ways that the area can be enjoyed by the visitor. Furthermore, most small villages have clean public toilets and *aires* – public spaces – for picnicking in the shade, and at a proper table with proper seating. Certain villages qualify as *villages étape* by virtue of the quality of their services (and if they have fewer than 5000 inhabitants and can be found beside a free – not toll – stretch of motorway, or dual carriageway), and these villages are clearly indicated on the highways and motorways that run past; in the words of the scheme's website, 'It's the village's life that's at stake'; 'a chance for development and recognition' (Village d'Étape, 2010). Beyond the village, France has 46 'natural regional parks' defined as 'inhabited, rural' areas in need of protection to preserve their natural beauty; nine 'national parks'; 327 nature reserves and numerous historical monuments (*monuments historiques*), classified sites of interest (*sites classés*) and thirty UNESCO World Heritage sites (UNESCO, 2010). The whole of France is, thus, way-marked for the tourist; at the entrance to small villages on both national and departmental roads, large signs display the amenities and attractions on offer; even huge hypermarkets advertise distinct regional produce. Rural and regional France, we observe, is both intrinsically appealing, and big business.

Such diversity is very much part of today's French national identity, even though, in reality, it exaggerates (for the purposes of business, the economy, and jobs) the extent of distinct regional identities in today's France. Yet, this is part of the picture in contemporary France, whereby protecting both rural and urban environments is in France, as elsewhere, an issue of rising political prominence that has provided opportunities for the politicization of special interests. Hunting, for example, remains a culturally significant and accepted activity in much of the French countryside, and some have fought politically to maintain it in the face of other agendas, including ecological movements and pressure from EU legislation to regulate such activities across the EU member states. Thus, the CNPT (*Chasse, Nature, Pêche et Tradition* – Hunting, Nature, Fishing and Tradition – movement) featured in French national elections in the 2000s (see Chapter 3), associating itself with broader arguments against the impact of the EU in France.

Nuclear Power, Food Scares and the Environment

In France, the matter of environmental protection is complicated by the fact that, for all its natural attributes, France is relatively poor in natural resources, especially fossil fuels. Currently, France relies on nuclear power to meet the bulk (over 75%) of its energy needs. A new generating plant is due to open in Normandy (Flamanville) in 2012, the development of prototypes of the next generation of reactors is under way; and, in 2005, a decision was taken to site the ITER project (the International Thermonuclear Experimental Reactor) for research into nuclear fusion technology in Cadarache, southern France. The beginnings of the French nuclear programme in the 1970s, at the time of a serious world oil price and supply crisis, gave rise to 'green' movements, but these were largely unsuccessful in withstanding the force of the French state in their day. However, now that the fight against climate change and for environmentalism have become significant preoccupations for governments of Europe and elsewhere, French authorities have themselves become markedly more active, particularly following a succession of challenges to environmental health and food safety. These have included the BSE (bovine spongiform encephalopathy) – 'mad cow' – epidemic that began in the UK in the mid-1980s, and damaged Franco-British relations for a decade; the prospect of genetically-modified organisms (GMO) crops (still partially banned in France); and what some see as the globalization of junk food – *la malbouffe* – and its consequences, real and imagined, for human health and the demand for local produce. José Bové, a well-known campaigner in France, has come to symbolize such arguments for green and 'slow' food following his imprisonment after having coordinated the dismantling of a McDonald's restaurant construction site in 1999 in Millau, south-west France.

Since 2002, notably, a 'Charter for the Environment' has been appended to the 1958 French Constitution, indicating the state's commitment, symbolic and legal, to the weight of the environmental factor when planning for economic growth (see Box 2.1). The Charter proclaims the right of all to a 'balanced environment'; and, in the 2007 presidential election, a popular ecological campaigner, Nicolas Hulot, applied pressure on his mainstream candidates for an environmentally-aware agenda. By 2008, a rolling programme of environmental debate and policy-planning (known as *le Grenelle de l'environnement*) was in place. Moreover, France signed the Kyoto protocol in 1999, and increasingly looks to the EU and the international stage to manage the environmental and climatic change, while gradually proposing a series of climate-friendly measures at home. These include the increasing use of electric vehicles in public transport schemes, including in Paris, and the ongoing development of France's leading expertise in nuclear energy technology; and the planning of further high-speed rail links. The 'Grenelle' initiative also launched a 'carbon tax' on individuals and companies. At the time of writing,

Illustration 2.4   Electric bus in Paris, la Traverse de Charonne in the 13th *arrondissement*

Another similar vehicle, the Montmartrobus, takes residents and tourists around the famous Montmartre area of the city.

however, this was first struck down by the Constitutional Council, and then suspended altogether following the poor results of the government in the 2010 regional elections. Thereafter, the whole 'Grenelle' initiative itself came into serious doubt.

The environmental agenda in France is, thus, driven by political considerations and cost-cutting measures, as well as a broader concern with the impact of climate change, and many actors and interests galvanize for and against change, making reform as difficult in France as elsewhere. Unsurprisingly, France has turned to international arenas to share the costs and responsibilities of tackling today's

---

Box 2.1   Charter for the Environment

'The French People

Considering that

Natural resources and equilibriums have conditioned the emergence of mankind;

The future and very existence of mankind are inextricably linked with its natural environment;

The environment is the common heritage of all mankind;

Mankind exerts ever-increasing influence over the conditions for life and its own evolution;

Biological diversity, the fulfilment of the person and the progress of human societies are affected by certain types of consumption or production and by excessive exploitation of natural resources;

Care must be taken to safeguard the environment along with the other fundamental interests of the Nation;

In order to ensure sustainable development, choices designed to meet the needs of the present generation should not jeopardise the ability of future generations and other peoples to meet their own needs;

Hereby proclaim:

Art. 1 – Everyone has the right to live in a balanced environment which shows due respect for health ...

Art. 6 – Public policies shall promote sustainable development ...

Art. 10 – This Charter shall inspire France's actions at both European and international levels.'

Source: National Assembly (2010).

deadly serious challenges to its environment, and the security and sustainability of its food and energy supplies.

Just as France is increasingly turning to its neighbours and seeking to maximize its influence in international forums to resolve its environmental dilemmas, so its identity as a nation cannot be divorced from France's international context. France, we have said, is a country open in 3D to forces and flows of all kinds. These include the movement of people, and the French population is, indeed, cosmopolitan and ethnically-mixed, the result of a long history of immigration. These characteristics have given rise to all sorts of public policy dilemmas in a nation where abstract ideals of national unity, and equality between its nationals whatever their ethnic origins, are increasingly hard to fulfil. Deciding who has the right to be on French soil and what they can do when they are there – work, marry, vote, receive welfare assistance, acquire nationality? – are all matters of public policy that can neither be made in isolation from France's neighbouring countries, nor from the EU or other international bodies – nor, indeed, from the developing world, many of whose inhabitants would literally die for the freedoms of France. The explicit link drawn by President Nicolas Sarkozy after his election in 2007 between immigration, on the one hand, and national identity, on the other, set off a particularly heated debate around the question of what it means to be French, and to live as part of the French nation.

Who Are the Twenty-First-Century French?

In the 1999 census, the total French population stood at 58.5 million, and was growing. By 1 January 2009, the estimated population size was 64.3 million, and still growing. These figures make France the second most highly-populated country in the EU27 after Germany (83.3 million inhabitants), accounting for around 14% of the EU27's total population. In 2007, for the first time in thirty years, the birth rate rose to an average of two children per woman, the highest in the EU along with Ireland, and far above the EU average of 1.48. At the same time, the French population is ageing, as in other European countries: French women, along with their Spanish counterparts, have the longest life expectancy in Europe, at 84 years (for men, 77). In 2007, just over 16% of the French population was aged 65 or over, with almost the same number of those aged under 20 years; whereas, in 1994, nearly 27% of the total population was aged under 20, almost twice as many as in 2007. Unlike most of its European neighbours, population growth in France is accounted for principally by an excess of births over deaths, rather than by immigration. Net immigration into France in 2006 was estimated to be in the order of 100,000, accounting for less than one quarter of the total growth in population, and far lower than the equivalent figures for, say, the UK.

Who's Who? Immigration and Nationality

France has a diverse population, and 'the French' have always been a mix of peoples: *at least* one in five French people is deemed to have *at least* one foreign ancestor in their family tree (Brame, 2006: 40). In 2008, France was home to 3.1 million people aged between 18 and 50 years who were born in France, (between 1958 and 1990, therefore) to one or two immigrant parents (INSEE, 2010b). This population constitutes 12% of all those aged 18–50 years in France, and 17% of all those aged 18–20 years. Of them, 40% were born to parents from North or sub-Saharan Africa; and 50% to parents of European descent. Of these children of immigrants, 32% live in the Paris region (the Île de France), compared with 21% of the entire French population aged 18–50 who live in this region.

To this figure of 3.1 million, Hargreaves (2007: 31) adds another five million individuals in France with one immigrant grandparent. In this context, 'immigrant' refers to individuals of foreign nationality also born abroad (elsewhere in Europe or beyond). Defined like this, immigrants (not their 3.1m children, born in France) were estimated to number five million in 2008, just over 8% of the French population, as against 4.3 million at the time of the 1999 census. By including people's origins (place of birth) in the counting as well as their nationality, it became possible, in 1999, for the first time in a French census, to distinguish which French nationals had been born abroad (foreign) and subsequently acquired French nationality. Of the 3.1 million children (aged 18–50, we said) born in France to one or two immigrant parents, most have acquired French nationality, especially those born to only one immigrant parent. However, immigration and naturalization policy in France is complex, and has changed many times in the past two decades, and the INSEE study (2010b) revealed that even some of its subjects themselves were unaware of the rules. Moreover, the rules have tightened, and the number of acquisitions of French nationality per year have been declining since 2000 (from 141,455 in 2000 to 129,152 in 2007) (INSEE, 2010c).

Box 2.2   French nationality and its acquisition

The rules of French nationality and its acquisition have undergone many changes in the course of the last one hundred years. Nationality is certainly not seen as a fixed characteristic of an individual. Laws have evolved in line with political thinking, itself linked to demographic and other social challenges as perceived by the government of the day. Nationality and citizenship have not always even been synonymous. At the time of the *ancien régime*, it was sufficient to pledge loyalty to the King to be deemed a 'citizen'. The vocabulary of citizenship itself emerged from the French revolution at a time when citizens were defined by their ancestry – their blood – and not by their country of residence – their 'soil'. Being a 'foreigner' did not preclude an individual from fighting France's wars. This regime was known as *jus sanguinis*, and lasted into the middle of the nineteenth century. Since then, and following new legislation in 1998, the principle has been that children born in France (on French soil) to foreign parents are French (*jus soli*), with some conditions.

- A child is born French if one parent at least is French, or if the child and one of its parents were themselves born in France.
- A child born in France of two immigrants who have not acquired French nationality is not born French. The acquisition of French nationality is automatic at the age of 18, if the child has been resident in France for at least five years since the age of 11. Since 1998, the young person is no longer required to specifically request to become French.
- In 2007, a total of 129,000 individuals acquired French nationality. In 2006, 3.6 million (non-naturalized) foreigners lived in France, representing 5.8% of the total population.

Sources: Data from Hayward (2007): 113–14; INSEE (2005).

France has long been a country of net immigration (with no significant tradition of emigration, unlike the UK, or Ireland, for example), which for the greater part it has engineered and welcomed for economic reasons, especially to fill jobs in the industrializing economy of the twentieth century. For half a century, the expectation was that these workers would return to their home countries in due course (when no longer needed). There was no specific attempt to build a nation around and including its immigrants and, in this respect, France is distinct from the USA. More recently, however – and, in particular, since the decolonization of France's North African and sub-Saharan African 'possessions' in the 1950s and 1960s –

immigrants increasingly have come to stay, and brought their families with them (and still do, naturally); family reunification, notes Hargreaves (2007: 25), is the 'single most important element in documented migratory flows during the last three decades'. Family reunification makes immigrants visible because they need mainstream, family housing (not just single males in basic hostels) and their children need school places. Accordingly, 'immigration' has increasingly, and especially since the 1980s, been treated by French governments as a 'problem' of public policy.

Most notably, immigrants have been expected, and explicitly so, to integrate into French society, and to assume a common identity – that of the French citizen. Moreover, French immigration policy *per se* has hardened in recent years, culminating in high-profile detentions and deportations of illegal immigrants in France, and their school-age children (and an equally notable civic backlash), the government having fixed itself an annual quota of over 25,000 deportations of illegal entrants and over-stayers. The plight of illegal immigrants (*les sans papiers* – without papers/undocumented) more generally has become a *cause célèbre*, supported by high-profile figures from the French establishment arguing for their right to remain in France, particularly when they have been working for employers preferring to turn a blind eye to their illegal status. Relations between France and the UK have been particularly strained at times in these respects, as a result of the transit route used by would-be illegal immigrants to the UK through France's Channel ports, although cooperation between the two countries is, however, the norm.

More broadly, France has seen a shift in policy towards the notion of 'selective immigration' (*immigration choisie*) on the grounds of the immigrants' usefulness to their communities, and to the job market. Such criteria may well be familiar to those applied in other countries, including the UK and USA, and they are increasingly in keeping with EU policy in this matter. But they are a departure from the traditional French image of the Hexagon as a safe haven for those fleeing harm and seeking a more humane existence, whatever their social status, professional qualifications or personal skills. Indeed, immigration policy in Sarkozy's France has stirred up much resentment and political opposition. Specifically, the bar for citizenship seemed to be rising ever higher. In this context, the decision in 2007 to create a new Ministry of Immigration, Integration, National Identity and Co-Development was seen by its

Box 2.3   Immigration and integration: changing the rules

French immigration policy in Sarkozy's France has been a clear political priority. It has generated a raft of legislative acts, as well as new language and charged rhetoric. In particular, from 2006, immigration into France is 'selective' (*choisie*), subject to a growing number of conditions and criteria. These relate, in particular, to an immigrant's capacity for 'integration' into French society. 'Good' immigrants will see their naturalization fast-tracked. In these expressions of state power in this matter, France is aligning itself with most other EU member states, and also with common EU policy in this domain. Combating illegal immigration is seen as a particularly high priority; cracking down on illegal workers is another. Implementation is a different matter, and what seems to matter the most is to maintain an uncompromising but highly symbolic language of repression and control. In 2010, in Calais on the northern French coast, French authorities destroyed the makeshift shelters built by migrants hoping to get to the UK; and planes were chartered to remove some illegal migrants to their home country, including Afghanistan. Penalties are stiff for non-compliance with the law for legal and for illegal migrants: from the withdrawal of state benefits to the removal of French nationality, if this has been acquired. President Sarkozy has taken a leading role in this activity, and made it a priority in his 2007 election campaign. Polls show that French opinion is divided on the President's priorities in this area. The issue over which consensus is greatest is that those living in France should behave according to French values and norms, in line with the Republican ideals set out in the French Constitution. Controversy has been greatest over proposals to DNA-test immigrants wishing to join family members already in France, and to remove the children of illegal immigrants from school to deport them with their adult family members. In the matter of EU nationals seeking to live or work in France, President Sarkozy has relaxed the rules, in line with EU rules and trends. France has also taken an active role in shaping EU policy in the matter of (im)migration, such as the 'European blue card' plans for work permits for highly-skilled individuals. Serious problems of people risking their lives and others' for a future in France and Europe remain.

critics as a totalitarian move by the state to legislate for national identity in the most exclusionary manner.

Migration: Europeans and the Rest

One specific aspect of these issues is the case of the European (EU) citizen on French soil. Since the 1992 Maastricht Treaty's provision for the creation of the European citizen, EU nationals, with very few restrictions, can move, settle and reside as they wish in the now 26 other member states. Once there, they are free to exercise the provisions of their EU citizenship should they so wish, including the right to vote (at local and European elections) and to stand in these elections; and also to work, seek health care and other welfare benefits, and so on (see Figure 4.1). Key dimensions of citizenship are, thus, divorced from nationality and, for some opponents of the nearly-defeated 1992 Maastricht Treaty in France, this was deemed a serious threat to national sovereignty. Prominent 'sovereignist' critics at the time even talked of the 'treason' of allowing non-French nationals any right to vote on national soil. This argument resonated as it did because of the ongoing refusal in France to grant voting rights to long-term, resident, non-EU nationals who also do not have French nationality. This group includes, primarily, France's post-colonial populations from North Africa. Most political parties have agreed that these populations should have the right to vote in local elections but, so far, they have lacked the courage to instigate the change. In 2010, the French Prime Minister François Fillon said that he thought it would occur in about ten years' time. In contrast, the former secretary-general of the government's majority party in Parliament, Xavier Bertrand, stated explicitly at the same time that 'foreigners' should never have the vote at local elections because the right to vote must be determined by 'citizenship, sovereignty and nationality'.

Being French: The 2009–10 'Great Debate' on French National Identity

Indeed, in today's France, the political problems of demography are no longer those of the past, when declining birth rates and total population size spelt a dangerous growth in the differential in population size between France and its enemy, Germany. Some of today's most politically explosive demographic issues, together with the difficulties of paying for the welfare of an ageing society (see Chapter 5), revolve around the link between racial, ethnic, cultural and religious identities, on the one hand and, on the other, definitions of national identity: what it means to *be French*. Here, legislation is frequently used as a blunt tool to manage these relationships. Indeed, in Nicolas Sarkozy's France, national identity has come to be determined through an increasingly narrow lens that links 'Frenchness' to ever more stringent criteria (see Box 2.3). At the same time, measures to identify and combat discrimination have found their way into the public policy domain, despite the fact that concepts such as the 'right to difference', 'minorities' and even 'communities' are alien to French political culture (as we see in Chapter 3). Namely, in France, all (legal residents) are guaranteed equality before the law by the Constitution itself, irrespective of race, religion or ethnic origin. Difference in these respects is deemed irrelevant from a political or policy perspective, and the state legislates to remove difference from the public policy equation: not only is there no special treatment, for example, for adolescent school girls wishing to wear the Islamic headscarf; in public (state) schools, they are banned from doing so (see Chapters 3 and 5). Such markers of personal identity have come to be deemed as signs of 'foreignness' in France and, the more visible the gap from the norm, the more potentially consequential for life chances. Hence, skin colour and surname have demonstrably gone hand-in-hand in France in recent years with discrimination in the job and housing markets, in police treatment, in opportunities for jobs in politics, and in the state more broadly. Is France a racist society? The question remains open and loaded, and, in a clumsy attempt to defuse it, the French government in October 2009 launched a 'great debate' on French national identity.

Polls suggested that a majority of French people were in favour of such a debate, and it was also undoubtedly a way for the government of making its increasingly tough immigration policies more palatable. It was also a political manoeuvre designed to appeal to voters who might otherwise be tempted by far right politics.

The Terms of the Debate

'What does it mean to be French?' 'What are the values of French national identity?' 'How better to spread the "values of national identity" to France's foreigners?' These were the questions posed by the French Minister for Immigration, Integration, National Identity and Co-Development, Eric Besson, in October 2009 at the launch of the debate. He reminded the French of the role of the state in forging national identity – a problem for his critics. He invited the country to think, individually and collectively, about the 'common project' that binds them and makes them want to live together as a nation. He stated that France's national identity seemed to be 'fading'. The initiative was to be conducted via the state's local representatives – the *préfets* in the regions and *départements* (see Chapter 4), and on the Internet with any citizen who cared to air their views. Of course, all this was also relayed by the media. In the first three months, there had been 350 public meetings, and 55,000 contributions to the debate on the Ministry site. At this point, February 2010, Eric Besson published a series of measures on the basis of the debate so far. What did the measures consist of, in summary? Overall, they seemed designed to encourage existing French citizens to renew their vows to the nation, and to raise the bar for those aspiring to nationality. At issue was the reaffirmation of 'Republican values'. By way of example:

- On the *spread of values*: a young citizen's *log-book* to record how they have personally upheld the values of the Republic; strengthen *civics teaching* in schools;
- on cultivating *pride in being French*: all children to have the opportunity to sing the national anthem, the *Marseillaise*, at least once a year; make the French *flag* obligatory in every school and the *Declaration* of the Rights of man in every classroom;
- on practising *Republican principles*: *respecting teachers' authority*;
- On 'welcoming' newly naturalized French (and legal aliens): more *ceremonial*, more *contractual*, more *obligations*.

The 'great debate' itself was dubbed a failure by its many critics and, beyond the implementation of these measures, not much further was expected from the process. Neither had it begun to tackle other dimensions of 'Frenchness' (beyond nationality and origins) which, in recent years, have come to be posed as problems of public policy. These revolve around the treatment, in French politics and society, of individual and group identities, and questions of discrimination on these grounds.

Beyond the Debate: Legislating for Identity?

The very language of what we might broadly call 'identity politics' – which is embedded in policy-making norms in certain other European countries, including the UK, and certainly in the USA – sits very uneasily with the French republican traditions that we explore at greater length in the following chapters. In many respects, even the notion of 'identity' itself, when applied not to the nation but, rather, to groups or individuals within it, is treated by much of the mainstream of French politics and society as unwelcome political correctness imported from the 'Anglo-Saxons'. The practice of ethnic monitoring, for example, used as a customary tool elsewhere for combating unfair discrimination (in the job market, in particular) on the grounds of subjective prejudices of race and ethnicity, is treated in France with suspicion; and even collecting statistics to compile records on

---

Box 2.4   Towards an anti-discrimination framework?

A web of laws, bodies and practices has emerged in France to identify and tackle discrimination and racism relating to ethnic origins. These developments are not without their critics. Moreover, positive discrimination, affirmative action and quotas are still problematic and potentially unconstitutional in France today.

Bodies

- CRAN (*Conseil représentatif des Associations Noires* – Representative Council of Black Associations). A pressure group, created in 2005, working towards the recognition of the 'wounds of History, slavery and colonisation', and for the 'fight against discrimination'.
- HALDE (*la Haute Autorité de lutte contre les discriminations et pour l'égalité* – High Authority for the Fight against discrimination and for equality). This body, set up by the state in 2004 as an independent administrative authority, has more teeth, but has courted controversy, and there is currently some doubt about its continued existence.

Legislation and best practice

- Laws outlawing Holocaust denial and anti-Semitic propaganda have existed since the 1970s, and, since the 1990s, have been extended to cover other racially-motivated behaviour, including on the Internet.
- The practice of the 'anonymous CV' received government backing in 2009. The idea is that companies cannot screen candidates (for skin colour, for example, or for address – which itself can denote a neighbourhood known for its ethnic minorities) from their CV alone. Big companies including Eurodisney and Accor have adopted this practice but, inevitably, it has its sceptics.
- In 2004, 35 big French companies signed up to a 'diversity charter'. This is designed to raise awareness and combat discrimination on ethnic grounds in the company, especially in France's small and medium-sized enterprises, which account for nearly three quarters of all jobs in France.
- In 2006, the government passed an 'equal opportunity' law (*loi pour l'égalité des chances*) aimed at improving the life chances, especially in the field of work, of people from 'difficult neighbourhoods' (*les quartiers difficiles*), particularly the young.

an individual's ethnicity is highly problematic. Indeed, the very terms 'ethnicity' – let alone 'race' – are, by and large, deemed as illegitimate categories of social difference by a wide spectrum of opinion in France. It follows that the idea of quotas or other forms of positive discrimination (or affirmative action) to achieve a more ethnically-diverse and representative body politic or labour force is anathema to most French – in theory. In practice, certain organizations (in the education system, as we see in Chapter 5) do find ways to level the playing field, taking an individual's neighbourhood as a proxy criterion for ethnic origin *per se*.

Yet, France does have a 'race' problem, particularly in association with its population of North African – ex-colonial – origin. In the 1980s, at the time of President François Mitterrand's Socialist Party governments, a head of steam built up in the form of social movements to combat racism directed at these populations in particular. Children of France's post-colonial immigrants, known as *les beurs* (slang for 'Arab'), involved themselves in the struggle. Such activity made the problem of prejudice in this context visible, but fell short of significant or systemic measures designed to combat its consequences. Neither did the *mouvement beur* prevent the rise of the far right as a political force (as developed in Chapter 3). In the following decade, and under pressure to implement a growing body of EU law, France began to tackle discrimination *per se*, more broadly defined. This remains a contentious public policy field, but a vital one, as evidence of discrimination comes to light. In this context, anti-discrimination legislation has been proposed, hotly debated and sometimes passed, and new public bodies have been established to feed and shape the debate, and to implement the law; pressure groups and watchdogs also exist outside the framework of the state.

Conclusions

In 2008, President Nicolas Sarkozy commissioned a report headed by one of France's most eminent female politicians and public figures, Simone Veil. The task was to investigate whether the diversity that characterizes the French should be written into the Constitution itself as an organizing principle of the French republic. 'Respect' for the diversity that constitutes French identity would have taken its place beside the existing statements in the Constitution that France itself – its *terre*, territory and *terroir* – shall be organized on a decentralized basis (Article 1); that its regional languages are part and parcel of the 'heritage' of France (Article 75-1); that it 'ensures' the equality of French citizens before the law, whatever their cultural, religious or racial origins (Article 1); that it formally 'respects' all religions (with the exception of some banned sects (Article 1)), and 'favours' one specific type of positive discrimination, namely the 'equal access' of men and women to elected political office, and to social and professional responsibilities (Article 1). The Veil Committee found that such a constitutional amendment, and the scope for positive discrimination that it would offer, were not necessary to fulfil the Constitution's existing commitments to freedom, equality and fraternity. For the time being, therefore, the acknowledgement of 'diversity' itself as a founding principle of the Fifth French Republic is apparently a step too far, for reasons and with consequences developed in our following chapters.

3

Politics and Political Culture

Introduction

Politics in contemporary France draws on a strong sense of history and culture, and French political identity is anchored in the past. In a society where the status quo is deemed to represent over two hundred years of democratic achievement and social progress, promoting change is a politically risky business. Following his election as French President in May 2007, however, Nicolas Sarkozy claimed that the French people were impatient for change, and promised for his part to make a clean break – a *rupture* – with what he saw as outdated political ideologies and practices of the past. This was a bold strategy, but it was also in the spirit of the Fifth French Republic itself, which was designed to tame French political life through the shock of new and revitalized institutions, and to marry France's colourful past to the demands of the present.

The chapter begins by surveying these core characteristics of French political culture, which revolves around the meaning of republicanism. This is a culture that has bred a sense of what is called 'exceptionalism' in French politics that, for its critics, can be seen as a brake on reform. 'Exceptionalism' has forged a strong sense of national identity that finds itself challenged in contemporary France as a result of domestic and external developments.

The chapter then reviews how political parties and voters alike have responded to these developments within a set of rules established in 1958 in order to generate political stability, as well as ensure political representation. We explore the meanings of 'left' and 'right' in a political system dominated until as late as the 1990s by the influence of Gaullism and Communism, and where the left did not come to power until 1981, nearly 25 years after the founding of the Fifth Republic. We assess the significance of the French far-right movement – the National Front, and its leader Jean-Marie le Pen. In 2002, le Pen came second in the presidential election, but in 2007 did less well, and in 2010 le Pen announced that he would finally be stepping down from the party leadership. Finally, we consider other forms of political action that are marginal to the mainstream of political life, but which wield social significance and political influence based around issues such as Euroscepticism; globalization; or the plight of sections of society such as the homeless, or immigrants, both legal and illegal.

The chapter closes with a brief assessment of the relationships between politics, the media and the judiciary, against a backdrop of recurrent high-level political corruption and scandal, and government emphasis on an agenda of law and order. The interplay between French politics and judges, for example, has historically tended to favour politicians and their state secrets over and above a duty to scrutinize and expose. The French media, for its part, is renowned for its observance of strict privacy laws, and for its overly deferential treatment of France's top politicians, certainly by Anglo-American standards. These French norms, however, are challenged in the present day by the openness of interactive, digital technologies that encourage new generations of voters to demand better access to their representatives. President Sarkozy himself, moreover, has actively courted the media, and has put his love life (or more accurately, love lives) on public display.

The picture of French politics to emerge from this overview is mixed: a society that in many respects is on the move, but a political class seemingly hamstrung by its traditional culture and historical inheritance, and noticeable even today for its ageing, masculine and culturally homogenous political class. Here, too, President Sarkozy promised ambitious change. His first governments, for example, included ministers poached from opposing political parties. By way of conclusion, we review French political culture in the light of developments that have led some in France to call for a Sixth French Republic, although President Sarkozy has demonstrated himself to be firmly wedded to the Fifth.

French Political Culture

French political culture is often described as 'exceptional'. This characteristic revolves around the French Revolution, and '1789' is, indeed, the key to understanding the emphasis in contemporary French politics on events that happened over two centuries ago – specifically the transition from the *ancien régime* of absolute monarchy, to the Republic.

Republican Democracy

Republicanism is at the heart of French politics and national identity, and, in the contemporary French context, denotes a nation of sovereign citizens whose 'general will' is served by the French state, under the leadership of the French President. The original republican ideal of direct democracy, symbolized in 1793 by the execution of the monarch Louis XVI, is encapsulated in the slogan enshrined in the current French Constitution of 'government of the people, by the people and for the people'. During the Revolution itself, the leaders of the 'Terror' under the First Republic were the first to pervert these new democratic ideals into a zealous and totalitarian form of rule, and, over time, French republicanism in practice has come to mean parliamentary democracy, upon which in the Fifth Republic is grafted a dose of direct democracy in the form of recourse to referenda, tolerance for the protest of the 'street', and a directly-elected President (see Chapter 4). French republicanism is a consensual political doctrine, and to be genuinely anti-republican in contemporary France is to be in an invisible minority.

The 'Godless Revolution': The Secular State or la laïcité

The anti-clerical nature of the Revolution involved the sweeping away of the 'Divine right' of the monarchs of the *ancien régime* in the form of the execution of the King, and the desecration of the property of the Catholic Church. These events laid the basis for what is still, today, one of the fundamental characteristics of French Republican politics, *la laïcité*. This term is notoriously hard to render accurately into English, but can be taken to mean the absence of an established state religion (such as the UK's Church of England or, in the French case, the Roman Catholic Church); and the removal of the 'religious factor' (Madeley, 2006) in public life. In exchange, French citizens have the right to uphold any and every creed (with the exception of certain banned sects) in their private life, with some material support from the state (see Chapter 5). Article 1 of the 1958 Constitution states that France is a 'secular' Republic; this crucial dimension of French republicanism was given legal status in 1905 by a law separating Church and State. Secular state education subsequently became available to all children, and the overt display of religious beliefs is outlawed from French public life, including and especially in schools. A new law passed in 2004 bolstered the century-old legal provisions by forbidding 'conspicuous' signs of religious belief in schools. In the context of the international 'war on terror' of the first decade of the twenty-first century, debate on the legislation revolved almost exclusively around the headscarves worn by some young female Muslim pupils in state schools; legally, however, it applied to other religions equally, including Catholicism.

Neither the ground-breaking law of 1905 nor the 2004 edict have led to the disappearance of religious conflict in contemporary France, where the issue of accommodating religious and cultural diversity is a major political issue. In question is the role of the state in respecting human dignity and the freedom of expression (*liberté*, or personal freedom), while simultaneously upholding its constitutional duty to *égalité*, the equal treatment of all individuals, and to *fraternité*, or solidarity (or absence of tension and strife), in this case between diverse religions and their organizations.

Political Style

Styles of political action that characterize modern France find their roots in the revolutionary legacy. Direct action by the French against their rulers was already a means of protest under the *ancien régime*, but the French Revolution legitimized such methods, and institutionalized them by means of the republican credo of *popular* sovereignty. The anarchist movements of nineteenth century industrializing France compounded these radical tendencies, and key social advances of the twentieth century, for example in labour law, can be linked to organized, popular protest. In contemporary France, direct action in the form of strikes or mass demonstrations are still as much part of the political process as parliamentary debate, as is the recourse to impassioned political rhetoric and oratory, reminiscent of the revolutionary patriots. This language is often flowery and abstract-sounding to non-native French speakers, and fiendishly difficult to translate. When, in early 2006, the French government was forced to withdraw controversial labour legislation aimed at easing youth unemployment, the actions of the 'street' were directly responsible for overturning the will of parliament.

National Identity: Myths, Symbols and Reality

Thus, the 1789 French revolution lives on in contemporary France in a style and vocabulary of politics that prioritizes equality and fraternity between French citizens, and the primacy of the secular, rational French state. This is an approach to the past that somewhat ironically relies heavily on the use of symbols and myths to suggest an uninterrupted and undisputed political history, in order to bolster contemporary French political identity. These include quintessentially French icons such as the French tricolour flag; the mystical *Marianne*, the allegorical female face (and bust) of France (found on certain French stamps and Euro coins, for example); and the Republican motto, enshrined in the 1958 Constitution and engraved since the late nineteenth century on many public buildings, of *Liberté, Égalité, Fraternité* (Freedom, Equality, Fraternity), as seen in Illustration 3.1. Such symbols and myths from the past are an important dimension of present-day French politics, because they give the sense of an undisputed, and continuous, national political history designed to unify a nation proud of its achievements and pedigree.

However, the 200-plus-year-old history of French republicanism has been punctured on many occasions by other non-republican regimes, including empire in the nineteenth century, and dictatorship in the twentieth (see Table 3.1). These reactions against republicanism have left their trace in the present-day regime in the form of provisions for strong leadership, reduced parliamentary powers, and the propensity for 'direct action'.

The truth, therefore, is complicated, and the legacy of the Revolution itself has been open to dispute amongst historians for many decades. In today's France, politicians discover on a daily basis that putting 'freedom, equality and fraternity' into practice simultaneously is problematic, and often contradictory. Ensuring fraternity, or solidarity, between France's different ethnic populations has, in the early twenty-first century, raised the prospect of policies of positive discrimination (seen in Chapter 2) which, in theory at least, runs counter to the principle of 'equality' for all. Even monitoring for ethnic origins – for example, in the national population census, or in the field of employment and recruitment – is highly controversial in France, although acceptance is spreading gradually. The 2004 law that banned school children from wearing conspicuous signs of religious belief – such as the Muslim headscarf – appeared to some as

The French republican motto (*liberté, égalité, fraternité*) is clearly visible, and is as symbolic of contemporary France as the tricolour flag, the Peugeot lion, the car park sign (*parking*) and the Chinese restaurant on the same street

Illustration 3.1   Municipal building in the 18th *arrondissement* of Paris

Table 3.1   200-plus years of regime change

Absolute monarchy	Louis XVI	1774–1792
First Republic		1792–1804
First Empire	Napoleon I	1804–1814
Monarchy	The Restoration	1815–1830
Monarchy	The July Monarchy	1830–1848
Second Republic		1848–1852
Second Empire	Napoleon III	1852–1870
Third Republic		1870–1940
The French State	The Vichy regime	1940–1944
Provisional government		1944–1946
Fourth Republic		1946–1958
Fifth Republic		1958–present

Note: In July 1989, France celebrated the Bicentenary of French Republicanism.

prioritizing equality (of treatment) over personal freedom (liberty), and left many uncomfortable. Similarly, the law of 2000 that imposed 'parity' between men and women on political parties' shortlists of electoral candidates was opposed by prominent feminists who, on principle, rejected 'unequal' treatment (and the provision was routinely flouted by France's biggest parties, at the price of fines). The feminists' argument was that republican values, such as equality, are *universal* in nature – that is, applicable to all, without exception. As we saw in Chapter 5, the principle of differentiated treatment for France's regions (such as Corsica) is also controversial, and riddled with barriers to implementation.

The political problems of the present, it would appear, call for solutions that are new. Nostalgia for the past, moreover, creates unrealistic expectations of the present.

The End of 'French Exceptionalism'?

For some, such developments constitute the 'normalization' (*banalisation*) of French political life: gone are the ideological battles over the existence of the republic itself; gone, even, is a sense of clear choice between political right and political left, since parties from both sides of the political spectrum have adopted similar methods to solve shared problems, such as adaptation to the European Union. The challenges posed by domestic and international developments to France's identity as an exceptional 'model' of republican democracy have led some to claim that the 'French exception' is dead, and this thesis has both its supporters and its critics.

For supporters of the idea of the 'end of exceptionalism', the very notion of a unique political culture implies that change is inherently destabilizing (if we change, we will no longer be unique, and therefore we will lose our identity). In contrast, those generating or embracing the 'end of exceptionalism' thesis in the mid-1980s were driven, in the main, by a desire to see France adapt more readily and constructively to the challenges of the global economy, and to adopt the sorts of approaches to multiculturalism more common in other European liberal democracies such as the UK. The complexity of the match between France's traditional political traits, on the one hand, and its contemporary identity as a 'normal' EU pluralistic, liberal democracy, on the other, is a constant theme of French politics that, today, combines a strong respect for the past with many of the characteristics of liberal democracy shared by its European partners and neighbours.

French Political Parties in a 'Bipolar' Party System

In 2007, the French electorate was invited to cast its vote on no fewer than four occasions in the space of less than two months. On 22 April and 6 May 2007, the two rounds of the presidential contest were held, followed on 10 and 17 June by two rounds of legislative elections. These elections were contested in a very specific context characterized by rising abstentionism, support for parties, movements and causes such as the National Front, the Trotskyite Left, and Euroscepticism; *alternance*, or the changing of government majority at every legislative election since 1981; and street protest and violence (such as the urban riots of October–November 2005, and the youth protests against reform of employment law) in the face of a seemingly powerless political class.

Notably, the presidential election of 2002 had suggested a party system in crisis, failing to supply credible candidates, or to ensure viable political alliances between parties, and generating voter distrust in the process; this was widely referred to at the time as a 'crisis' of political representation; and, in 2010, polls suggested nearly 70% of the French mistrusted their politicians. In 2002, the candidates of the main parties on left and right – the incumbent Prime Minister (Lionel Jospin) and President (Jacques Chirac), respectively – had polled extremely badly (16% and 19%, respectively), drained of popular support by contestants from smaller movements to their left and right (one quarter of votes in the first round in 2002 were cast for candidates who won less than 5% of the vote). Prime Minister Jospin of the Socialist Party did not even win his way through to the second round of voting, making way instead for Jean-Marie le Pen, leader of the French far right, who was subsequently beaten in the second round by President Chirac by a preposterous 82% of the votes. Abstentionism at 30% was also unprecedently high, as was the proportion of spoilt ballot papers, at nearly 4%. By way of comparison, in the first presidential election in 1965, the first-round winners, President de Gaulle and François Mitterrand, polled 76% of the votes between them.

The outcome of the 2007 elections was in stark contrast to this backdrop, leading to claims that the cycle of negative and destructive voting behaviour had been broken, and that party politics had become rational again. For the first time in nearly thirty years, the French electorate returned a sitting majority party, the UMP (Union for a Popular Movement – *Union pour un mouvement populaire* – by then, taken over by Nicolas Sarkozy); it voted in very high numbers (a turnout of 84% at both rounds of the presidential contest), underlining the underlying appetite in contemporary France for political engagement; it concentrated its votes in the first round of the presidential contest on the contenders from the two main French parties, ensuring a left–right contest in the second and final round; and in that vote, it returned a decisive victory for Nicolas Sarkozy of the UMP.

Table 3.2   France's main party political players

Party label	Comment
UMP	**Centre-right**. In power in the presidency, government and National Assembly. Successor party to the Gaullists.
PS	**Socialist party**. Divided over its core principals and its leadership. Holds all but one of France's 22 mainland regions.
FN	**National Front party** led by Jean-Marie le Pen. Not merely a protest party. No seats in National Assembly; 3 seats in 2009 European Parliament legislature, and a strong vote (over 11%) in the regional elections of 2010, translating into the election of a total of 118 (out of 1880) regional councillors.
UDF	**A federation of centrist parties** formed by former President Valéry Giscard d'Estaing in the 1970s. In the National Assembly (2007), split between *MoDem* (Mouvement Démocrate) under the leadership of François Bayrou, and *Nouveau Centre,* part of the government's parliamentary majority.
PCF	France's once-powerful **Communist party**. Through alliances, has representation (4 seats in European Parliament; 15 in National Assembly).
NPA	**Anti-capitalist party** formed in 2009 by its leader, postman Olivier Besancenot. Besancenot fights presidential elections (score of around 4% in 2002 and 2007).
Europe-Ecologie	**Grouping of green parties** under leadership of 1968 rebel Dany Cohn-Bendit. Formed for and did well in 2009 European Parliament elections (14 seats and 16% of the votes) and the 2010 regional elections (262 out of 1880 regional councillors).

In the ensuing legislative elections, the French electorate voted in an absolute majority of UMP deputies, sealing the new French President's institutional power.

The 2007 elections, therefore, suggested that French party politics and French voting behaviour had obeyed the logic of party and electoral politics in the Fifth French Republic, designed to produce a 'bipolar' contest between political alliances on the left and right, where the alliances – or 'poles' – accommodate France's multiparty tradition, but funnel it into workable political majorities. The 2007 results also suggested that French political parties *were* fulfilling their representative role. A closer look at French political parties, voters and key political issues, however, allows us to challenge this picture of contemporary French politics.

Winners and Losers on the French Right

The 2007 elections marked a significant achievement for the main party on the French right, the UMP. Formed in haste after the presidential elections of April/May 2002 by former Prime Minister Alain Juppé in order to beat le Pen in the second round of the presidential election, and to contest the June legislative elections of that year, this successor to the RPR (Rally for the Republic – *Rassemblement pour la République*), in the very unusual circumstances of the 2002 election aftermath, found itself able to unify much of what previously had been a rather fragmented centre-right ground. Thus, not only did the party win an absolute majority of parliamentary seats in June 2002, it was able to replicate this success in 2007, when its candidate, Nicolas Sarkozy, also won both first and second presidential rounds with strong scores (see Table 3.2).

This was a important development for a party that had grown out of the Gaullist movement, and had uneasily accommodated or co-existed with the numerous traditional 'families' of the French right, ranging from liberals to authoritarian and nationalist movements towards the far right of the spectrum.

The Gaullists: From the RPR to the UMP

President de Gaulle relied primarily on the support of the majority of the French nation, which he tested in a succession of referendums, rather than on a single party, and he resigned when he lost his fifth plebiscite in 1969. His supporters organized themselves into 'rallies' and 'unions' dedicated to defending the new Republic and de Gaulle's vision of a restored French identity and unity (and the UMP's title today – a *Union* – pays homage to these roots). Party organization was secondary to these aims; indeed, de Gaulle blamed the party politics of the Fourth Republic for rendering the National Assembly incapable of producing durable government majorities, and the Gaullists consequently defied classification. Their politics were the restoration of France as an independent global player via a strong currency, economy and image.

The 1965 presidential election, in which de Gaulle had to fight a second-round contest against François Mitterrand (subsequently leader of the left), demonstrated that even a 'great' leader such as de Gaulle required some sort of party machinery (known as an *appareil*) in order to mobilize the electorate. For de Gaulle's successors, the need for a supportive party was even more pressing, since they could not, by definition, rely on de Gaulle's unique aura and authority for the votes of the French. On the death in 1974 of Georges Pompidou, de Gaulle's immediate successor, and the election as President of a centrist, liberal, Atlanticist politician, Giscard d'Estaing, an ambitious Jacques Chirac reformed the Gaullist movement into its most organized structure yet under the name of the RPR. Its members sought to differentiate themselves from Giscard's supporters – the Independent Republicans – by a shift to a more independent – Gaullist – foreign policy line, and an emphasis on the traditional economic statism of Gaullist politics. The uneasy relationship between the RPR and Giscard's later new federation, the UDF (Union for French Democracy – *Union pour la démocratie française*) was a contributory factor to the defeat of the right in the 1981 elections in favour of the French left.

Under Chirac's leadership during the 1980s, the RPR nevertheless began to look more like other west European conservative parties, with an emphasis on free-market economics, and attempts to oppose and curb the social liberalism of the ruling French left; this was, in a specific economic context, characterized by France's commitment by the mid-1980s to the EC's goal of completing the single European market by 1993 (see Chapter 7).

Nevertheless, 'Europe', the market economy, and matters of society continued to hamper unity within the RPR, and made it vulnerable to splinter groups, and to completely new political opponents.

Jean-Marie le Pen and the National Front

One of the unique characteristics of the French political right is, indeed, the existence of a far-right movement in the shape of the National Front under the leadership of Jean-Marie le Pen. This movement was largely dormant in the Fifth Republic until the 1980s, but its roots can be traced back to the anti-Semitic, authoritarian and militaristic ideas and groups of the early twentieth century, and to Petain's Vichy regime of the '*État français*' (French state) intended to turn the clock back on republicanism to a mythical time of the traditional values of '*travail, famille, patrie*' – work, family and country (see Chapter 1). Today's National Front, therefore, has long intellectual and political roots that have, to an extent, tapped into latent fears of moral decline, social *anomie*, and the cultural irrelevance of France on the world scale. Le Pen himself, moreover, developed into a startlingly effective, indefatigable, rally-style political leader capable of rousing, manipulative political rhetoric.

Despite the National Front's internal problems (which in 1998 led to a break away in the form of the MNR (National Republican Movement – *Mouvement national républicain*) led by le Pen's former lieutenant, Bruno Mégret), and the party's ever-shifting ideological stance and policy positions, (which makes it very hard to classify by traditional labels such as populist, radical or extreme), the French National Front rose to political prominence from the early 1980s to the point where, by the 1997 legislative elections, it could legitimately be described as France's third biggest political force (Shields, 2007) after the UMP and the Socialist Party, and the second biggest component on the political right, ahead of the UDF.

The political context that established itself from the 1980s onwards was an important contributory factor to le Pen's rise. This included, in particular, the tepid or inept opposition of the mainstream right to key policies of the left at the time, including its commitment to European integration; and its social liberalism (the end of the death penalty, a softer immigration policy environment, the tolerance of cultural differences, the promotion of cultural diversity, and the fight against racism). This setting provided the FN with an opportunity, apparently, to offer a genuine alternative to mainstream wisdom. The repeated occurrence of cohabitation (a President and Prime Minister from rival political parties, with the President opposed by the parliamentary majority) between left and right (1986–88, 1993–95, 1997–2002) only provided further scope for le

Pen to depict the mainstream left and right as converging around a centre ground of politics designed, in his terms, to drag France into a multicultural, globalized mire. The decline of the French Communist Party (*le Parti communiste français* – PCF) at this time, and the failure of other new entrants to the political game (such as the ecologists) to organize sustained opposition to the traditional left–right politics (of the 'Big Four', as le Pen called the PS, the PCF, the RPR and the UDF) was grist to the mill of a talented leader and orator such as le Pen who, at a time of rising unemployment, played shamelessly on people's fears for their jobs, their neighbourhood, their safety, their identity, even their life.

During this period, the FN succeeded in influencing the political agenda in matters not only of immigration and cultural identity, but also, albeit to a lesser extent, regarding France in Europe, and the economy. The rules of the VR political game kept le Pen away from power at the national level, since neither the RPR nor UDF were prepared to treat the FN as a constant ally (with some aberrant exceptions at local and regional levels). The party's electoral successes were limited to those contests fought under full or partial proportional representation (European elections, regional elections) and to a handful of municipal victories in its stronghold in the south-east of France (in the mid–late 1990s, four towns were controlled by the FN). In addition, le Pen polled between 10% and 20% in the presidential elections of 1988, 1995, 2002 and 2007 – representing approximately four million French voters. The nationwide implantation of the FN and the strength of its electoral support, however dispersed, ensured that, in the 1997 legislatives, it was able to maintain candidates in many second-round contests alongside the mainstream left–right opponents (so-called *triangulaire* contests), a fact that split the right-wing vote and contributed to the unexpected success of the left in those elections. These achievements brought le Pen and the party visibility and, just as important, resources in the form of broadcast airtime, and media attention in general, public funding (at national and European Parliament level), and the opportunity at local level to try out its policy of *la préférence nationale* – the preferential treatment of 'native' French people regarding welfare and other benefits.

In comparative terms, the FN's core voters are ambivalent about the party's more extreme nationalism and racist excesses, and the prospect of him becoming President in the 2002 elections was one step too far. The FN has conclusively exerted influence over the

French party system and party politics itself but in the current political system its prospects are uncertain, particularly in view of the apparent unity of the UMP at the end of the first decade of the twenty-first century, and the sustained significance, for voting behaviour, of issues on which le Pen's discourse was least convincing,

Illustration 3.2   Regional election posters, Paris 2010

particularly the EU and the role of the state in the global market economy.

'Sovereignists', Centrists and Liberals

The 1992 referendum in France, in which the electorate was asked to accept or reject the terms of the EU's Maastricht Treaty (see Chapters 7 and 8), constituted an opportunity for a certain strand of thinking on the right in France to express itself forcefully. The so-called 'sovereignists', led by RPR heavyweight Philippe Séguin, argued that the Treaty eroded the French republican notion of national sovereignty on at least two accounts: the Treaty created 'European citizens' with voting rights in other EU member states, so detaching citizenship from nationality; and it involved a transfer of powers from Paris to Brussels in monetary policy, in preparation for the introduction of the single European currency in 2002. Their arguments were eloquent and, although the RPR's leader, Jacques Chirac, voted in favour of the treaty (his ambition to be President trumping his 1970s' Gaullist opposition to European integration), he did not exhort his party to do the same. The centre–right split on the issue and the referendum was barely won (by 51% of the votes), 'sovereignism' having its supporters on the left as well.

Subsequently, a sovereignist rump broke away from the RPR to contest the 1999 European Parliament elections, and the climate encouraged similar-minded individuals such as Philippe de Villiers to break away from the pro-European UDF and campaign, henceforth, on a very narrow anti-European, anti-immigration and anti-Islam platform. In this way, the 1990s were problematic for the RPR, which could not speak for all of its leading figures, let alone electorate, on a matter as important as France's future role and influence in the European Union.

Simultaneously, the RPR, seeking dominance within its camp, or 'pole', had to find a way to coexist with so-called market liberals such as Alain Madelin's *Démocratie libérale* members. These people thought and behaved more like European conservatives in their desire to cut back the French state in favour of a more open and free market economy. Another group, centrists, was led by François Bayrou, heir to France's Fourth Republican Christian Democratic tradition. Bayrou represents a conviction that the centre ground of French politics could lead an autonomous existence. His alliance with the RPR, in and out of government, was conditional at best, fractious at worst. By 2007, neither the liberals nor the centrists had succeeded in establishing a strong electoral presence outside an alliance with the UMP, leaving the UMP dominant in a – by definition – unbalanced 'pole' on the right, leaving French politics at this end of the spectrum at this point looking more 'bipartisan' than 'bipolar'. The politics of the French left, on the other hand was, in 2007, far from a mirror image, making for an unbalanced left–right divide.

Identity Politics and the French Left

Where Gaullism has shaped the identity of the contemporary French right, so Communism has been a key factor determining the state of the French left in contemporary France. During the course of the Fifth Republic, today's biggest party on the French left, the Socialist Party (PS – *le Parti socialiste*) has been tied both ideologically and systemically, via electoral alliances, to the fortunes of the French Communist Party. The dramatic electoral decline of the PCF in the first decade of the twenty-first century, combined with the difficulties experienced by the PS leadership in settling on a doctrinal direction for the contemporary era; and the fragmented nature of other political movements on the French left, has diminished the appeal and success of the French left as an electoral force, in an electorate that in the post-Cold War years has shown a gradual but definite shift to the right, together with its tendencies to vote against mainstream parties of government, or to abstain altogether.

Socialism and Communism à la française

French Socialism and Communism first took shape in the early twentieth century in response to domestic industrialization and the communist revolutions in the first decades of that century in Russia. The two movements split in 1920 over their differences regarding the Bolshevik revolution and their own willingness to work within the electoral politics of the Third Republic. The experience of World War II was crucial in lending the PCF a form of credibility in response to the active part played (or claimed to have been played) by many Communist party members in the resistance of the Free French to the German occupier. Relations between de Gaulle and the PCF however, then, as in the VR during the Cold War, were undermined by de Gaulle's suspicion of the PCF as a Soviet satellite (the party did not ever explicitly convert to 'Eurocommunism') and by the PCF's hatred of a regime and President who they branded as dictatorial, and the Communists' rejection of the emerging mass consumer, capitalist society. Yet, the PCF was a stronger party than the Socialists for much of the Fourth and Fifth Republics, in part due to stringent internal party discipline and widespread nostalgia for their revolutionary message – in particular, regarding the sharper edges of the capitalist economy.

The Socialists' fortunes were revived at the start of the 1970s by the arrival of François Mitterrand. Under Mitterrand's leadership, in 1981 the PS was able to win the presidency from the political right, and to win presidential majorities for all but four of Mitterrand's 14 years as presidency, which lent him and the PS considerable authority and power. Mitterrand's success in gaining power was due in no small part to the tactical deals he made with the PCF; these ranged from an uneasy 'common programme of government' in the 1970s to including Communist ministers in his government from 1981–88. Socialist Party Prime Minister Lionel Jospin, from 1997–2002, similarly brought Communist leaders into his *gauche plurielle* – a 'pluralist' left alliance. But Mitterrand's biggest triumph was to persuade the Communist and Socialist constituencies in the French population that he, Mitterrand, was the single leader of the left; and that Communist followers' only chance of representation in the republic was to vote for him as President.

Mitterrand's victory came at a high cost for the PCF and, ultimately, for the PS itself. In this way, he compounded the decline of the PCF arising from factors external to France, especially the ending of the Cold War in the late 1980s, and from internal problems such as the party's reluctance or inability to update its ideology. In distinction to the PCF's maintenance of its original ideological principles, the PS under Mitterrand's leadership underwent significant ideological change. After a largely failed 'Socialist experiment' from 1981–83 (see Chapter 1), Mitterrand pinned his political survival and career on adapting French socialism, and France, to new rules, especially those of the expanding and deepening European Economic Community, as it then was. By 2003, this course had led to crushing defeat.

In the 2007 presidential election, the candidate for the PS was not even the party's leader, François Hollande, but his partner-in-life (they split after the elections), Ségolène Royal. This was a candidate who squarely won the party's primary for the nomination, and also embodied change by virtue of her age, gender, interest in participative democracy and, paradoxically, her lack of roots and experience within the party. That factor meant that she was less divisive of the party leadership than the other heavyweights, in particular former Prime Minister Laurent Fabuis. But this was a short-term strategy that, in 2007, failed to convince the electorate in sufficient numbers and so, for the third consecutive presidential election, the PS, France's second largest party, was unable sufficiently to overcome its internal identity crisis to swing France back from right to left.

The questions of doctrine that continued to plague the French Socialist Party in the early twenty-first century revolved principally around what is called the 'French social model', referring to the relationship between state and market in delivering social goods (health, welfare); regulating the economy; and redistributing resources in accordance with the republican principles of, specifically, equality and fraternity (see Chapter 7). This is a debate that occurred in the broader context of a globalizing world economy and the striking of a balance, at this level, between 'rampant' capitalism on the one hand, and regulatory bodies, at state and international level, on the other. This was a playing field where the PCF rejected compromise, its identity revolving as late as 2008 around a 'break' (*rupture*) with capitalism, and where the PS had, in practice, moved far away from the similar *rupture* that Mitterrand promised in 1981, now to embrace and foster most aspects of a deregulated, Europeanized and globalized economy in which the role of the state was limited.

The PS itself was divided on such matters. Former Socialist Party Prime Minister Laurent Fabius went so far as to campaign against the EU's Constitutional treaty, and thereby against his party line, in France's 2005 referendum. By aligning himself with the 'no' vote, Fabius was part of the resounding defeat of the government's and President's position in favour of the treaty. This 'no' turned on a diffuse set of demands and fears within the French electorate regarding the EU's faltering role in taming the excesses of globalization. Certain of these concerns were represented by, and representative of, other partners and forces that comprise the contemporary French left.

The Far Left

The level of support for political formations to the far left of the PS was at its highest in the 2002 presidential elections, when far-left candidates attracted between them over 10% of the votes that might otherwise have gone to the PS candidate, incumbent Prime Minister

Lionel Jospin, and which thus cost him a place in the second round of those elections. Some are movements and personalities with a long life in the VR; Arlette Laguiller, for example, leader of the *Lutte ouvrière* (LO – Workers' Struggle) stood in every presidential election since 1981 until her retirement from politics after the 2007 presidential vote. Olivier Besancenot emerged in the 2000s, leading the *Ligue revolutionnaire communiste* (LCR – Communist revolutionary league). In 2009, Besancenot renamed the LCR as the *Nouveau Parti anticapitaliste* (NPA – New Anti-capitalist Party), thus removing all mention of 'communism' from its title in the hope of broadening its appeal. The NPA's message revolved around the sort of challenge to France's Europeanized, globalized economy that, formerly, the PCF would have articulated on behalf of, principally, those implacably opposed to the opening of national trade borders, and deeply committed to challenging the domination of capital over labour. Unlike the FN, the electorate for these movements is very small; like the FN they are kept away from political power by the system's play of majoritarian elections and electoral alliances; they are also fragmented, rejecting any systematic alliance on this end of the political spectrum. Neither has the far left, to date, proved that it has the agenda-setting capacity of the FN on the right, in that the policy of successive governments, of left and right, towards the EU in particular and the globalized economy in general, has not been deflected or even inflected. They do, however, have high visibility and the capacity to mobilize popular protest.

In contemporary France, as elsewhere in Europe (and the developed world more generally), 'post-materialist' values have emerged to influence voter behaviour alongside more traditional factors such as class, religion and gender; these latter are cleavages whose salience holds for a decreasing proportion of the French electorate, although they are far from defunct. Age, in particular, showed itself to be a determinant of voting behaviour in the 2007 presidential election, when the majority of the post-Cold War generation, voting in 2007 for the first time, cast its votes for Royal, with Sarkozy the favourite of those aged 35 and over, and particularly popular amongst pensioners.

Post-materialism implies a set of demands and behaviours oriented away from the satisfying of individual needs and interests and towards collective efforts bent on improving society and the world at large. It encompasses causes ranging from interventionist humanitarianism to more diffuse concerns of environmental protection, and the protection of cultural and ethnic difference in human rights regimes at home and abroad. These are just some of the problems of French politics in the current day.

French Politics and Twenty-First-Century Problems

Within the left–right divide, therefore, French politics offers a multiplicity of political groups, movements and parties that are structured in their competition and in their representative function by the rules of the political game of the Fifth Republic (electoral, funding, broadcasting), intended to produce stable governmental majorities, and to encourage left–right differentiation. The rules both encourage small groups to label themselves as parties – thereby ensuring some access, for example, to public funding (such as the case of the CPNT in the 1990s and 2000s: the movement for the defence of Hunting, Fishing, Nature, and Tradition, a group campaigning for the preservation of rural tradition) – and to deprive them of the opportunity to represent their electorate unless part of a larger electoral alliance *and* sufficiently concentrated geographically.

The 2002 elections suggested that a point of 'crisis' had been reached, represented by signs of a rejection of the political process *per se*, and of the parties of government, of left and right, in particular. Five years later, the 2007 electoral results suggested the contrary. These developments and processes can more accurately be seen to indicate broader and deeper issues of liberal democracy to which France is not immune, revolving around the questions of the legitimacy and credibility of 'politics as usual'.

Thus, we have seen that the traditional left–right divide in French politics can no longer contain or adequately represent issues at the heart of French national identity. Of particular note are that:

- the question of European integration remains problematic for all party players;
- French people have repeatedly expressed their distrust and dissatisfaction with their leaders in opinion polls and at election times, and their sense of distance from the political elite;
- the *alternance* of 1978–2007, combined with nine years of political cohabitation between 1986 and 2002, brought relatively little political change, in comparison to hopes and expectations, particularly of the left in the 1980s;

- the class cleavage that structured French political competition for much of the twentieth century has, in France as elsewhere, been diminished by the rise of the salaried middle classes, growing individualism, and the decline of the blue-collar electorate;
- geographical mobility has blurred the relevance of geographical location as a key determinant of voting behaviour;
- the decline in religious practice has also undermined a traditional determinant of French electoral sociology.

To these developments, we can add more spontaneous and unpredictable developments arising from social and technological change. Thus, the rise in the twenty-first century of digital, interactive media has created new opportunities for citizens to take political action and exert influence. The 'no' campaign in the 2005 referendum, for example, was characterized by an effective use of interactive media such as blogs and chat rooms, and this was a development positively welcomed and promoted by PS presidential candidate Ségolène Royal in 2007, but to limited effect. Over and above their effectiveness as political tools for politicians is the fact that such interactivity has created new demands for participatory politics, which, in turn, has the inevitable effect of challenging the social hierarchies that characterized twentieth century French society and in which the political class was a distant elite. Virtual worlds such as 'Second Life' offer the electorate, but also politicians, the opportunity to break down the codes of traditional hierarchical deference, contributing to an irreversible evolution of French political culture.

Grass Roots

This is a political climate, moreover, that lends itself to the activities of France's vibrant *vie associative* (seen in Chapter 4), and other groups organizing high-profile action around specific issues and campaigns. Thus, the 1980s saw significant social movements organizing against racism (*Touche pas à mon pote*) and poverty (Colluche's *Restaurants du Coeur* – soup kitchens). The 1990s and 2000s saw particularly tenacious and well-organized campaigns against homelessness (*Les Enfants de Don Quichotte*) and the expulsion of illegal immigrants and their children (in 2006, *le Réseau autogéré Education sans frontières* (RESF)); and, in the lead-up to the 2007 presidential campaign, various groups set out to mobilize new voters to register on electoral lists and inform themselves appropriately; all with a view to preventing a re-run of 2002's second-round appearance of Le Pen.

The Environment

In the case of the *environmental* factor, the French green movement is characterized by its small size and influence, certainly in comparison with its German counterparts. From their early days in the 1960s as protestors against France's vast nuclear energy programme and in opposition to France's land-based nuclear missiles, and via attempts in the 1980s to challenge the very relevance of the left–right character of political combat (and which led to a succession of splits within the movement), today's French Greens are predominantly to be found operating as reliable allies to the French Socialist party, to the extent that the Greens won ministerial positions in Prime Minister Jospin's government between 1997–2002, and enjoy representation in the French National Assembly. In 2009, a new arrangement of green forces, *Europe-Ecologie*, did surprisingly well in the European Parliament elections. Moreover, 'the environment' as a political issue has been incorporated into the French constitution itself in the form of a 'Charter for the Environment' (as seen in Chapter 2). In the 2007 presidential elections, a well-known French television presenter, Nicolas Hulot, placed pressure on the front runner candidates by asking them to sign an 'ecological pact', or face the prospect of him running as presidential candidate himself.

Euroscepticism and 'Alter-Globalization'

The question of France's commitment to European integration and its role in shaping global rules of trade, aid, defence and development has grown in salience to occupy a very visible and vocal place in French political life. Yet, it is also of rather limited electoral impact, certainly at the level of presidential and legislative contests. Simply put, it is politically fashionable and expedient for France's leading politicians to maintain a discourse that is critical of the process whereby nation-states are capped in their ability to alter and shape global flows, particularly when and because these flows affect domestic lives – and political chances and ambitions. Thus, Nicolas Sarkozy, in his victory speech on 6 May 2007, declared that he would work to ensure that French people were 'protected' from undue global forces. He subsequently challenged the notion that 'undistorted competition' is a founding principle of the European Union (which it is and has been since 1957), claiming that the EU had fallen prey to the 'dogma' of the competitive market to the detriment of aspects of the 'social model' that France aims to practise at home and to upload to the European level.

The relationship between France and the European Union, and between the EU and what we can term in shorthand as globalization, proved to be at the heart of the French political landscape in the first decade of the twenty-first century, and spilled out of the left–right divide. For decades accustomed to believe that the EU was a stage for French interests to play themselves out further afield and to preserve the integrity of a 'European' way of life, in distinction to an imagined 'Anglo-Saxon' socio-economic model, the French electorate in the 2005 referendum on the EU's Constitutional Treaty demonstrated a loss of faith in the capacity of either the French state or the EU to exert influence on the shape of the global market, or to attenuate its negative consequences for workers unable or unwilling to take up the opportunities afforded by an open world for personal mobility, for example.

Where 'Europe' had habitually been presented to the French by their politicians as the answer to – a form of protection against – globalizing markets and culture, and although the levels of support in the French public for France's central role in *la construction européenne* were still relatively high, the French deplored its weak-nesses, and expressed increasing fears about the capacity of the French state to direct its orientation. Anti-globalization gained visi-bility through French figures such as José Bové, a farmer-lawyer who risked prison to demonstrate and resist what he saw were threats to the French way of life (agriculture) and culture (from the Americanization of markets); indeed, such anti-globalization pres-sure, also articulated by the pressure group ATTAC, was frequently channelled into anti-US sentiment or reasoning. Bové argued for 'alter-globalization': the alteration of the terms of global trade in food, culture, goods and capital. Within the politics of the left, the former government minister Jean-Pierre Chevènement for two decades represented a Eurosceptic current to the left of the Socialist Party, arguing in terms of defending France's republican identity and independence; by 1997, Chevènement was prepared to serve in Jospin's 'plural left' government; and, ten years later, declared his support for Royal's presidential campaign for the PS.

Scandal and Corruption

Alongside these developments, French democracy has numerous and significant blind spots. France is notorious for the tight, interlocking relationships that exist between its leading elites in many layers of French society: politics, administration, business, education, the media and so on. The traditional media, to the present day, is overly-deferential to the political class, lacks the investigative teeth of its counterparts in other western democracies, and is constrained by strict privacy legislation. The reach of the French state is also part of this phenomenon through patronage; and many of the elites are trained at the same exclusive set of higher educational establishments (*les grandes écoles* – see Chapter 5) where they develop fierce loyalties and a shared outlook, particularly with those who share their political beliefs.

Widespread and large scale corruption has been one of the consequences of these characteristics and, as elsewhere in Europe, these aspects of politics have undermined trust in the system and the credibility of its leaders. They have also fuelled Jean Marie le Pen's rage against the established parties. 'New' media of a more investigative type than was traditional have exacerbated these trends, gradually eroding any notion that high-ranking public figures are somehow above the law, that financial corruption is not a crime, or that the proximity of French elites across the establishment hampers transparency in the democratic process.

Money, Mistresses and Lies

The case of François Mitterrand's undeclared terminal illness is a case in point here, not to mention his long-standing relationship with mistress Anne Pingeot and their daughter, Mazarine: both cases were open secrets kept by a press in the know from the general public in the dark (see Chapter 2). Furthermore, Mitterrand was discovered to have fostered a culture of secrecy in which wire-tapping and covert intelligence operations were routine. The Rainbow Warrior case was infamous in these respects. In 1985, a Greenpeace ship, the *Rainbow Warrior*, was sunk in Auckland, New Zealand as it readied itself to protest against French nuclear testing in the region. One photographer lost his life in the incident. Subsequently, it emerged that French secret agents were behind the sabotage, and that President Mitterrand had most likely approved the operation. Accusations of this order extended to his family members: Jean-Christophe Mitterrand, the

President's eldest son and Africa advisor, was accused of involvement in illegal arms deals in Angola.

Mitterrand's personal and state secrets were not the only scandals to emerge from the last decades of the twentieth century in France. Many instances of financial corruption – such as insider dealing and lack of disclosure inside major, state-owned financial institutions (the case of the bank, Crédit Lyonnais) – and illicit party funding across the party political spectrum also came to light during these years. Jacques Chirac became notorious whilst still President for, earlier, allegedly corrupt dealings designed to enrich his party (the RPR) and to enhance his own chances of success in the 1995 presidential election. These all related to his lengthy service as Mayor of Paris (1977–95). Immune from questioning whilst in office as President of the Republic, he was subsequently investigated over a range of activities by which he was alleged to have made money for the RPR (fake jobs at his Paris headquarters, the *hôtel de ville*; kickbacks from works contracts and the like) as Paris mayor. These accusations did not turn on personal enrichment, although the Chiracs were known to have spent lavishly whilst in power in Paris and also, later, in the presidential Elysée Palace.

Just as notorious, in the late 1990s, Roland Dumas was tried and found guilty of large-scale corruption, but subsequently cleared of all charges. Dumas was a very prominent political figure of the Mitterrand years. Between 1988 and 1995 he had been François Mitterrand's Foreign Minister; and from 1995–2000 – until his trial, in fact – he was President of France's highest legal authority – the Constitutional Council (see Chapter 4). The case related to Dumas' role, a decade earlier, in accepting cash bribes from France's then state-owned Elf-Aquitaine oil company in the context of controversial arms deals involving Elf; Elf was also accused of having a vast slush fund for just such eventualities. Dumas's mistress at the time, Christine Deviers-Joncours, was deployed as a conduit for some of the money that was explicitly to be spent on entertaining Dumas in style. In the trial and in print, she memorably labelled herself the 'whore of the Republic'.

Investigating Crime: The Judges and the Judiciary

The Dumas and Chirac cases, each assisted by a media agog with such colourful news, brought into the limelight the limitations of France's judicial system, and the controversial role of the institution known as the 'investigating magistrate' (or judge). The French judiciary, defined in the Constitution as an 'authority' rather than as a branch of government in its own right, is known to be subject to greater political control than in comparable west European countries, and is weak in comparison to the executive branch of government. The judiciary, for example, does not have a role to play in matters of state; that is the remit of a dual system of administrative justice (see Chapter 4). Historically speaking, moreover, judicial power has been held in deep suspicion by kings, dictators and presidents alike. There is no tradition of jurisprudence, case law or judicial review, and investigators have found themselves accused, within the political establishment, of waging politically motivated crusades in celebrity style to uncover 'the truth'. Some have even been blocked in their efforts to bring high-profile individuals to court.

Indeed, the French system of civil and criminal justice is based upon the inquisitorial principle whereby the 'truth' is discovered by means of 'logical' investigation, and the results presented in court to a presiding judge who exercises considerable discretion. In this system, the presumption of innocence is weak, and the opportunities to present the case for the defence, structurally limited. Cases are prosecuted by lawyers (the *procureur*) appointed by the state (by the Ministry of Justice), but the investigations themselves are conducted by independent judges – the *juge d'instruction*. This institution is something of an anomaly in legal terms, in that the *juge* is asked to collect, interpret and present the evidence as part of the process of bringing a case to trial. Indeed, the Dumas and Chirac cases became known for the zeal with which the investigating judges constructed their cases and pursued their prey. Eva Joly, in the case of the Dumas trial, and Eric Halphen in Chirac's, found themselves subject to intense scrutiny, and subsequently left the profession. Joly was a particular *cause célèbre* by virtue of being a woman, foreign-born (Norwegian) and lacking any natural deference to (male) authority.

Corruption in French politics persists despite the investigating judges – whose very existence has come under threat of abolition during Sarkozy's presidency – and despite the 'intrusion' of the popular media. President Sarkozy has not been above suspicion, and members of his government had to resign in 2010 when their lavish expense accounts were brought to light. Sarkozy himself was directly implicated in a complex scandal in 2009 known as the 'Clearstream' affair. The most prominent aspect of this case involved alleged smears against Sarkozy made by a political rival, former Prime

Minister Dominique de Villepin, against the backdrop of arms deals dating back to the 1990s and kickbacks in hidden bank accounts. De Villepin was cleared of all charges of smears and conspiracy, but remained a bitter political rival of the President despite occupying the same political camp. In all these respects, France is far from alone in Europe. These structural weaknesses undermine the government's effectiveness in dealing with one of its most prominent agendas in the present day: law and order.

Security and Insecurity: The Politics of Law and Order

In twenty-first century France, security has risen to the top of the political agenda. The context is complex, and not limited to France. Internationally, the 'war on terror' has stigmatized Islamic and Muslim communities throughout the west. In Europe, governments and the EU itself have proved themselves incapable of preventing terrorist atrocities – in London, in Madrid – perpetrated by 'home-grown' Islamic terrorists. In France, public policy problems of deprivation and disorder in outer city environments known as *la banlieue* (suburbs) have created an ever more repressive law and order regime.

La banlieue – The Suburbs
The term '*la banlieue*' has become synonymous in France with urban and outer-city strife in a context of social and economic deprivation and high concentrations of ethnic minority populations. The literal meaning of the term suggests banishment outside city limits, to the wrong side of the tracks, and, in real life, these are typically (but not exclusively) areas of high-rise social housing, typified by a concentration of ethnic minority populations and extremely high unemployment. In some cases, gang culture is rife, the violent intimidation of women is proven, and particular *cités* – housing projects – have become no-go zones for the police. The 1995 acclaimed film *la Haine (Hate)* portrayed these facts of life in particularly grim and pessimistic detail at a time of notorious uprisings in *banlieues* outside Paris and also France's second largest city, Lyon.

In this context, and as Minister of the Interior in 2002–04 and 2005–07, Nicolas Sarkozy had already gained notoriety for his plain, often crude-speaking tactics, and for a series of policies seeking to reassure the public that the government was capable of imposing law and order across its own territory. In particular, he drew a link between immigration followed by faulty integration into society on the one hand, and law and order on the other, as expressed in Sarkozy's 2006 sound bite, 'love France, or leave it'. This connection, sensationalized by most media, had come to light in the 2002 presidential and legislative elections when le Pen and his party had done better than ever on an ultra-nationalist platform.

These were developments that set in train a series of tough immigration laws alongside measures designed to stigmatize and penalize those deemed guilty of poorly integrating into French society (see also Chapters 2 and 5). The extremely serious riots of autumn 2005 in *banlieues* across France, sparked by the electrocution of two French youths fleeing the police in the Paris suburb of Clichy-sous-Bois (not that they had committed a crime but, rather, feared an identity check and its possible repercussions), suggested that such policies had missed the point. Public policy failures across the board were subsequently found to have incited the violence that followed the Clichy incident, and gripped and shook the whole of France (tens of thousands of cars were burned, at least) for over a month. By far, the majority of the protagonists were found to have been motivated by frustrations bred by failures to fit into French society, and not a rejection of France on extremist or separatist grounds, religious or other.

But, as President, there was no toning down of the language, and no reprieve for the principal targets of Sarkozy's security crackdown. These, primarily, were (illegal) immigrants, foreign-born, naturalized French citizens deemed to be acting unpatriotically, French citizens deemed guilty of un-Republican behaviour (such as wearing the full Islamic face veil in public); and young offenders – branded as delinquents – from France's *banlieues*. The measures included curfews for those aged under 13 years, the extension of CCTV surveillance equipment throughout France's, stiff penalties for 'outrage' committed against the French flag, and the gradual tightening of immigration policy, as seen in Chapter 2.

Added to a domestic environment in which relations between society and the police are notoriously poor – where France's police forces will not escape the public sector cost-cutting measures associated with Sarkozy's presidency, where France's prisons suffer a shocking reputation, and where the infamous provisions for detention following arrest (*la garde à vue*) were declared unconstitutional in 2010 – the provision of law, order and security in France is set to remain a public policy challenge of the highest order.

Conclusions

It would appear, by way of conclusion, that France is far from immune from the political developments characteristic of twenty-first century Europe. These include the rise of single-issue interests such as the environment and human rights; the persistent presence of the far right and their nationalist, if not xenophobic agendas; sceptical attitudes towards the EU's free-market economics; an increasingly disaffected middle class; the advent of new technologies to challenge traditional ways of 'doing politics'; and the seemingly intractable problems of contemporary democracy that range from high-level and large-scale corruption to the stirrings of disaffected citizens and would-be members of the nation. Politics and politicians alike, struggle to command credibility, legitimacy or trust. For the time being, nevertheless, French democracy looks set to be delivered within the institutions of the Fifth French Republic that, for over half a century, have proved themselves remarkably resilient to political developments of all kinds.

4

Government, Policy-Making and the Republican State

Introduction

Like other liberal democracies, contemporary France is governed by formal political offices and their incumbents, and by bureaucratic policy-making processes and the staff that service them. Governing France is also a question of accommodating specific norms, customs, practices and perceptions in a country reputed to be conflict-ridden and, on past occasions, ungovernable. French government is characterized by a pervasive tradition that only a strong state can guarantee the republican ideals enshrined in the 1958 Constitution; this is the pact between the state and its citizens. Hence France, by tradition, is a *secular* state, designed to unite diverse faiths into one republican nation; it is a *centralized* state, concentrating power tightly around the core executive in Paris by means of an extensive administrative apparatus; France sustains a costly *social welfare* state, the policy expression of solidarity between citizens of the nation (old and young; employed and unemployed; rural, urban and suburban); and Paris takes its place in the international arena as a *nation*-state whose citizens are bound by their nationality – their Frenchness – and whose state is *sovereign* over its own decisions.

Contemporary developments such as European integration, the globalization of markets, and the growing ethnic, religious and generational diversity of the French have placed this model of government under strain, as have the costs and demands of running a country as large, diverse and as open to outside influences as France. These challenges have led to change that is incremental – as is the case of the decentralization of power, controversial – in the case of the ongoing transfers of power to the European Union, and, above all, difficult to reconcile with tradition. Public expectations of the French state are still high, and what are perceived as repeated policy failures to meet them have created persistent distrust on the part of the French electorate in the first decade of the twenty-first century. Expectations that the state will provide 'public service' – the delivery of key public goods – is particularly sensitive in today's France; the costs and deficits of doing so have led successive governments to trim the scope of its public service, but not expectations. There has been no cultural revolution where the French state is concerned, but there has been reform, and it has been challenging.

This chapter, first, tackles the subject of 'government' in the narrow sense of France's central, Paris-based, political institutions which form a 'semi-presidential' regime where political power is highly concentrated around the president of the Republic, the Head of State. In this respect, France is still in the present day a *Gaullist* state, shaped around the preferences of its founder president, Charles de Gaulle: to challenge these foundations could be construed as destabilizing the Fifth Republic itself. The 1958 Constitution has outlasted its early critics, and the semi-presidential regime has become a new form of parliamentary democracy in its own right. Yet, in France, semi-presidentialism can still have the air of a temporary, stop-gap measure, and talk of a Sixth French Republic in France is serious and respectable. Two of the three leading contenders for the presidency in 2007, Ségolène Royal and François Bayrou, explicitly supported a Sixth French Republic; they lost. President Sarkozy, winner of that election, indicated instead his intention to consolidate the Fifth Republic as a system of government centred on the presidential role, and went on to clarify the 1958 Constitution in that respect.

Second, we expand our definition to include the complex of actors, processes and mechanisms that constitute the French policy-making environment at national, regional and local levels; this is best defined as 'governance'. Here, our discussion seeks to establish the extent to which France can still, today, be classified as a 'state-centric' model of administration in comparison with a more pluralist model. We ask how far French public policy is upholding French republican principles in the present day, with particular reference to the unity of the French territory following the decentralization reforms of the past quarter of a century; and we assess the sovereignty of its policy-making powers in the face of half a century of French commitments to the European Union.

The Semi-Presidential Regime of the Fifth French Republic

'Semi-presidentialism' is the term coined specifically to describe the government of the Fifth French Republic, whereby a politically powerful President is grafted onto a Westminster-type parliamentary democracy, and where the executive branch of government is top-heavy. The origins of this regime lie in the circumstances of 1958. Faced with army rebellion in Algeria, the government of the Fourth Republic called upon Charles de Gaulle, who drafted a new Constitution designed to restore stability and strength to the French Republic. This settlement was, therefore, negotiated in a very specific set of circumstances; namely, the collapse of the political authority of the Fourth Republic under the weight of the doomed fight for *l'Algérie française* (see Chapter 1). These events provided de Gaulle with an opportunity to return to power and implement his ideas of government, which immediately after World War II had been rejected as too authoritarian.

The 1958 Constitution was ratified overwhelmingly by referendum on 28 September 1958. It forms the framework for contemporary French government by acting as the fundamental law of the Republic. It draws its principles from the 1789 Declaration of the Rights of Man and the Citizen, the Preamble of the 1946 Constitution, and the 2004 Charter of the Environment. The 1958 text defines the powers and roles of each of the central institutions of French government. It is also fundamentally ambiguous, and owes its survival to a process of interpretation by Presidents and by courts, and by multiple amendments, to the point of internal contradiction (between 1958 and 2007 there were 23 'revisions' of the Constitution, 15 of which occurred in a 12-year span between 1995 and 2007). It was de Gaulle's own incumbency of the presidency for the first 11 years of the regime (1958–69) – and his unconstitutional but successful amendment of 1962 providing for a *directly*-elected presidency – that shaped, in practice, the power relations between the core institutions and, in particular, between President and Prime Minister.

Who's in Charge? Power and Political Leadership in the French Dual Executive

The 1958 French Constitution provides for simultaneous political leadership by both President and Prime Minister. In this system, a directly-elected President co-exists with a Prime Minister appointed by the President and who 'directs the actions of' a government nevertheless chaired by the President. Both Prime Minister and government are responsible to parliament and, until 2008, the President was banned from the parliamentary chambers. Now, '[h]e may ... take the floor before Parliament convened in Congress for this purpose' (1958 Constitution, Article 18). This is the separation of powers, French-style. When the President and Prime Minister both represent the majority in the National Assembly (the directly-elected lower house) – usually, but not necessarily, this is when they both emanate from the majority party – power and powers are divided between them on the basis of a unique pact dependent on their personalities, and the political circumstances of the time.

The stronger of the executive duo in terms of the overall policy-making agenda – and certainly in terms of public visibility – is usually the President, and all Presidents have certainly seen this as the true spirit of the constitution. It is, in any case, the President who at all times retains the constitutional upper hand by having the right to call new elections (Article 12), appeal to the electorate via referendum (Article 11) or, in very extreme cases – the last resort – decreeing a state of emergency (Article 16).

It is also France's Presidents who are the international face and voice of France: contemporary France's most famous statesmen (there have been no female French presidents) have been its presidents, particularly Charles de Gaulle (1959–69), and François Mitterrand (1981–95). Moreover, the French President is, in formal terms, the Head of *State*. In all other EU countries this is a ceremonial role, but in France it is a politically powerful role underpinned by the popular legitimacy of direct election. However, by the same token, French Presidents can, and do, become extraordinarily unpopular over time. Article 5 of the 1958 Constitution has been interpreted by all Presidents since 1958 as a licence for the President to decide upon foreign policy in relative isolation from government, parliament or electorate. France's international partners, on the other hand, can be disconcerted when both President and Prime Minister attend the same summit-level gatherings.

In practice, a President's actual (as opposed to constitutional) power can be curtailed by a lack of party political support in the National Assembly. This happened five years into each of François Mitterrand's seven-year presidential terms, at the end of the National Assembly's five-year mandate, in 1986 and 1993. These were

Box 4.1   Presidential power? Article 5

'The President of the Republic shall ensure due respect for the Constitution. He shall ensure, by his arbitration, the proper functioning of the public authorities and the continuity of the State.

He shall be the guarantor of national independence, territorial integrity and due respect for Treaties.'

Source: National Assembly (2010).

Mitterrand's mid-term elections, which he lost on both occasions, forcing him to 'cohabit' for the remaining two years of the presidential term with a Prime Minister and government nominally of his choosing, but politically his opponents. The third period of cohabitation to occur since 1958 forced President Jacques Chirac into cohabitation for five years with his Socialist Prime Minister Lionel Jospin (1997–2002). This blow was self-inflicted by the President, who ill-advisedly called and lost early elections only two years into his first term of office. By the time of Chirac's re-election as President in 2002, the 1958 Constitution had been amended to reduce the presidential term from seven to five years; this shortened term is known as the *quinquennat*. Presidential elections are now held at five-yearly intervals and are immediately followed by legislative elections, the function of which is now to confirm the President in post by means of a parliamentary majority; to date, such elections have gone to plan. Thus, in May 2007, Nicolas Sarkozy was elected President of the Republic and, in June the same year, the legislative elections returned a majority for the party over which he presided before his campaign, the UMP.

This electoral sequence links the President far more explicitly than before to his parliamentary majority, which becomes the linchpin of the system, and yet also raises the profile of the Prime Minister, whose job it is to manage this majority in order to support the presidential policy agenda. As the President's appointee, the Prime Minister more often than not serves the function of drawing any political poison (unpopularity, failed policy) away from the President into the prime ministerial office, culminating, if necessary, in the appointment by the President of a new, fresher Prime Minister destined to fulfil the same purpose. Such instrumentalization of the office of Prime Minister is not a constitutional right of the President, but a practice that has become a norm of French political life, to the detriment of political accountability at the top of the executive.

The Prime Minister does play the vital role of running French government by heading the ministries and machinery of daily administrative life, with the lion's share of the nation's administrative resources at his disposal. But even here, the Prime Minister is rivalled by the President, who has the right to appoint his own staff in the Elysée Palace (site of the presidential office). Thus, in 2007 President Sarkozy appointed powerful figures to his team to offer foreign policy and general advice without reference to the Prime Minister or government. President Sarkozy also indulged his appetite for presidential power by calling for a succession of 'commissions' charged with proposing reform to a range of aspects of French government and policy-making (constitutional reform, economic competitiveness, defence and security). Nevertheless, the legitimacy of the Prime Minister derives from his constitutional powers and functions, and his administrative resources, not to mention his and his ministers' right to their own political staff (their *cabinets*); whereas the President relies far more heavily on the more tenuous tools of popular legitimacy and personality, and the quality of his advisors.

Scrutiny of the French Executive

French Parliament

The French parliament is a bicameral institution, comprising the National Assembly and the Senate. The National Assembly is the lower house: it is a directly-elected chamber, whose 577 members are called 'deputies', and who represent their constituencies. The upper house is known as the Senate, whose 343 members are voted in by an electoral college composed of National Assembly deputies, and locally and regionally-elected figures such as mayors and councillors. Within this legislature, the National Assembly is the more influential of the two houses; significantly, its members have the right to initiate legislation of their own on an equal footing with the government. The Senate provides legislative oversight – for example, by amending legislation brought before it – and it enjoys a legitimacy derived from the stability of its membership (nine-year terms; only one-third of its members renewed at a time); its powers of patronage (its President nominates three of the nine members of the Constitutional Council, as does the President of the National

Assembly); and its ranking in institutional protocol; the Senate's approval is also required of any constitutional reform. However, the 1958 founding text severely curtailed the power of the legislative branch as a whole, and the fifty years of the Fifth Republic's existence have confirmed this balance of power. The Constitution (Articles 34 and 37) confines parliamentary involvement to designated statutory domains, with all other areas being matters for government regulation and decree.

Furthermore, the government has priority over the bulk of the parliamentary agenda, and it can force parliament's hand by means of the 'blocked vote' or 'package vote' of Article 44-3 of the Constitution, whereby deputies have to accept or reject an entire legislative package on the basis of government amendments. Moreover, under the terms of Article 49-1 and 49-3, the government can call for a vote of confidence on its general policy programme or on specific finance bills. Confidence is considered granted unless the deputies can muster a vote to the contrary. The provision is frequently invoked by governments seeking to hurry along their legislative programme, or to bully an unstable majority to support government policy, but the Assembly has never seen a successful motion of censure under this procedure since 1962, and it is unpopular.

The President's control of foreign policy and his prerogative to call national referenda creates the potential for important matters of national policy to bypass parliament as a decision-making body. The same constitution, however, does confirm parliament's right of scrutiny and debate. In EU affairs, for example, the National Assembly in the 1990s and 2000s won the right to be consulted and informed, and to vote resolutions on government policy, but these are not binding. Neither do the National Assembly or Senate delegations, despite their expertise, have the resources fully to expose or influence government policy towards the European Union. Following the entry into force in 2009 of the EU's Lisbon Treaty, however, these delegations were upgraded to standing committee status, thereby gaining a more formal role of scrutiny. The National Assembly has also won the right to longer sittings than was provided for in 1958, to a ministers' 'Question Time' and to a vote on the social security budget bills. These alterations are best understood as attempts by successive governments to preserve the uneasy balance that lies at the heart of the design of French government; namely, to preserve the prerogatives and power of the executive, and especially of the President, within the framework of a parliamentary democracy.

The Constitutional Council
The evolution of the role of the Constitutional Council, created in 1958, is part of this broader picture in which the executive branch finds itself exposed to greater scrutiny which, nevertheless, falls short of transforming the power balance within France's institutions of government. The Constitutional Council is composed of nine members for one nine-year mandate, plus former Presidents of the Republic who sit (or not) *ex officio*. All members are political appointees: three members and the President of the Council are appointed by the President of the Republic; the other six by the Presidents of the National Assembly and Senate. The Council's function is to rule on the constitutionality of legislation *before* it is promulgated, and to ensure that elections are conducted constitutionally.

The Council is increasingly called upon by opposition deputies in the National Assembly (a minimum of sixty is required) as a way of raising public awareness of the nature of government legislation and, increasingly, the Council finds itself engaged in matters of human rights and individual freedoms. Following a historic reform passed in 2010, for example, individuals involved in legal proceedings have the right, via the appeal courts, to challenge the constitutionality of legislation *after* it has come into force (Article 61-1).

In these ways, the Council can intervene in the policy process in a way unintended by Charles de Gaulle. He saw the Council as a mechanism for exposing *parliamentary* forays into government prerogatives, and could not have imagined how it could 'harass' the government instead. There is no appeal against a Council decision, and its evolving role is to be seen as part of the process of the judicialization of French politics, and the taming of the French state.

The State and the Republic: Grand Ideas into Policy

One of the key features of French government that is not immediately obvious from the 1958 constitutional text is the centrality of the French 'state'. The meaning of 'the state' is not fixed, and it does not denote a finite set of discrete institutions, although at its core are administrative bodies, and at its head is the President of the Republic. Just as important are the connotations attached to the meaning of the 'state' in French political culture and discourse. Namely, politicians across the entire political spectrum allow themselves to convey the notion that the state must be strong, in the sense of powerful and

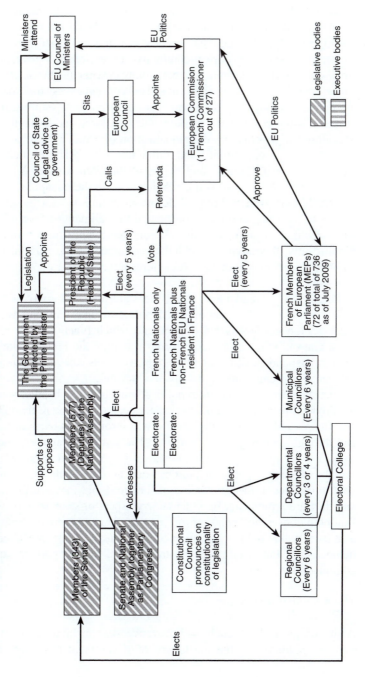

Figure 4.1 **Outline of the structures of French government**

unfettered. This is a perception that is wildly at odds with reality, but it persists and, to an important extent, puts a brake on reform.

Significantly, 'the state' has become equated in France with the nation itself, and its historical continuity. It therefore follows that a weak state would undermine and potentially threaten the fabric of the nation itself, with potentially negative consequences for social harmony. Contemporary developments – such as European integration, the rising costs of the welfare state, the logic and dynamic of decentralized government, the globalization of economic exchanges and of cultural opportunity and influence – have all resulted in changes to the institutions and norms of the French state. All EU member states have faced similar challenges, but these responses are invariably portrayed in political debate in France as attacks on or threats to the state, and have contributed to a climate of fear, crisis and 'decline' in the first decade of the twenty-first century. Significantly, this environment has undermined public trust in the ability of politicians to bring sufficient resources to bear on society's problems.

Perceptions of and ideas about the state are, thus, part of the policy-making environment in French politics to an extent that distinguishes France from its neighbours, and which functions as a real constraint on policy and state reform. In reality, the French state is more robust and flexible, but these objective facts can get lost in the subjective and emotional terms of such 'debate'.

The state, finally, is far from politically neutral. The head of state, the French President, is in the twenty-first century an intensely political figure, and interprets the general will through this partisan lens and through patronage *à la française*. The state apparatus – principally, its millions of public employees – is for its part expected to promote French republican politics such as *laïcité*; these are not neutral policies in the strict sense of the word, but they are French, and they are republican. In all and every aspect of state activity, we find both conservative and reformist forces in contemporary France as it faces public policy challenges confronting all of Europe's liberal democracies, but within the constraints of a unique political and administrative culture.

The Administrative State

At its simplest, the French administrative state or civil service (*la fonction publique*) is the machinery of government (bureaux and bureaucrats) that lies directly behind government decision-making, and brings decisions to life at the national and sub-national levels. Its officials are *fonctionnaires* (functionaries), and the most senior of these are the *hauts fonctionnaires*, a very prestigious career label in France yesterday and today. The term implies both the notion of the British civil servant, working in the public interest, and also denotes the specialization and professionalization of functions.

This is especially, but not only, the case in the higher echelons of the French bureaucracy where the state is organized into prestigious and respected 'great bodies' – *les grands corps*. These are responsible for the main sectors of public policy (local government, infrastructure and public works, hospitals, education, and so on); this is France's policy-making elite. The system is underpinned by the ideal of meritocracy whereby the equality of opportunity provided by education and qualification should trump chance, luck and individual qualities. This characteristic of French bureaucracy has fed into a society reputed to cling to a hierarchical social structure whereby pecking orders and fierce *esprits de corps* co-exist with incontrovertible evidence that social class and distinctions are reinforced and reproduced by an education system typified by a strata of elitist and specialist establishments, particularly at the level of higher education (Chapter 5). Following World War II, attempts were made to attenuate some of the rivalries within the administration that in certain cases are centuries-old. General civil service statutes now exist that unify France's public service, to a point, and by 2010 some of the most prestigious of the *corps* were undergoing painful mergers. The 'old schools' still exist today. One of the most iconic is the *École polytechnique* for public sector engineers, which is run on a military regime, and whose students are salaried. But the postwar reforms in turn created their own elitist channel for France's most ambitious and fortunate graduates. In particular, France's famed 'school for national administration' – *l'ENA* (*l'École nationale d'administration*) – was founded in 1945 precisely to professionalize the French civil service, and to produce generalist senior elites to go on and work in senior administrative bodies such as the *Conseil d'État* and *Cour des Comptes* (Council of State and Court of Accounts); the French diplomatic corps; the tax inspectorate and the prefectoral staff, who top the state at the local level. *L'ENA*, in time, became a stepping stone in its own right for would-be politicians seeking the highest office. Most Presidents and Prime Ministers of the Fifth Republic have been graduates (*énarques*) of this school. Thus, a characteristic of the French administrative state is its politicization, and the interlocking of its various elites (administrative, political, commercial and media) via these elitist schools and their networks. President Sarkozy made much of the fact that he, by contrast, did not move through these worlds in order to gain his lawyer's qualifications.

'Deconcentration' and Diversity

The French state is hardly immune, however, from the pressures of cost and fashion that permeate Europe's liberal democracies and, in the twenty-first century, the French state has undergone change and reform. For example, state employees – not all of whom are *hauts fonctionnaires* but, rather, are more lowly public employees supposedly infused with a public service mission – have, since the 1980s, found themselves 'deconcentrated'. This refers to the ongoing process in France whereby state functions have been delegated to the 'field' or locality, and given more autonomy from the Paris-based government ministries for matters such as the maintenance of law and order, emergency and disaster relief, the arbitration of labour disputes, the implementation of EU policy on the ground, and the more prosaic but vital functions of tax collection and administration.

The presence of the state in the regions and localities of France nevertheless remains a powerful symbol of the historical role of the French state in forging the nation; immigrants seeking residents' permits, for example, must still appear in person at the *préfecture*, or *sous-préfecture* of their *département* where the 'prefect' and his/her adjuncts are the gateway to the rights and duties of citizenship, and a historically key conduit between the state and its citizens. Similarly, no marriage is legal unless sealed in a ceremony conducted by the local mayor (see Box 4.4). Marriage is a *civil* contract in France, and the mayor on these occasions (as with births and deaths) is quite literally the face of the state in even the smallest hamlet of mainland France or the most remote municipality in the overseas French territories. That, indeed, is the point: that the nation coheres across physical and cultural borders and boundaries by virtue of the uniformity of the state. In reality, variation (of service provision and delivery) is as much a feature of French administration as the fabled uniformity.

Despite this overarching principle, recent decades have seen reforms designed specifically to accommodate the diversity that characterizes contemporary France. Elitist institutions, such as *l'ENA*'s 'Paris-based feeder school known as *Sciences Po* (School of Political Science), have experimented with programmes designed to achieve what in the UK would be known as 'widening access'. This involves admitting bright pupils from socially disadvantaged localities (and by extension, backgrounds), by means of a differentiated admissions process (see Chapter 5). At the national level, attempts have been made to provide for a degree of administrative 'experimentation' in regions such as Corsica, while stopping short of ceding the degree of autonomy afforded to France's overseas territories. The balance has proved virtually impossible to achieve – certainly in the high-profile case of Corsica, where separatist claims to regional identity are strong. Here, attempts to transfer a minimum of law-making powers and to attribute 'special status' to the island in regulatory matters have, for the time being, remained a dead letter.

In keeping with the times, moreover, the French state has taken significant steps to discard its notorious reputation as the land of red tape and faceless bureaucracy. Timely access to administrative services can still be a frustrating experience, as it can be elsewhere; but the overall interface between state and citizen was overhauled in the wake of the Internet revolution of the late twentieth century. In today's France, for example, the websites of the country's leading institutions prioritize audio-visual media and social networking sites as the primary means of providing information, doubtless in the hope of presenting a friendly face to the public – providing they have access to a computer and the Internet.

Such developments have favoured the development of what we might recognize in Anglo-Saxon political cultures as a 'civil society', despite centuries of state suspicion of such 'intermediaries' between itself and its citizens, such as 'associations' (see Box 4.2).

*The '*État de Droit*' – The Rule of Law*

There are strong historical reasons for the French state to be suspicious of what we call 'civil society', and notions of the public good trump individual or group interests in French republican theory. In comparative terms, the traditional French state is neither corporatist nor pluralist, but uniquely statist. However, while state secrets (*le secret d'État*) for state-given reasons (*la raison d'État*) are hardly a thing of the past in France, they are more open to challenge and liable to exposure in the present day context of Internet news, 'citizen-journalists', and the influence of legal norms and precedent

Box 4.2 Associations

Associations are very much part of the fabric of French society, and a resource for government. They are non profit-making organizations run mainly by volunteers for the benefit of their members, although some bigger associations also employ paid staff. An association is defined as 'a group of people organized around an idea, project or activity', where at least two people enter into a contract to pool their knowledge or activity with 'another purpose than profit'. It is estimated that today there are about 1 million associations in France, run by some 12 million volunteers, and 1.5 million paid workers.

Most French people will belong to at least one association, and associations spring up whenever there is a cause to defend or an activity to organize. Associations usually ask their members for dues and, if the association registers with the local authorities, it is usually subsidized by public money (often minimal sums), and is eligible to use local facilities such as the village hall. Associations are independent from local authorities, but often work with them for the benefit of local people. Some associations are nationwide, often created in defence of the most vulnerable (the homeless, the poor, refugees and others otherwise excluded from mainstream society); most bring people together locally around shared sport and cultural activities, and many make important contributions to the life of the village, community or neighbourhood.

Historically, the French state has feared any form of group or gathering that could act as a rival magnet for popular loyalty. Church and workers' organizations were banned in the aftermath of the French Revolution: if people associated, they might have undermined the revolutionaries and tried to bring down the new regime. For more than one hundred years, governments remained suspicious of groups that might have had 'subversive' goals – such as campaigning for better wages, or supporting the Church. It was not until 1901 that the law changed in order to give them official recognition and access to resources – and keep an official eye on them. The expression '*la loi 1901*' (the 1901 law) is often heard in France to refer to an officially-registered association.

Today, associations play an important role in France, for the individual wanting to join in and be part of the local community to the activist trying passionately to influence government policy. The French authorities have come to rely on associations for the part they play in holding society together; and call on their expertise as partners in the policy-making process when making decisions about people's lives. This is *governance* in action, part of a picture that normalizes France's statist model of policy-making along more pluralist lines, and which coincides with broader policy trends in favour of the liberalization of society whereby the rights of the individual find themselves championed, if not pitted, against the historical dominance of the state.

imported from the European Union's legal corpus, known as its *acquis*. Indeed, individual or even group rights increasingly find themselves championed in contemporary France by organizations empowered to challenge the traditional pecking order of politics above the law. The most significant of these are the bodies at the highest echelons of France's unique system of administrative law – the administrative courts – which have instituted a French version of judicial review; and bodies with independent regulatory powers, as in many other European countries (see Box 4.3). The administrative courts are part of France's dual justice system, where administrative cases are hived off from what is known as 'ordinary' justice,

---

Box 4.3   The judicialization of the French state: key bodies

- The *Conseil d'Etat* (Council of State) is the most prestigious of these bodies. It is at the summit of France's unique system of administrative courts and tribunals that runs in parallel to the civil justice system, hearing final appeals. The court rules on the legality of state administration, acting as court of appeal for administrative law; it also, nevertheless, acts as the government's legal advisor. All government bills and decrees are submitted to the Council of State for opinion before going before Parliament; the Council's decision is non-binding but influential due to the legitimacy conferred by the body's status.
- The *corps des comptes* (Court of Accounts) oversees the efficiency of public spending and ensures its transparency by means of audit and the certification of accounts. Its members are administrative judges and can sit for life.
- The *défenseur des droits* (defender of rights, or ombudsman) is a post given constitutional status in 2008, unlike the previous 'Mediator of the Republic'. It is a presidential appointment. Article 71-1 of the 1958 Constitution states that 'The Defender of Rights shall ensure the due respect of all rights and freedoms by state administrations, territorial communities, public legal entities, as well as by all bodies carrying out a public service mission.'
- *Independent regulatory authorities*: these are numerous, and provide regulatory oversight of public policy domains and issues such as the freedom of the press, audio-visual policy, immigration, civil liberties, anti-discrimination; and competition.
- French governments also make frequent recourse to *ad hoc* consultative *committees* (usually known as *commissions*) for the provision of expertise and advice, presumably to legitimize subsequent policy. President Sarkozy instructed his Prime Minister, François Fillon, to establish a rash of these in 2007–08, on institutional reform, the teaching profession, and economic growth.

meaning civil and criminal law. The state, in other words, prosecutes the state, protected from the judicial branch of government.

State Reform

The Fifth Republic was, to all intents and purposes, grafted onto pre-existing structures of state administration and processes. Unsurprisingly, reform has been piecemeal and, given the historical symbolism of the state tradition, frequently painful. In twenty-first century France, and certainly following the election of President Nicolas Sarkozy in May 2007, a leitmotif of French public administration has been the pursuit of rationalization and modernization via reform. For Sarkozy, change itself appears to be a treasured value and policy goal for its own sake. Such trends are also driven by considerations of cost and the quest for value for money, as in other EU member states. New policy ideas and fashions are, moreover, themselves the product of new environments in which French public policy is made and which French policy-makers share with their European counterparts, including the political system of the EU itself.

Thus, the last twenty years in France have seen a succession of battles to trim the costs of French public service, all the while maintaining a discourse of absolute belief in the right of each and every citizen to a generous and efficient set of public services. Shortly upon Sarkozy's election as President, notably, a comprehensive programme of public sector reform was launched under the name of the RGPP (*la révision générale des politiques publiques* – general review of public policies). In addition, specific and difficult conflicts have been waged over the 'special regimes' – generous pension provisions – enjoyed by certain groups of public sector workers; and the drive is ongoing to harmonize pensions provision in the private and public spheres (see Chapter 7). Trades unions are strongest in the public sector (education, transport) and the battles here have been fierce. President Sarkozy also campaigned on a pledge to scale back the numbers of public employees in certain public services by replacing only a fraction of those who would retire as France's postwar baby-boomers came of age. French policy-makers have long looked to the private sector for the provision of public services (such as the management of the motorway network) and, as noted earlier, the 'agencification' of French administration has become a norm. Alongside all these aspects of gradual change sits the so-called *grande affaire* (big idea) of the 1980s, which has most directly transformed the lives of France's *administrés* (its 'administered' citizens); namely, by the ongoing process of political decentralization. This, too, has proved complicated, and change has been incremental.

Decentralization and Local Democracy

Local and regional government in France is complicated, by any standards, with a bewildering range of bodies, actors, powers, resources and duties, most overlapping. Arguably, this situation is also a perfect reflection of the complexity of a country with as strong a tradition of both *pays* and *État*. The 1958 French Constitution tells us that France is an 'indivisible' Republic and also that, since 2002, it is organized 'on a decentralized basis'. This apparent contradiction means, in practice, that the drive in France since the early 1980s to disperse power, resources and political responsibility across the French territory into regions, towns and villages has its limits. Namely, France is very unlikely ever to become a federal or a multi-national state.

The 'Big Idea': Twenty-Five Years of Decentralization

Decentralization in France has been a piecemeal process answering to no single institutional or ideological blueprint. Today, it is both irreversible and incomplete, but France's territorial units are finally 'self-governing' in letter and spirit. The principle of loosening the grip of Paris over the entirety of the French territory, at home and overseas, was uncontroversial from the first decade of the Fifth Republic. However, it was not until the 1980s that the idea took shape in the form of the 'big idea' (*la grande affaire*) of President François Mitterrand's first seven-year term from 1981 to 1988. The timing was not coincidental: the generation of the social 'revolution' of May 1968 was coming of age; key members of the French Socialist Party, by now in power, had long supported the idea; it fitted with Mitterrand's agenda of modernizing and liberalizing French systems and society; and it was played out in a specific context of higher EU spending at regional level, for which more flexible structures and responses were required. There were to be limits, nonetheless: not too much individual *liberté* in comparison with equality and solidarity: this was not a liberal but, rather, a social state agenda.

Nearly two million (approximately one third) of France's public servants work at one of the local levels, and roughly half a million elected representatives exercise decision-making power in the name of local populations.

A key characteristic of the 1980s decentralization legislation was that decision-making – executive power – would be transferred to local authorities at a variety of local levels, none of which would be hierarchically answerable or superior to any other, and all of which would co-exist in the shadow of central state oversight. Functions – called 'competences' – were also transferred *en bloc*, along with certain revenue-raising powers (such as car tax), block grants and some staff and buildings.

Over time, the decentralization agenda has altered to account for new imperatives and objectives in keeping with the broader political context. So, in the 1990s, new legislation was linked to the drive to trim the fat off the state and, in response to the EU-wide 'governance' drive, to take decisions at the smallest possible unit of government. The state still invests heavily, nonetheless (for example, in trains, or in policing), and the traditional officers of the state on the ground locally (the *préfets*) are still there to advise, guide and approve *post facto* decisions taken by elected authorities at the local level. In addition, the mayor officiates for the state, and is also an official elected by his or her peers. At the same time, the scope of local authorities to raise revenue and exercise autonomy has grown, as has the scope for gaps to appear (in wealth, in creativity) between parts of France, in a context of population drift to large cities, especially in the south and west of France.

Moreover, a new layer of representative government was created by the 1980s laws. This was the region that, along with France's largest cities, has gained over time from the decentralization agenda. Regions, for example, are important actors in the raising and spending of EU funds, in partnership with the state. A definite trend also exists in contemporary France towards the rationalization of local decision-making. This takes the form of incentives for authorities to group together in ever larger structures, both in urban and rural settings. At the same time, the French state has acknowledged persistent demands for ever-greater scope for local democracy and political participation. Voting at regional level, for example, is by proportional representation (but stacked to favour the winner); and proposals for local referenda were included in the decentralization legislation of 2002 in the form of a law on 'democracy and proximity'.

Decentralization brought the political competition characteristic of national level politics into local government which, in turn, links the local back into national politics. Local and state interests in France have, in any case, never been remote, given the strong and enduring tradition of the *cumul des mandats*, whereby office-holders may accumulate more than one post, most usually mayor and National Assembly deputy – or even mayor and government minister. Thus, in the 2008 municipal elections, several members of the government stood for local election as mayor; several lost the election, but all kept their government post. These are relationships intended to benefit both political careers and local authorities – particularly the big towns and cities – which stand to gain by virtue of being an important political stake for a national-level politician. However, the *cumul des mandats* tradition remains controversial and subject to reform. Local elections, finally, increasingly function as second-order, mid-term judgments on national government; the regional elections of 2004 and 2010, and the municipal elections of 2008 were a case in point – in both examples, the majority UMP party lost seats and councils to the left, in opposition at national level.

Local Power in Practice

The coexistence in France of state presence and local politics is played out on a map that has changed remarkably little over the centuries, with many boundaries and local administrative entities – such as the *commune*, the smallest administrative entity but the biggest in importance for the daily lives of most French citizens – having their origins in pre-revolutionary times. The 1789 Revolution and the first Napoleonic Empire subsequently marked out an administrative map of France that remains remarkably intact still today.

The Department (le Département)
The provinces of the *ancien régime* were abolished in the revolutionary years and replaced by the *département*. There are 96 *départements* in mainland France today, plus five overseas *départements* which are also regions in their own right, namely Guadeloupe, Martinique, French Guyana and Reunion Island and, most recently, Mayotte (see Chapter 2). French *départements* have average populations of between 200,000 and 700,000 inhabitants. Each *département* is neutrally named, usually after a predominant geographical feature such as a river (for example, the Seine and Marne, Bas Rhin, Haut

Rhin, or Dordogne departments); or a mountain (for example, the Pyrénées Atlantiques, the Pyrénées Orientales and the Alpes de Haute-Provence departments). The idea behind these names was to erode the memory of tribal and sub-national identities. Each department, moreover, has a unique number that still features in postcodes and, until 2009, on car number plates.

French people profess attachment and loyalty to their *département*. It is also the core unit around which the state organizes its local services, and it has a symbolic value as a reminder of France's surge into modernity in the early nineteenth century. Thus, periodic proposals to scrap the *département* on the grounds of the costly duplication of administrative functions have, to date, failed to find sufficient support. Napoleon Bonaparte created the *prefectoral system* and, until the decentralization laws of the 1980s, the *préfet* was the chief executive officer of the *département*. This is a role now held by the president of the departmental council (known as *le conseil général*). The *préfet* retains responsibility for policing at departmental level, and oversees policy decided by the elected council. The departmental council's main policy functions (having benefited from the lion's share of 'competencies' transferred in the 1980s decentralization legislation) are in social services (such as co-financing with the state and dispensing certain welfare benefits; preventative health policy), public sanitation, transport, roads and the upkeep of secondary schools. Amongst the *départements*' tax revenues is the French version of the UK's council tax, the *taxe d'habitation*.

The Commune *(la Commune)*

Contemporary France is divided into nearly 37,000 *communes*, of which all but 200 or so are in mainland France. The vast majority of these *communes* are small and rural in nature, and over half of the total has populations of under 500 inhabitants. At the same time, Paris is a *commune* in its own right, as are other of France's major cities that are the driving force of dynamism in the French economy. The *commune* (also called *municipalité*) has historic resonance, predating the French Revolution which nevertheless deposed the priest and installed in his place the mayor, the best-known of France's elected officials (see Box 4.4).

Inter-Communal Relations

Since the *commune* is far from being the most rational unit of administration in terms of cost and infrastructure, a distinct trend in French governance has been towards the organization of 'inter-communal' structures with the authority to raise revenues and deliver services (such as waste management), especially in urban areas. Thus, France is home to numerous *communautés urbaines* (urban communities, such as *le Grand Lyon* – wider Lyon); and *communautés de communes* (communities of *communes*), which are also to be found in rural areas. The staff of these organizations is for the time being indirectly elected, but pressure is building for direct elections to what are, in some cases, key and highly resourced posts.

*Le pays (*area*)*
This unit was created in 1995 with the intention of encouraging inhabitants in areas where there are perceived to be shared historical or cultural interests to cohere around ideas or projects designed to develop the area. The *pays* so conceived is a very weak echo of the historical territories and identities that comprised France before it took its present-day shape.

'PLM': France's Largest Cities
Paris, Lyon and Marseille are France's three biggest cities. Paris and its surrounding area are home to nearly 10 million inhabitants, and Lyon and Marseille to well over 1 million each. Lille and Toulouse now also have over 1 million inhabitants. Paris, Lyon and Marseille are administered according to the 'PLM' law, which divided the single *communes* into *arrondissements* (districts) *municipaux* (Paris with 20; Lyon, 16; and Marseille, 9); each has its own *mairie* and *conseil* which elect representatives to the city's municipal council. In addition, Paris is unique in that it functions simultaneously as both a town *commune*, and as a *département* (known by its number of 75), meaning that its council covers the policy functions of both of these layers of government. By 2010, plans were under way for a *'Grand Paris'* – a greater Paris conurbation designed to replace the existing departments, and to concentrate economic activity and opportunity. Proposed by President Sarkozy, the ideas met with considerable opposition, and were watered down. They would have constituted yet one more layer in an already dense network of local government.

The Region
France's 22 regions were the last administrative units to benefit from the powers of decentralized government. They are disparate in terms of their population, resources and dynamism. French regions are not

> **Box 4.4   The French mayor: the French state and locally elected figure combined**
>
> The mayor is a central figure in French local government. Paris, other large cities and towns, and the smallest of villages all have their mayor. Mayors are authority figures, and can have a great deal of power. The former mayor of Paris (1977–95), Jacques Chirac, went on to become President of the Republic, and the present mayor of Paris, Bertrand Delanoë, wants to build new skyscrapers that would irreversibly change the skyline of his city. These mayors are career politicians who rely on a political party for their position.
>
> The vast majority of France's mayors, however, are involved with much smaller communities, and so are more concerned with people's daily lives than with high politics. Over 90% of France's *communes* have fewer than 3500 inhabitants, and over 50% of them have fewer than 500 inhabitants. Therefore, most mayors represent a very small population and will be well-known to their population. French people often identify with their *commune* and with their mayor, and this aspect of French government has not been reformed in hundreds of years.
>
> In today's France, mayors play two different roles. On the one hand, the French mayor is the official representative of the state in his or her *commune*, and is overseen in this capacity by the *préfet* (prefect) sitting, usually, in the largest town in the *département* in a building known as *la préfecture*. When a French mayor registers births and deaths, and conducts marriage ceremonies, he or she is officiating on behalf of the French state. The mayor's other function is to *decide* on what should happen in his/her *commune* with regard to aspects of daily life, such as the maintenance of roads and of primary school premises;
>
> ➜

intended to resonate with old historical identities, and certainly not with the regional provinces and parliaments of the *ancien régime*, which were early casualties of the French Revolution. They were given no new electoral constituencies under the decentralization laws, and electoral turn out is notoriously low by French standards. The French term '*la province*' is, nevertheless, an extremely common way for French speakers to designate those parts of France that are not Paris or its 'island', and regions such as Alsace and Brittany are home to flourishing local identities, including local dialects.

The prime function of the French region is to boost and organise economic growth, innovation and development. For the purpose of attracting tourist revenues, French regions certainly capitalize on what they claim are their local specialities, especially the gastronomic. The brown signs adorning French motorways offer artistic representations

➜
and the organization of cultural events and facilities. Here, the mayor has his or her own resources – mostly raised by local taxes – and is supported by a team of councillors. This team is the *conseil municipal* (municipal council) and is directly-elected every six years. The mayor is elected by the members of the council, and chairs the council.

The voting system for the council team is complex, especially in the smallest villages (different electoral rules apply depending on the size of the *commune*). Here, teams tend to represent different local interests rather than traditional party politics of the left/right variety. In villages with fewer than 100 inhabitants, the total number of seats on the council will be nine (in contrast to *communes* of over 300,000 inhabitants, which have 69 councillors, or Paris with 163), and the system in practice is complicated. The mayor will put forward his or her list of candidates, and there may or may not be an opposing list. The mayor's own list might contain the names of people who oppose him or her, officially at least, but who cannot put together their full list of people. These are neighbours, remember. The list might have more names than there are seats on the council. Voters can add names to the list, if they want to vote for someone who does not feature on the list; this is called *panachage*. Voters can also cross out names on the list, on their own ballot paper.

Notably, EU residents are entitled to vote in these local elections, and stand for election as council members. They are not allowed to stand for election as mayor, however. As regards gender parity, this principle applies only to larger *communes*, where lists must be composed of alternating male and female candidates; in small councils, this does not apply, and men still dominate. Until 2008, fewer than 10% of all mayors in France were women; that figure is now closer to 14%.

of such attractions for the curious motorist. The Paris-centred Île-de-France, and the Lyon-centred Rhône-Alpes are by far the richest regions in mainland France, and are critical to the French economy overall. The region works in close partnership and in contractual arrangements with the French state in core economic sectors such as the provision of higher education, professional training and transport. It is a key actor in the raising and expenditure of European Union funds and, if it wishes, it can intervene in other policy domains (such as the environment) – as can any level of local government.

The region is run by a directly elected regional council (*le conseil régional*) whose president is indirectly elected by the councillors and who, like his/her counterpart in the *département*, co-exists with the state's representative – in this case the regional *préfet*, whose main role is to facilitate the coordination of national government and

The panoramic picture displayed on the sign outside the offices emphasizes the natural beauty and favourable climate of the area, as well as the opportunities it provides for outdoor leisure pursuits. Cyber-base means that these offices provide Internet access.

Illustration 4.1   The offices of a *communauté des communes* **in Navarrenx,** *Pyrénées orientales* **department**

regional council policy. President Sarkozy's desire to see the departmental and regional councillors merged into one role – the territorial councillor – had not, by 2010, won parliamentary approval.

Co-existing, finally, with all these layers of government are the complex and dynamic relations that exist between France's domestic institutions, offices and structures and those of the European Union.

France in Europe, Europe in France

French political leaders find themselves increasingly obliged to justify to the French public the impact of EU membership on French politics and government. A popular perception is of French politicians unable to tackle serious domestic problems such as unemployment, and forbidden to spend generously on public services, because of the constraints imposed by the EU. This seriously underplays the extent to which French governments and presidents have successfully shaped EU rules and norms, but it is an impression that successive generations of French politicians have seemed unable or unwilling to correct. The outcome has been disappointed voters, electoral instability and some social unrest, all of which were typified in the 'no' vote (54% against) in France's 2005 referendum on the EU's then 'Constitutional Treaty'.

The fact of the matter is that the leading role taken by France in *la construction européenne* is a text-book case of the 'European rescue of the nation state', as per Alan Milward's powerful thesis (2000). In the 1950s, France was a founder member of the first communities (the European Coal and Steel Community – the ECSC, and the European Economic Community – the EEC) that symbolized the French commitment to modernity in matters of economic and social policy. In the 1960s, President de Gaulle's insistence on a Common Agricultural Policy was the *sina qua non* of the survival of French agriculture and its millions of *paysans*, albeit with a new, industrial-look dimension. Again, in the mid-1980s, the European Community offered France a genuine alternative to President Mitterrand's failed 'socialist experiment' for the modernization of its public sector, and the internationalization of its economy in overall terms. In the early 1990s, the Maastricht Treaty extended the level playing field between France and the now-united Germany to include monetary policy, and secured German commitment to, one day, shouldering its part of the burden of defending Europe along the lines of France's strong preference for an *Europe puissance*: a regional power with its own military capability (see Chapter 8).

A Europeanized France?

In the present day, moreover, interaction between French and EU-level institutions occurs on a permanent, continuous basis, and is just as much part of France's structures of governance as is the interface between the state and France's local authorities. As EU member states voluntarily relinquish control over more and more policy domains where there are shared incentives to tackle problems jointly, France inevitably finds that public policy processes are subject to the pressures and norms of 'Europeanization'.

Thus, EU law (its treaty provisions, plus secondary legislation) has primacy over domestic French law (as it does over the law of all its 27 member states) and takes direct effect. However, the *Conseil d'État* (for administrative law) and the Appeals Court (*Cour de cassation*) for criminal and civil law took several decades to acknowledge and adjust to this fact of European Community life, and France still lags behind its EU partners in the matter of transposing secondary EU legislation into national law. On the other hand, France is reputed for its well-coordinated routines for the formulation of French proposals to the European Commission, for its formidable negotiating tactics at decision-making time in Brussels, and for the authority that the French President enjoys over his government colleagues and parliamentary scrutiny provisions in European affairs.

These features of French government all constitute strengths when it comes to the 'uploading' of French policy preferences to the EU level, such as in matters of the Common Agricultural Policy, the world trade in 'cultural products' (such as motion pictures; see Chapter 6), and the limits to the deregulation of public services. On the other hand, the same features have created a domestic climate in which failures to win support at EU level for French preferences (in defence, in competition policy, in the governance of the single currency) have contributed to rising Euroscepticism in a profoundly pro-EU nation, where concerns revolve around a number of specific ways in which France's commitment to EU membership (and leadership) challenges the capacity of the French state to honour its republican pact with the citizens of France as outlined at the outset of this chapter.

The 'Problems' of Integration for the French State

The Sovereignty Problem

The 1958 French Constitution explicitly states that the French people are sovereign. EU membership – and, in particular, the extension of EU-level policy competence – has required equally explicit 'transfers of power' to be written into the Constitution in the form of constitutional amendments under the provisions of Article 89. This procedure, particularly when Presidents Mitterrand and Chirac put the matter to public referendum (1993, 2005), has turned EU membership into a political matter that has disrupted traditional party cleavages, and revealed the French population to be divided in its attitudes to Europe and to the 'outside world' in general.

The Citizenship Problem

The Maastricht Treaty of 1993 included provisions for 'EU citizenship' (as seen in Chapter 2). Under the terms of the treaty, EU nationals have certain rights in any member state of the EU, including the right to vote and stand for election in local and European Parliament elections but not, in France, to stand for mayor or deputy mayor (see also Figure 4.1). This was a controversial clause in France, derided by the 'sovereignist' opponents of the Maastricht Treaty. Thanks to this development, the *French* people are, indeed, no longer exclusively sovereign over their own affairs: a British municipal councillor in rural Normandy, for example, has just as much decision-making power as his or her French counterpart. Furthermore, the measure exposes a long-lived reality of French political life; namely, that the French body politic is composed of more than one *nation*. Not only may EU nationals now reside in France with virtually identical rights to their French neighbours, but *their* rights contrast starkly with the paltry and discriminatory rights accorded to France's resident *non-EU* nationals (such as first generation Maghrebin immigrants; see Chapter 2).

The Liberalism Problem

France proclaims that it is a 'social Republic'. An important aspect of this ideal is that the state accepts as its duty the protection of its citizens, particularly in their guise as workers, from the excesses of the capitalist economy. Since the EU's single market initiative of the mid-1980s, and the staged transition to Economic and Monetary Union (EMU) in the late 1990s, the scope for state intervention at the national level in competition, industrial or monetary policy is strictly regulated. EMU has removed exchange rate control from domestic governments and required them to adhere to strict financial discipline in the form of low inflation and public deficit targets. These 'Maastricht criteria' have become associated in France with austerity measures or, more accurately, cut-backs in state spending (on state employee pensions, for example). In practice, developments such as EMU have provided tactical opportunities for successive French governments of both left and right to scale back the public ownership of economic and industrial resources, making way for privatization deals of considerable financial benefit to the state coffers (see Chapter 7). These developments have been controversial in a country where the notion of 'public service' is closely associated with state activity, and where political support for economic liberalism is virtually non-existent.

An additional dimension of this 'problem' lies in the clash we find in mainstream French political discourse between the values of 'Anglo-Saxon'-style capitalism in comparison with what French governments are apt to call the 'European' social model, which claims to 'humanize' market forces better to balance the interests of capital and labour. French governments are periodically accused of 'economic patriotism' when they seek to intervene in market decisions deemed detrimental to home-grown enterprise (see Chapter 7). Similarly, French leaders have had some success in 'uploading' national preferences into EU-level policy; the 1997 Amsterdam Treaty, for example, bears the French stamp in its recognition that 'general interest' services play a role in promoting social and territorial cohesion, and accordingly may qualify for state aid. The reality is that EU economic policy is predominantly guided by neo-liberal economic values that inherently challenge the ideal of an active, expensive state role in the market economy. President Sarkozy came to power in 2007 armed with the high-risk intention of bringing France into line with reality on this all-important dimension of French public policy.

French politicians used to justify the sacrifices involved in adjusting to 'Europe' by arguing that EU membership bolstered France's identity as a modernized postwar nation-state; that French leadership of the EU fulfilled France's ambitions to be a world power of global significance; and that *la construction européenne* – as European integration is invariably referred to in French – buffered France from the forces of globalization. President Sarkozy depicts the European Union, still, as a 'Europe that protects'. Here, however, he is referring principally to the scope for joint action in the face of truly global questions and dilemmas, such as the future of energy supplies, the human tragedies of forced and unregulated migration, and the need to defend Europe militarily in a world of nuclear proliferation. These are legitimate ambitions for EU-level action shared by many member states, and successes for France in shaping international policy in these domains may compensate for the growing fear amongst French voters regarding the economic costs of EU membership, and the distrust of the political class that this has engendered – a trend not unique to France.

Conclusions

Contemporary French government in 2008 is marked by the traumas and events of its past, both distant and of living memory. The Fifth

Republic and its Constitution were themselves born out of the Algerian debacle, which continues to pose policy challenges in today's France. The administrative map of France, as prosaic as it may seem, testifies to the large-scale political conflicts of eighteenth- and nineteenth-century France, and represents the triumph of what are seen as modern values of democracy, human rights and progress. At the same time, we have seen that contemporary French government has been marked by permanent and ongoing change, and by its permeability to external influences, and the current period is no exception. French government is significantly shaped by the successes and excesses of the postwar experiment in supranational policy-making at the European level, and it is hard to see how this process could be reversed, even though it raises many questions about the very foundations of French national identity. France in the last fifty years has demonstrated its capacity for change and its resilience, but also its propensity to resist serious departures from the past for fears of losing vested interests and a sense of identity. Thus, change management remains a politically risky and tricky business in France, where interests and tradition are habitually defended by means of conflict.

5

A Social French Republic

Introduction

The Constitution of 1958 states that 'France shall be a *social* Republic', and maintaining the 'social cohesion' of the French nation is a goal of French politicians across the political spectrum. In question is the state's ability to implement the principle of solidarity (in French, *fraternité*) that, along with *liberté* (liberty) and *égalité* (equality), constitutes the famous motto of the French Republic. The first vehicle here is the welfare state, especially what is known in France as *la sécu* (*la sécurité sociale*) – the social security system that delivers health care and most social benefits. This took shape over the decade between 1944 and 1954, to foster national solidarity after the traumas and destruction of World War II, and is a key pillar of contemporary French society. The second instrument here is the state education system, and particularly its schools. Shaped by centuries of political upheaval, the school system is designed to socialize young minds into the ways of the French republic, win their loyalty to the nation, and overcome inequalities of class and social background through the implementation of meritocratic and democratic ideals. A key aspect of this vision forms a third pillar of French society; namely, its secular identity, known as *la laïcité*. Since the French Revolution of 1789, and especially since the 1905 law separating Church and State, education in French state schools is characterized by the rigorous exclusion from school premises of what Madeley (2006) has called 'the religious factor' (seen in Chapter 3). This includes a ban in state schools on the wearing by a pupil in a state school of any item of clothing deemed by the school authorities to constitute a conspicuous religious symbol. In twenty-first-century France, the secular state, the welfare state and the state education system are all creaking under the strain of adapting to sociological, demographic and economic change in a society where vested interests defend themselves with notorious vigour, where expectations of the state remain high, and where public policy is anchored by the revolutionary ideal of universalism.

Universalism, in the French context, is a political philosophy whereby individuals are deemed to enjoy innate and natural characteristics that transcend differences, whether of gender, or nationality, for that matter. This ambitious perspective translates into the notional equality of all citizens and, vitally, a commitment to the equal treatment of all (by the state in particular), whatever their identity in terms of gender, race, ethnicity, religion or sexuality. From this perspective, what many Anglo-Saxon and Nordic countries understand as minorities (cultures, religions, races and so on) are traditionally not recognized as such by French public policy; neither, accordingly, is there a tradition of group or community rights. From this abstract perspective derives the reputation of the French Republic as blind to differences and so, also, to discrimination; for example on gender or ethnic grounds, which, in reality, can characterize and blight daily lives. Some inhabitants of France live as second- if not third-class citizens; this is especially true for those without French (or other EU member state) nationality; or those perceived as foreign because of the colour of their skin, or their accented French. This is a situation that undermines the fabric of French society, on some occasions fuelling serious violence. Accordingly, the question of 'diversity' and its accommodation has risen to the top of the political agenda in Sarkozy's France.

In this chapter, we first review the social structures that typify contemporary France – matters of family fabric, gender and age, for example – and consider how the state has fulfilled its duties to a population less bound by these markers of social convention than in the past. Under this heading, we review the French welfare state (and especially *la sécurité sociale*), which is reputed to offer some of the best health care in the world, but at the cost of crippling public finances, in particular as a result of high consumption rates of medicines and medical services. We evaluate provisions for other social services intended to prevent what is known as the 'social exclusion' of those lacking basic resources (such as housing, a job and/or educational qualifications), and to foster national solidarity (such as social housing and measures against poverty). We look at the legislation designed to account for the growing diversity of French society with regard to marriage and the family in traditional and non-traditional forms; and we review the broader debates that frame and contest these developments, such as discourses on women, gender and the family.

We then examine the realities of France's secular society, framed by the concept known as *la laïcité*. *La laïcité* is declared but not defined or guaranteed in the Preamble of the French Constitution (see Box 5.1); and all religions and faiths in France coexist within the boundaries of this secular state. *La laïcité* therefore refers to the constitutional and legal framework that separates religious affairs from public life in contemporary France. This system is supposed to guarantee the freedom of expression and conscience, and deliver equality of treatment. By separating the private and public realms in the matter of religious belief, this radical interpretation of secularism has, for its opponents, led to discrimination on ethnic grounds – for example, by targeting the wearing of the 'headscarf' (*le foulard* or *le voile*) by young Muslim women attending state schools; and it can certainly be construed as an assault on personal freedoms (*liberté*) and individual autonomy. The agenda of *la laïcité* is complex, but where it overlaps with ethnicity, France is some way from meeting its universalist aspirations.

Finally, we investigate the education system. This is designed to improve an individual's opportunity to lead a life that is both fulfilled (or 'examined', to borrow from Jean-Paul Sartre's existentialist vocabulary) and economically productive, and to knit a peaceful, thriving, prosperous, democratic and French society. In this sphere, too, France has a history of strong state intervention whereby the state has sought to integrate children into a single, French nation with a strong republican and secular identity. Primary school education in France has been free, compulsory and secular since the end of the nineteenth century but, by the middle of the twentieth century, schooling beyond the age of 14 was still, by and large, confined to a social elite. Fifty years on, however, by the turn of the twenty-first century, the French education system has 'democratized' itself to the point where a large majority (nearly two in three) of all 18-year-old French pupils take and pass their *baccalauréat*, which is subsequently their entry ticket to higher education or, more specifically, the university system. At this point, the impact that social origins – and, just as important, their aspirations – still have on people's opportunities and professional chances in today's France are at their most obvious, and takes the form of a parallel network of higher education

> **Box 5.1   A Social Republic**
>
> Article 1
>
> 'France shall be an indivisible, secular, democratic and social Republic. It shall ensure the equality of all citizens before the law, without distinction of origin, race or religion. It shall respect all beliefs. It shall be organized on a decentralized basis.
>
> Statutes shall promote equal access by women and men to elective offices and posts as well as to positions of professional and social responsibility.'
>
> *Source*:   National Assembly (2010).

establishments that still, to a large extent, train and reproduce a social – and political – elite. We look here at the attempts by the French state and other actors to address and redress ongoing inequality in this respect.

In all these matters of health and wealth – physical, material and psychological, the real picture is as complex as we would expect from a west European country, especially one with such a large population: we saw in Chapter 2 that France is the second largest EU country in population terms, with nearly 62 million people living on the French mainland (including Corsica). Despite its aspirations to national solidarity and equality of treatment, French society is as typified as its European counterparts by the individualism that is so characteristic of a mass consumer society, where materialism is becoming ever more entrenched, and by the social inequalities and inequities of imperfect social policy. We bring the chapter to a close, accordingly, by identifying the trends in contemporary French debate in this field – in particular, the recognition by public policy-makers of the significant *diversity* of French society, and the tentative steps taken to combat the intolerance of difference.

Social Structures and Social Policy

France, along with other European nations, has experienced the breakdown of traditional social structures and norms that took root in the nineteenth century with relation to religion and class, age and gender. These structures once forged a society that was deeply conservative, Catholic, and with a strongly Mediterranean and rural character. Only thirty years ago, these identities regulated individual choice and behaviours to a higher degree than in many comparable west European countries. British novelist Lucy Wadham (2009) gives a funny but thoughtful first-hand account of how, amongst some social groups in France – such as the young, Parisian middle classes – contemporary behaviours and attitudes regarding family, money, sex and other pleasures still bear strong traces of France's Catholic past. This, she contrasts with the puritanism of more predominantly Protestant cultures such as the UK and the USA. Nevertheless, France today is a society that is extremely open – economically, technologically, linguistically and culturally – to influences from the rest of the world, making it diverse and cosmopolitan. In terms of individual morality, furthermore, France, in the present day, is a markedly more liberal country than at any time in its recent past, with more children born out of marriage than inside it, and alternatives to marriage both popular and state-sanctioned.

Family and Friends

The family remains central to France's social fabric, but the typical French family today is increasingly likely to be less nuclear, more 'recomposed' (*la famille recomposée*) around second or third marriages, step-children, half-siblings and ex-partners. In 2005, nearly three million children aged under 25 in France (amounting to nearly 18% of all children of that age group) lived in single-parent families (*les familles monoparentales*), and over one million in *familles recomposées*. The vast majority of the single-parent families are composed of mothers and children, and are amongst the most vulnerable to economic downturns. More children are born to non-married than married heterosexual couples in France; and more heterosexual than same-sex couples avail themselves of the official alternative to marriage, the *Pacs* (*pacte civil de solidarité* – civil solidarity pact). At the same time, procreation, according to the civil code, is still the point of marriage. At their wedding ceremony, for example, couples are issued with a *carnet de famille* – a family book – specifically in order to record their children's births; and family policy has traditionally encouraged large families (*la famille nombreuse* – three children or more – of which there are currently around 1.7 million), as well as stay-at-home mothers, who could rely on universal (not means-tested) social benefits. The civil marriage ceremony conducted on behalf of the state by the mayor (see Chapter

4) cannot wed a same-sex couple; it is the court's duty, instead. Same-sex couples cannot, for the time being, adopt children in France (although this has been challenged by the European Court of Human Rights, and reform is virtually inevitable); but single-parent households can.

The number of marriages conducted in France in 2007 (266,000) was twice the number both of divorces and *Pacs*, but is still in the steady decline that began with the liberalization of divorce laws in the 1970s; the age of first marriages is rising too, to age 30 on average. The decline in the rate of marriage compares to a steady rise in the rate of divorce, and in the number of *Pacs* concluded (in 2007, 100,000 Pacs compared with 77,000 in 2006; particularly between heterosexual couples, confirming this as an alternative to traditional marriage). The drive to '*pactiser*' is generally a practical one, where partners are concerned with important matters of rights and duties, particularly in the event of the death of one partner, when the other becomes the legal heir (as was the case, for example, of Pierre Bergé, the *Pacs* and business partner of Yves Saint Laurent, and heir to his fortune on Yves Saint Laurent's death in 2008). For the time being, however, France has certainly stopped short of allowing so-called 'gay marriage' (with Nicolas Sarkozy, before his election as President in 2007, having declared himself implacably opposed to any change in this respect).

Families in France today are smaller than in the past, and old people cannot necessarily rely on their extended family, or even their children, to care for them in their old age: the summer heat wave scandal of 2003, where elderly mortality rates far exceeded normal figures, showed this with tragic effects. Yet, France, as elsewhere, has an ageing population that is growing in size, wealth, health and, therefore, influence. Neither can families necessarily sustain young people much beyond their coming of age at 18, although the family remains a very important social framework for young adults; most French university students, for example, live at home. However, the younger generations that will be coming to the end of their working lives in the 2030s face gloomy prospects of inheriting today's public debt, bankrupt *sécu*, and ailing pension provisions. The birth of the 'teenager' as a specific social identity coincided, in France, with both the social movements of May 1968 (as seen in Chapter 1) and the economic boom in consumerist and materialist behaviours; and French youth today finds itself torn between its identities as consumer, social revolutionary and productive worker. In this dilemma, they are not at all dissimilar from their counterparts in other countries. In France, therefore, age is less and less predictive of attitudes and behaviours, but is considerably less complex than gender, particularly with regard to belief systems and policy responses.

Gender and Sexuality

Family structures and relationships are closely linked to questions of gender and sexuality. Here, stereotypes have proved to be strong and resilient: the mistress lives on, for example perfectly illustrated by the revelations on his death in 1996 that former President Mitterrand had maintained a mistress and their child for much of the duration of his 14-year presidency. This had been an open secret, as we saw in Chapter 3. By and large, it is still socially acceptable in France to stereotype individuals according to their gender, unfettered by any overpowering sense of political correctness in this respect. In any case, the Anglo-Saxon terminology of women's 'liberation', or 'battle of the sexes' misses important points about dominant notions of femininity and sexuality in France; and feminist discourses have been complicated and fragmented by differing interpretations of French republicanism within the feminist movement. Legislation has gathered pace since the 1980s in favour of closing gaps between men and women in terms of their pay and professional opportunities (see Table 5.1), but as elsewhere in Europe, the gender gap is still a matter of daily life. Wadham's observations of Parisian life amongst wealthy, high-flying twenty-somethings in the 1980s and 1990s led her to observe that 'France seemed to have been bypassed by the feminist revolution' (Wadham, 2009: 39); and that French society was 'unreconstructed by feminist ideology' (*ibid.*: 234).

In many objective respects, and along with other European nations, France has seen a sharp decline in the patriarchal *structures* inherited from different times in the country's past; we would therefore expect *attitudes* to evolve in time. The feudal rule of primogeniture – where the first-born son inherited all a family's wealth – was swept away in the wake of the French Revolution; but the Napoleonic code of 1804, and the enduring influence of the Catholic Church in the nineteenth century, nevertheless fostered structures that, in practice, subordinated wives to their husbands. Most of these are now past history. Since the 1970s, women have had access to abortion and contraception, and no longer need their husband's permission to get divorced or open a bank account – and the stigma of divorce itself is definitely fading, as separation by mutual consent has been made faster and easier: it is possible that no one – not even the woman! – is to blame for the breakdown of a marriage. The very notion of an 'illegitimate' child has disappeared and, along with it, much of the former stigma; and children no longer need to bear their father's surname. There are legal frameworks for gender equality in the labour market – and family policy has gradually evolved to encourage women into the workplace, as is the norm in EU societies – and for 'parity' of women's equal access to 'to elective offices and posts as well as to positions of professional and social responsibility' (see Boxes 5.1 and 5.3).

The free-floating Bridget Jones character – the 'singleton' edging unmarried and childless into her mid-thirties – nevertheless remains something of a alien notion in France, certainly outside the bigger cities. At the same time, the association made between extreme youth and attractiveness in women is not as pronounced in France as in, say, the UK or the USA: older women in France can be sex symbols too (actress Catherine Deneuve being an obvious example here). Indeed, contrasting notions of femininity and female gender continue to divide French feminists. There is an inherent tension between, on the one hand, 'mainstream' feminists who are deemed by their opponents to uphold conformist, white, male, French ideals of femininity and sexual desirability and availability; and, on the other hand, those more radical voices whose point of departure is the diversity that characterizes 'the female experience'.

Such a clash derives much of its force from the very specific context of the universalist principles described earlier (see p. 123). Some of the most vociferous opponents of the parity reforms of 1999–2000, for example (see Table 5.1), were feminists who believed that any form of affirmative action for women undermines the universalist principle of equal treatment for all citizens, irrespective of their (self-defined) social identities. Proponents of women-friendly legislation of all kinds, on the other hand, have typically argued that French republicanism is, in fact, 'gender-biased' against women, and must be corrected by legislation.

These are arguments that overlap with and draw on broader discourses of diversity: how should the state respond to such challenges in a social policy environment marked by high costs, both financial and in terms of the political risk of reform? The management of the population's health and well-being from cradle to grave illustrates these vexed aspects of the quest for solidarity and inclusion.

Table 5.1   Legislative milestones on the road towards gender equality

Date	Development
1944	Women get the vote; Women eligible to stand for election.
1946	Equality between men and women written into the 1946 Constitution.
1965	Married women can work without their husband's permission.
1967	Contraception legalized.
1970	Principle of equal pay established.
1975	Abortion legalized up to 10 weeks Divorce permitted by mutual consent.
1999	The principle of parity in politics written into the 1958 Constitution.
2000	Law on equal access to electoral office and elective positions. Political parties were obliged to present an equal number of male and female candidates on electoral lists. In 2003, this was amended in line with electoral reform in regional and European Parliament elections: men and women candidates must now be alternated on the electoral lists. In 2007, the provision was extended to municipal elections (in *communes* of 3500 inhabitants or more), and to the councils of these *communes*, and of the regions.
2001	Law on professional equality between men and women.
2006	Law on equal pay for men and women.
2008	Constitutional reform extends the principle of parity ('equal access') beyond politics to women in 'positions of social and professional responsibility'.
2010	By 2010, the situation was mixed. In politics, 18.5% of National Assembly deputies were women (compared with 10.9% before parity was introduced). This figure still puts France in 19th place in the EU27. Nearly half of all France's deputies in the European Parliament (44.4%) are women, putting France into 6th place in the EU27, and compared with 30% in 1994. Of regional councillors, 48% are women, but only 7.7% are council presidents; 35% are municipal councillors, but only 13.8% are mayors. In 2010, one third of the government was composed of women. In the workplace, women's salaries are still, on average, nearly 20% lower than men's in the private sector, and nearly 40% lower in the public sector (including part-time work).

Source: Data from L'Observatoire de la parité (2010).

Social Security: Health, Wealth and the Limits of Solidarity

La Sécurité sociale, or *sécu* for short, is the overarching system that delivers welfare to the French population. In 2009, the budgetary deficit (or *trou* – hole – as it is usually known) of the *sécu* was expected to reach €20.1 billion, twice that of the previous year. All of the principal 'branches' of welfare provision were expected to be in shortfall; namely, health care (*l'assurance maladie*), old age pensions (*les pensions vieillesse*), and family benefits (*les prestations famille* – maternity and childcare payments).

Health care provision and other key welfare benefits, such as old-age pensions and family benefits, are principally resourced by what are known as 'social contributions', in a system of social insurance. Unemployment benefit (which has its own structures distinct from *la sécu*, and was created in 1951) also operates along similar lines. The 'social contributions' (known as *les charges sociales*) are made by workers and their employers, from their pay-packets and payrolls respectively, through occupational 'regimes' which, in turn, are run by workers' and employers' representative bodies known as the 'social partners' (see also Chapter 7).

This is solidarity in action, but it is flawed. 'Social contributions' are both inadequate to meet welfare costs, and costly to employers, themselves under pressure to control their costs and make profits. The assumptions on which the welfare state was created in the postwar *trente glorieuses* (particularly full employment) no longer apply, and welfare dependency is an expensive luxury, as in most European countries. In particular, the *solidarity* it aims to create between the generations, and between workers and the unemployed, is no longer sufficient to provide for the aged, the chronically-ill, or the long-term unemployed, which are as much part of the fabric of contemporary French society as the welfare state itself.

The state, accordingly, has had to step in and, unsurprisingly, is engaged in a war on cost. But tackling and trimming the French welfare state is political dynamite, and attempts to do so have typically either failed, or been limited in scope and effectiveness, however symbolically innovative. In terms of revenue, payslips now show deductions in the form of generalized income taxes such as the CSG (*la contribution sociale généralisée* – general social contribution). This tax removes just over 1% of an individual's income, including investments), and is specifically ring-fenced to fund 'universal' welfare payments for the low-paid or unemployed (over one third of health care spending is now met from the CSG). In today's France, similarly, unemployment benefit is firmly linked to job-seeking; and today's workers can no longer fund today's pensioners in the pay-as-you-go schemes of the past. Raising the retirement age, raising taxes and, more generally, levels of personal responsibility are the challenges currently facing French society and its policymakers, if the 'French social model' of welfare is to survive into the second decade of the twenty-first century and beyond. But since the welfare state is a pillar of French republican identity itself, attempts at reform are fraught with political danger.

Health Care
The French population is healthy by international standards. The smoking ban that came into law in 2008 – and was enforced – and the introduction of speed cameras onto French roads since 2002 to reduce the rate of fatal road traffic accidents from an annual average of just under 10,000 are recent attempts to improve matters still further. But France is not immune from the obesity-related diseases associated with other national cultures, and its ageing population suffer from similar rates of Alzheimer's and cancer as its neighbouring countries.

In its health care provision, *la sécu* has traditionally placed a high premium on the patient's right to access and consume drugs, services and specialisms based on the right to choose between a range of alternatives and, if so desired, to replicate this choosing until satisfied (but not necessarily cured). This emphasis on choice and on consumption has created a health care system that is renowned for being humane, high-quality and patient-centred, but at the cost of duplication, wastage and high cost. In France, in 2000, health care accounted for 9.6% of GDP, 1.5% higher than the OECD (Organisation for European Cooperation and Development) average.

Most health care professionals in France, such as general practitioners, are known as 'liberal professionals', meaning that they charge for their services at rates (mostly) set by the state. Accordingly, most individuals (patients) are expected to take out medical insurance policies with private, but non-profit-making organizations (called *les mutuelles*) to cover the shortfall between the total cost of this health care provision, and the amount that the state will reimburse; those on low incomes can expect 100% of their costs to be covered. In addition, and in recent years, the state has clamped down: medical professionals are no longer allowed to dispense medicines that are either not known to work, or known not to work; or, rather, the state will no longer refund the costs of such drugs if a 'generic' drug is proven to work better. Patients must now make a small, non-refundable contribution towards prescription charges, and ambulance and hospital transport (up to €50 per annum), as well as a non-refundable payment of €1 per visit to the doctor and towards blood tests and x-rays (again, to an annual total of €50).

Pensions

Systematic state provision for old age in the form of pensions post-dates the French health and unemployment benefits systems, but is run along similar, social insurance lines to those regimes. Crucially, France operates a pay-as-you-go system, whereby today's workers (in the form of social contributions and taxation) provide for today's retirees, and where private pensions are far from the norm; and the activity rate (in the job market) for those aged over 55 is below the EU average (see Chapter 7). Just as critical, France is an ageing society like its EU counterparts, with nearly one quarter of the population estimated to be over the age of 65 by the year 2030; it is also a society marked by exceptionally high longevity for women, with the figure for men just on the EU average (as seen in our Introduction).

State pensions provision is the product of a mix of general and occupational (complementary) pensions on the one hand, and means-tested, universal benefits drawn from general taxation on the other, especially where an individual's employment-linked contributions are minimal or non-existent. Over 10% of France's GDP currently goes into its state pensions, an above-average figure in EU terms. Thus, high unemployment brings the state ever further into a system that is already even more politicized than the health system; and reform here has been incremental, politically painful, and slow. A specific challenge has been the discrepancy between provision in the private and public sectors, with many state employees enjoying generous pensions after only relatively short, and not necessarily physically arduous, working lives (in the education system, for example). Successive governments have chipped away at such privileges; the Balladur reforms of the early 2000s, for example, began to align the length of pensionable service in the public sector with that of the private sector (forty years' of contributions), and to discourage early retirement. Sarkozy's governments have successfully dismantled the 'special regimes' enjoyed by a small minority of public sector workers, not all of whom work in physically demanding occupations; and more recent proposals have included the raising of the retirement age (currently set at 60 years; see Chapter 7).

'Precarity' and 'Exclusion'

These reforms are part of an agenda to reduce the public deficit; and they occur in the broader policy-making context of the European Union, which applies pressure on member states to trim their public expenditure (see Chapters 7 and 8). They also fit into a French political environment of shifting priorities in matters such as poverty, exclusion (from society – the opposite, therefore, of *solidarité*), and 'precarity' – living hand-to-mouth on either benefits and/or short-term, low paid employment contracts. 'Exclusion' has come to refer to 'the increasing number of people who have no social protection against sickness, unemployment and old age, and who are marginalised as a result' (Kelly, 2001: 90). Poverty, exclusion and precarity are socially visible and politically-charged questions, as are the 'withouts' (known as *les sans*; those without housing, for example, are referred to as *les SDF – sans domicile fixe*). French governments have found themselves lobbied by vociferous and often 'celebrity' groups from civil society campaigning on behalf of the disadvantaged (as seen in Chapter 3). Such actions invariably occur in the name of solidarity, making it impossible for the state to look away without being seen to undermine a very pillar of society. In reality, its responses, as in the matter of health, pensions and education reform, are as much a matter of symbolic and partial progress as evidence of life-changing or radical reform.

A Secular State in a Diverse Society

In the same way as welfare spending in France must increasingly account for the diversity of French society, even at the expense of universalist ideals, the secularism at the heart of French society is challenged by a society that is ethnically and religiously diverse. Individuals in France enjoy the freedom of expression and the right to practise their faith without persecution or discrimination, providing they do so in the private sphere, such as the family home (see Box 5.1). French history, we saw in Chapter 1, featured periods of extreme religious persecution and discrimination, and freedom from these is an important ideal and pillar of French republican society.

Religion may not structure society and individual behaviour as it did in the nineteenth or even twentieth centuries, but it certainly still shapes political debates.

There is no established Church in France, by virtue of a process that began with the French Revolution and culminated in the 1905 law separating Church and State. From 1801 until 1905, Napoleon's *Concordat* with the Catholic Church had ensured that the French state paid the salaries of Catholic clergy while appropriating their property and controlling their activities, and it recognized Catholicism as France's first religion. The 1905 law formally separated Church and State and overturned the *Concordat* regime, with the exception of the *départements of* Haut-Rhin, Bas-Rhin and Moselle which, in 1905, were part of Germany; here still, today, religion plays a bigger part in school and university curriculums than anywhere else in France.

The majority of French people today declare themselves to be Catholics – although this does not necessarily extend to attending church (probably fewer than 10% of all Catholics attend church on a regular basis). Moreover, Mendras and Cole (1991: 67) have shown how a 'fundamentally Catholic mentality' continues to shape French society in the form, for example, of demand for places at Catholic schools, and the ongoing emphasis on the family as the key social structure of French society. There is also a clear bias in French society that testifies to the symbiosis of the Catholic Church and State for many centuries. Thus, the holiday calendar in France revolves around Christian holidays (Easter, Christmas, and many others: France has more public holidays than most other EU countries thanks to Christian festivals; and every day of the year is associated with a saint's day). Visitors to rural France cannot help but notice the statues and shrines to the Virgin Mary on the outskirts of French villages, along with listings of the times that Mass and Holy Communion take place in the village's Catholic church. Moreover, the French state subsidizes private Catholic schools that contract to teach the national curriculum.

Nearly 20% of French schoolchildren are educated in private schools, nearly all in Catholic schools, and virtually all in schools 'under contract' with the state to teach the same curriculum as state schools. Other faiths can also benefit from such provisions (which have strong public support), and over 200 Jewish schools and one Muslim school in mainland France (the *Lycée Averroès* in Lille) do so. Up until very recently, parents were obliged by law to name their children after Christian saints (or figures that were symbolic of French history); traditionally, finally, time has been set aside in the school week (usually Wednesdays) for children in state education to take religious – Catholic – instruction outside the school. Nevertheless, nearly 80% of school-age children are educated in state schools in France where the principle of *laïcité* is applied with increasing rigour. Children are taught the history of France, and take the study of the French language – and philosophy – throughout their entire school life. No significant or systematic accommodation is made for any cultural or religious practices or beliefs (unlike in the UK, for example), and there is no religious education or instruction.

In today's France, there is also strong 'competition' to the Catholic Church in the form of other religions and belief systems, and this includes atheism. France has more Muslims than any other EU country (figures vary wildly and are usually between three and eight million); Judaism is the country's third most followed religion, and Protestantism is fourth. Buddhism and Scientology have their followers too; but the state reserves and practises the right to outlaw cults (*sectes*) it deems dangerous to public order by dint of 'brainwashing'. The French state has institutionalized dialogue with the Jewish and Muslim religious communities, although, in the case of the *Conseil français du culte musulman* (the French Muslim Council), the Muslim community is itself divided (as in most countries), and this has undermined the effectiveness of the relationship. To date, however, the over-riding state response to such religious pluralism has been to stiffen the law on *laïcité*, primarily at the expense, it is argued by critics, of Islam and its French followers.

In 2004, a law was passed in France that banned the wearing of 'ostensible religious insignia' in state schools; these 'insignia' include Jewish skullcaps, Christian crosses and the Muslim headscarf (*le foulard*) worn by many practising Muslim young women. The 'problem' of young girls wearing headscarves in school had been an issue for at least a decade before the law was passed (unanimously: *laïcité* is no longer a matter of left–right political battles), and, up until that point, head teachers were given the discretion to decide whether or not such symbols were disruptive of class discipline, or whether they were being worn defiantly, in which case the child would be obliged to remove the item. When former President Jacques Chirac began the process of hardening the rule that led to the 2004 law, he said it was because *la laïcité* was 'non-negotiable'. This was in the international context of the international so-called 'war on terror', and strong domestic support for Jean-Marie Le Pen, leader of France's National Front party that opposed any formal tolerance of minority ethnic and religious behaviours and practices (see Chapter 3). The law, in practice, still left it up to head-teachers and their staff to interpret what constituted defiant behaviour; some have allowed the *foulard* or *bandana*, which leave the neck and ears visible, but others have not; most have banned the *hijab*, which hides the hair, ears and neck from view

Five years later, in 2009, President Nicholas Sarkozy extended the debate regarding such symbols of religious affiliation out of the school to include the wearing of religious clothing in public. The *niqab*, he said 'was not welcome' on French soil, and he supported a parliamentary enquiry into its significance in French society. This, in turn, led to a 2010 law outlawing the wearing of the item in public. The *niqab* is usually referred to in English as the *burqa*, but they are not exactly the same: the *niqab* has a gap for the eyes between the headscarf and the fabric covering the rest of the face, whereas the *burqa* – associated with the Taliban regime in Afghanistan – hides the eyes too, behind a fabric mesh, and are worn in public by a tiny minority of France's Muslim women. Sarkozy's argument referred to this latter form of veil, and claimed that this was not an item of religious clothing, but a cultural practice that forced women to compromise their freedom, dignity and identity behind the 'grille' of their clothing. This was an opportunity for President Sarkozy to make explicit the distinction between the respect of all *religions* that is the basis of *laïcité à la française*; and the tolerance of different *cultures* – which, for Sarkozy, clearly has its limits (in this case, when cultural habits are deemed degrading to women). *Liberté* – in this example, apparently derived from a subjective interpretation of what constitute a woman's freedom – has trumped *égalité* (the freedom for *all* to dress how they like), and has challenged French Muslims to define the line dividing culture from religion.

The so-called 'headscarves affair', the 2004 and 2010 laws, and Sarkozy's statements half a decade later all point to the difficulties France experiences in reconciling the realities of its multicultural and multipath society with its theoretically universalist principles. France does not define itself as multicultural and, by the application to everyday life of philosophies such as *la laïcité*, attempts to downplay the differences between people, at least in public life. Some French intellectuals see the US and the UK, for example, as too 'politically correct' towards their minorities, by playing up their differences at

Table 5.2   *Laïcité* and the law

Date	Development
1801	The Napoleonic regime recognized and controlled the Catholic Church by Concordat.
1882	Jules Ferry laws instituting secular primary education.
1905	Law separating Church and State ('the law neither recognises nor remunerates nor subsidises any religion'. Some support is available for 'cultural' activities.)
1946	*Laïcité* is declared in the Constitution ('the people of France proclaim anew that each human being, without distinction of race, religion or creed, possesses sacred and unalienable rights').
1958	The Constitution states that France shall be a 'secular Republic'.
2004	Law banning 'ostensible religious insignia' in state schools.
2010	Law banning the wearing in public of clothing 'designed to conceal the face, in particular the "integral veil"'. The National Assembly approved the law by 335 votes to 1. In 2009, a young woman was evicted from a swimming pool in the Paris region for wearing the sports version of this veil, the 'burkini'. In 2010, a young woman was fined for driving whilst wearing a full veil.

Sources: Observatoire de la parité 2010; National Assembly (2010); Legifrance (2010); France Diplomatie, *Label France*, No. 60 (2005) (Paris).

the expense of society as a whole: this perspective on political correctness – as an Anglo-Saxon import – is contentious, and fuels intellectual and political debate. The result is that differences get ignored, and discrimination arises. This, in turn, has led to serious problems of social integration and unrest in France (as seen in Chapters 2 and 3), and to ongoing reform in the education system, the pillar of society designed to flatten out, if not equalize, differences of origin of social, ethnic and religious kinds.

Education, Class and Opportunity

French state schools are not only a battleground for the expression of personal autonomy over and above religious beliefs; they also shape life chances, or are supposed to. They are expected to do this in the manner of a social elevator (known as the *ascenseur social*) that moves in one direction only: from the basement to the top. French children, on average, stay at school for longer than their counterparts in any other OECD country (nearly 17 years in full-time education), and France spends slightly more of its GDP (6%) on its overall education budget than the OECD average. Many French children from the age of two months attend a state day nursery (*crèche*); and both child-minders (*les assistante maternelles*) and after-school care (*la halte-garderie*) are similarly regulated by the state. Virtually 100% of all three-year-olds go to nursery school (*la maternelle*) and stay in full-time education until they are 17 or 18. Of young people aged between 17 and 29, 80% currently are in full-time education; and over 60% of a generation (over 500,000 pupils) attempt the high-school leaving examination, the *baccalauréat* (on average at age 19) each year, in comparison with only 10% in 1960, and 5% in 1950. Pass rates at the *baccalauréat* are high: over 83% of entrants passed the exam in 2007, 83.5% in 2008, nearly 86% in 2009, and 85.4% in 2010. Yet, school failure and dropping-out is common (as they are in the early years of university education, where between 40% and 50% of students fail or leave after their first year); 17% of young people left school in France in 2004 with no qualification whatsoever; unemployment rates in France for those aged between 16 and 24 are persistently high; qualifications are gradually being devalued on the job market; and, unsurprisingly, reform of the French education system is both endemic and politically troubled.

Democratization

The state education system in France today is based on the principle of equality of access, treatment and opportunity for all children. It underwent a rapid democratization and massification process from the 1950s onwards but, inevitably, the system is far from perfect. Historically, education in France was based on a clear hierarchy of social classes, and structures of hierarchy and elitism still character-ize education in France today, albeit in more subtle and changeable forms.

The Ferry laws of 1881 and 1882 dictated that primary school should be universal, obligatory, free and secular; indeed, the teachers of the Third Republic constituted an important and vociferous source of support for the regime and its republican ideals. The Catholic Church, however, was still allowed to teach at secondary level; and secondary level education itself was still reserved to a small elite. The secondary *lycée* establishment and its leaving examination, the *baccalauréat*, were founded under the Napoleonic regime in 1802 specifically to train elites, along military lines, for the state bureaucracy; entry to both the *lycée* and the teaching profession itself was reserved largely to the wealthy middle classes, irrespective of merit.

Part of France's post-1945 transformation included a succession of attempts by the government to democratize education. Fees for secondary school had been abolished in the 1930s, but entry to the prestigious *lycées* and their *baccalauréat* was academically difficult, and most children ended their formal, primary education aged 14 (with or without a leaving certificate – *le certificat d'études primaires* (CEP) – a passport to employment and, possibly, a career), at which point they were available to work for their family or, perhaps find work in training as an apprentice. Harvard academic Laurence Wylie's sociological account of living in France with his family in Provence in 1951 provides an excellent account of the high stakes of the CEP, as well as a summary of the contents and grading system of the exam itself (Wylie, 1964: 91–7).

The Berthouin reforms of 1959 extended compulsory education to the age of 16, and channelled all 11-year olds into 'secondary' schools (*le collège*); this was a concerted drive to raise the educational standards of the whole population. In 1975, the Haby reforms transformed the *collège* into what it is today, by and large. This is known in the UK as the 'comprehensive system', and in France as *le collège unique*. It is intended to standardize all pupils' experience of secondary education, and thereby raise the chances of equal access for all to the *lycée*, aged around 15, and thereafter to higher education. By means of the *collège unique*, moreover, children should *not* 'know their place' in society but, rather, see themselves as equal, and be treated as such. But a combination of the historical hierarchies inherent in French society and its education system on the one hand (where the teacher knows best), and the diversity of French society on the other, have undermined the egalitarian ambitions of these reforms. Many factors dictate and structure different outcomes for different children through the state school system, where early choices (of subject, stream and so on) can seriously narrow subsequent career prospects. Public policy, here, seeks a balance between the pursuit of equality, and the goal of equity (fairness), by compensating for the social factors that make school failure more likely.

Although success in France's meritocratic system is in theory confined only by ability, in reality it is also conditioned by more structural factors. These include gender, as well as, crucially, a child's origins and identity in regional, social and ethnic terms – which form the child's cultural 'baggage' or 'capital' that, in turn, influences their ability to access the resources made available to them. In reality, schools can reproduce these inequalities and fail to lift their charges beyond the ground floor; and, if a child fails at school (there is even a specific term for this experience – *l'échec scolaire*), they are likely to fail in society and find themselves excluded (from jobs, housing, health and wealth), or at least marginalized from it. Failure at school and failure to get the 'right' qualifications matter greatly in a job market where qualifications definitely trump personal (or even professional) experience, and where jobs and careers are still thought to be for life. On paper, this may well be a fair system, but it struggles to accommodate inequalities of birth and early childhood, which can be left to mutate into a second-class educational and career trajectory – or long-term unemployment. French society is less structured by class than in its past but, as in other countries, subtle and not so subtle distinctions apply, and affect everyday lives in real ways.

Of such factors, gender is perhaps the least significant, since girls are as numerous and successful as boys right through school and into higher education, although girls are over-represented in so-called 'soft' subjects (such as literature) at the *baccalauréat*, and their glass ceiling comes later in professional and domestic environments where gender stereotyping can work against them. More pertinent than gender is the matter of a child's social origins defined by class. Class means different things in different societies; in France, it is very closely correlated with occupation. Class consciousness is historically high – particularly amongst the working classes, whose identity was transmitted throughout the twentieth century by the French Communist Party, now virtually defunct. But other occupations in France have developed strong class identities. We saw in Chapter 2 that farmers, and especially *paysans*, carry a cachet of their own; so do *artisans*; for example, craftsmen and women in regulated professions (from bakery to builders) for whom the *artisan* label is a badge of status and, probably, quality. Similarly, independent professionals and the more-wealthy, leisured classes once known as the *bourgeoisie* have their place in the French social pecking order. The decades after World War II in France (as seen in Chapter 1) brought about a rapid decline, first, of the *paysans* and then of industrial workers as distinct classes. In their place came the rise of a new class, the *cadres*, white-collar workers with managerial responsibilities in large organizations in the public and private sectors. These were the architects of France's postwar socio-economic transformation and the bedrock of what is today, in France, a sprawling middle class that extends from menial white-collar workers (*les employés*) to include senior managers and civil servants, and large-scale agricultural owners. As in other European countries, it is predominantly the middle classes that worry about the loss of distinction and the devaluation of their status – in particular, on the job market. Accordingly, strategies to maximize their children's opportunities in the school system are commonplace, and map on to hierarchies in schools that perpetuate and compound differences arising from children's social origins, as well as their innate abilities and motivations.

So, for example, not all *baccalauréats* are equal; neither, more to the point, are *lycées*, and attempts by parents to get around the rule of attending the closest school are commonplace. The 'general' *baccalauréat*, especially the stream emphasizing maths and science (*série S*), is still prized more highly than its 'technological' and 'professional' alternatives, which were created after the 1960s. The 'technological' *baccalauréat*, for example, includes subjects relating to the tertiary and industrial sectors of the economy; and a 'professional' *baccalauréat* would be a logical route for a young person seeking to work in the (growing) services sector. Yet, in 2007, only 16.8% of all *bacheliers* studied for the technological *baccalauréat*, and fewer still for the *professional* version (12.8%); and success rates on these two routes are around 10% lower than for the general *baccalauréat*, although the gap is closing. Who takes the 'general' *baccalauréat*? Around 33% of its pupils are the children of *cadres* or 'higher intellectual professions' (such as doctors and lawyers) compared with approximately 12% children of blue-collar workers (*ouvriers*). In contrast, one quarter of those studying for the 'professional' *baccalauréat* exams are the children of *ouvriers*, and only 8% are children of *cadres*. Similarly, parents can get around the confines of the catchment system (*la carte scolaire*) by opting for schools offering specialist classes (in languages, for example), hoping to stack the odds early in their child's favour; they can also, if they wish, send their child to a private school at their own cost. Since the election of President Sarkozy in 2007, moreover, the French government is committed to extending parental choice by relaxing the requirement of the *carte scolaire* that children attend their nearest school; and, it claims, by forcing schools with a high demand for places to favour local children from disadvantaged backgrounds, over children from other localities with pushier, middle-class parents.

Meritocracy and Elites

This scrambling to preserve middle-class privileges of social and cultural 'capital' or resources perpetuates itself into higher education. In 2007, 22% of all young people took their studies at least two years beyond the *baccalauréat*, compared with only 8.6% in 1982. These figures mask disparities according to the parents' profession, since only about 15% of these had a father who was worker or farmer (*ouvrier*; *agriculteur*) and, although the number of students from these backgrounds is rising, it is doing so at a slow rate, and from a low point. The French higher education system, moreover, offers very distinct routes to very different career outcomes, where a student's social and cultural background and confidence are at a premium.

The university system itself (France currently has 83 state universities) is based on the principle of access for all young people who have passed their *baccalauréat* exam, however well or badly, and who pay minimal tuition fees. The universities are, therefore, chronically overcrowded, and failure after one year is commonplace. Moreover, French universities are under-funded and 'uncompetitive' in terms of attracting international students. They are also prone to repeated and often prolonged industrial action on the part of both students and staff with pronounced, usually ideological, vested interests in the status quo. The most obvious of these concerns is the entrenched principle that universities should not select their students on any criteria other than the possession of a *baccalauréat* pass (at least, not until they have completed three or four years' study). This is unlikely to change and, to date, reform of the French university system has been incremental; even the overhaul after the 1968 events, which created many new universities, was limited in effect.

In contrast, the French state heavily funds what are known as its *grandes écoles*, of which there are over two hundred. *Grandes écoles* exist explicitly to train elites; historically, these were confined to the teaching, military and engineering professions. In today's France, however, many *grandes écoles* specialize in business and management studies; and, since 1945, the 'national school of administration' – *l'École nationale de l'administration* (*l'ENA*) – has become a virtually indispensible rung on the ladder to high office in politics, government or the state bureaucracy (President Sarkozy being a notable exception here; see Chapter 4). These schools, particularly the best of them, are renowned for their strong *esprit de corps*, which translates in their working lives into powerful alumni networks of influence and patronage.

Notions of elites and elitism are nothing new in France. From the nobility of the *ancien régime* to the lawyers of the French Revolution, the military and bureaucratic leaders of Napoleon's Empire, and the political and intellectual elites of postwar France, France has maintained an innate sense of social hierarchy that can be experienced in everyday life in France. The entry ticket to the *grandes écoles* (a system with strict hierarchies of its own) is itself high, although most *grandes écoles* operate a system of means-tested grants for poorer pupils. The prestigious, Paris-based Political Science Institute (*Sciences Po*), the feeder school for *l'ENA*, has, for a decade, implemented a form of positive discrimination in favour of pupils from unconventional and disadvantaged neighbourhoods who are allowed to by-pass the competitive entry exam. Results suggest the experiment is a success, and it has gained momentum, spreading to other establishments (see Illustration 5.1). The barrier separating universities and *grandes écoles* is also gradually becoming more permeable, with movement from one to the other a possibility. In general, however, the degree of cramming required to pass the competitive entry exams (usually in special preparatory classes that last up to two years after the *baccalauréat – les classes préparatoires aux grandes écoles –* CPGE or *'classe prépa'*) works against students with what Keaton (2006) calls 'cultural deficits', for whom the 'school canon' of Franco-French literature, history and language jars with their own ethnic and cultural backgrounds; and for whom intensive cramming and studying aged between 17 and 20 may simply not be an option.

French education reform is politically contentious, and the past decades are littered with failed attempts and a succession of ministers at the helm of the education ministry. But the themes tackled by reform are constant: how to address rising levels of violence and 'incivility' amongst school pupils? How to improve opportunities for euphemistically-called 'new' pupils from minority ethnic or social groups? How to respond to what is widely seen as a decline in deference and in respect for authority in the family, and its repercussions on society at large? How to improve the employment prospects for children from ethnic minorities, proven to be worse than those of other young people in France? And how to conduct reform in a field – education – where beliefs in the abstract principles of French republicanism are high, and where interests are entrenched precisely,

This is one of the most prestigious *lycées* in the capital, situated in the heart of the Left Bank district. In 2006, the school launched a scheme to widen access to its *classes préparatoires*, the crammer years for France's notoriously difficult and highly competitive *grandes écoles* entrance exams. The idea was to admit pupils bright enough to try for these exams, but disadvantaged in terms of their cultural baggage, their family and educational experiences.

Illustration 5.1   The Henri IV lycée in the fashionable 5th *arrondissement* of Paris

thanks to a system that prizes so highly the 'right' qualification (as a teacher, for example) as a passport that remains valid for the rest of one's working life no matter, often, how one performs? These issues take us back to the general questions addressed in the course of this chapter.

Conclusions

All EU member state governments find themselves under pressure to trim the size and the cost of the state. Welfare and education provisions are not immune from this exercise. In France, the task is complicated by the framework of historical and political battles that constitute today's French republican culture. French governments find themselves under some obligation to translate 'grand principles' into everyday policies. In the case of social policy, this means the encouragement of solidarity between citizens, on the understanding that the state will treat its citizens equally. Amongst political and intellectual elites there is considerable attachment to this interpretation of republicanism and, in particular, to the notion that it constitutes a 'model' of society that is admirable, exceptional and exportable.

Long before iconoclast Nicolas Sarkozy came to power as French President in 2007, citizens and politicians alike in France were confronted with the stark realities of the differences, diversity and discrimination that characterized French society, just as much any abstract notion of the 'universal' citizen. Social contributions (the practice of solidarity) fell short of funding welfare provision. The hardening of *laïcité* legislation brought *culture* into a relationship between state and society that is supposed to govern religion only. The meritocratic and egalitarian principles underlying the state education system have allowed inequalities to take root and distort individuals' experience of society at crucially formative stages of their life.

President Sarkozy's approach to change includes a willingness – or, to his critics, a dangerous determination – to introduce new ideas and language into the state–society relationship. In January 2008, for example, he called for 'diversity' to feature alongside 'pluralism' in the Preamble to the 1958 Constitution, to signal the modernization of French republican values. So far, constitutionally, this has remained a dead letter, but it has sparked debate and generated new language. Sarkozy, for whatever reason, has dared to challenge many of the taboos and icons of French republicanism to the point of deconstructing the French 'model' of society itself. From this perspective, French national identity in the twenty-first century is not dependent on abstract notions of solidarity or equality that, in practice, are impossible to implement fairly across a large and diverse population. Similarly, in this view, Sarkozy's France has no real need for a ban on headscarves or full veils, because the battle between Church and State has been won. Cultural battles are a different matter entirely, and the recognition of 'cultural diversity' remains a contentious political issue in France today.

6

Culture and Identity

Introduction

Contemporary France is renowned for its culture, and culture is a patently obvious aspect of French national identity. French art, literature, cinema, fashion, film, cuisine, wine, photography and theatre have all enjoyed periods of epic and global status. French ideas are the backbone of much contemporary philosophy, and the French language is treated by French governments as a vehicle for challenging the 'Anglo-American' (Hayward, 2007) orthodoxies of the world. Cultural diplomacy – the promotion of French culture and language across the world – is an important dimension of French foreign policy, and France periodically engages in cultural 'wars' with US administrations in defence of home-grown French assets such as Roquefort cheese, champagne and art-house cinema. France champions these cultural 'products' against alternatives – often Anglo-American in origin – deemed inferior, homogenized, or both. Typically, these battles end in triumphs for quantity and quotas, and are matters of trade and competition as much as tradition.

Indeed, French culture is indisputably a commercial affair. The manufacture and export of the famous, luxury, so-called 'Paris' goods – such as perfume; and *haute couture* from the small, extravagant fashion houses of Chanel, Dior, Givenchy and (by 2009, bankrupt) Lacroix – are just as important for the French economy as for national pride. Moreover, France is the world's most visited country (with almost 80 million foreign visitors in 2008), and Paris receives the most tourists per year (nearly 30 million) than any other city on earth. Disneyland Paris is the most popular of all French tourist attractions, with about twice as many visitors annually as the Louvre (16 million and 8 million, respectively) (see Box 6.1). Annually,

France welcomes flocks of tourists whose spending, representing over 5% of French GDP, is critical to the economy's balance sheet. The aesthetics of French design fuel lucrative French business in fields as diverse as fashion and automobile construction. History and heritage are economic commodities, as are France's architecture, gastronomy and natural attractions. French cultural successes in film, literature and art owe as much to the market and its demand for entertainment and popularity, and to the exceptions to trade regulations that are made for 'cultural products', as they do to traditional norms of art, taste and refinement.

Alongside its glamorous image and exports, moreover, daily, domestic French ways of life – food, drink, conviviality, pastimes, leisure activities – are integral to the quality of life for which France is renowned, and contribute to its culture in the popular sense. This is the famed, French *art de vivre*. 'Popular culture' say Mendras and Cole (1991: 221) 'lays great emphasis on activities as ends in themselves', as opposed to 'means to ends'. To take French President Sarkozy as an example, he may jog for the pleasure of jogging, or – by all accounts – to get fit. More broadly defined, popular culture in France is just as important to national identity as the projection abroad of French cultural success and creativity. How French people spend their free time and their spare cash, and how they seek to 'cultivate' themselves – or not – constitute significant dimensions of French society and national character.

The facts suggest that 'culture' is both more prominent in French society, and more democratically enjoyed, than at any other time in France's history, although social origins still shape people's cultural habits. Which newspapers which French people read; how much they spend on books, and how many of them they actually *read*; how often they go out, and to do what; how many hours they spend in front of the television (in 2008, three hours and 25 minutes per day, on average, and falling amongst the young, who spend around two hours per day on the Internet), and what they watch are all choices that shape contemporary French identity. 'Consumption' of the television, and the Internet in particular, has narrowed traditional gaps in French lifestyles, such as that which once existed between urban and rural dwellers, or between bourgeois and working-class lives. Differences in cultural behaviours do still exist, nonetheless, between men and women, between people of different ages, and between individuals according to their educational attainments, as in many developed societies. Parisians, unsurprisingly, 'consume' more culture than their counterparts in the 'provinces'. Inevitably, not all culture in France is mainstream; and pluralism – the respect for, the incorporation into policy, and the encouragement of difference and diversity – is a professed goal of politicians of left and right in matters of culture, as well as in social affairs more broadly.

French cultural health in all these respects – diplomacy, trade, social cohesion – operates as a bellwether of national well-being, and for centuries it has been official policy to place culture at the heart of nation-making. French kings and Presidents from the *ancien régime* to the present day have conducted themselves as arbiters of taste and fashion, and the state has always spent heavily on culture, even in lean times. The grandest buildings of Paris, new and old, and the *châteaux* of the Loire Valley, to cite only a few examples, are permanent reminders that, in the history of France, appearances matter, and heritage (known as *le patrimoine*) has pedigree.

As a colonial power, furthermore, France sought to 'civilize' native populations overseas by cultural means, including language (as well as religion), and its model for the integration of its minorities in France today still echoes the traditional goal of assimilation, by immigrants, of the dominant national culture, principally expressed through the French language. Thus, nation-building in France has at times involved the systematic repression of regional languages and identities, and sustained state spending on and intervention in cultural matters. In France, today, culture is increasingly decentralized, with local authorities spending the lion's share of public monies on cultural matters; and with regional identities, while having relatively little political significance, playing an important role in the French tourist trade, and contributing to the make-up of French national identity.

Indeed, in the present day, France's cultural identity encompasses the diversity inevitable in a population as cosmopolitan as the French. Ethnicity is as vital a source of cultural creation in France as is youth, or the expression of differences such as gender, sexuality and lifestyle, or the quest for tourist revenue. Much that is iconic for the tourist visitor to France, especially in Paris, is typically bound up with traditional images of France, and is liable to be expensive at best, disappointing at worst. But it is part of the variety that makes up French cultural identity and, in this respect, is as authentic as the literary canons, regional country cooking and ethnic music forms. Cultural life in France is as much a local as national affair, and the state periodically intervenes to ensure that this is so: the so-called 'democratization' of culture has been an objective of each and every President of the Fifth Republic. From a cultural perspective, there is no one 'real France', just as we saw in Chapter 2 that there is no *France profonde* beyond nostalgic imaginations and sentiment. It would be an exaggeration to claim that there are significant sub- or counter-cultures in today's France, but there are diverse ways of speaking French, especially amongst the young (as in most cultures), and a strong demand for music other than the traditional French *variété* (pop) or *chanson* (lyrical song), by way of example. French national and local authorities, by and large, attempt to support 'cultural diversity' at home, but critics – in the fields of contemporary literature, for example – argue that anti-establishment voices on France's cultural scenes are left out in the cold.

In what follows, first, we explore the politics of culture in contemporary France: culture is definitely political, and has been for as long as modern France has existed. This revolves around the role of the state, especially 'the Ministry', in fostering, regulating, promoting and protecting cultural norms and 'commodities' at home and abroad. We emphasize the examples of language and cinema to illustrate our arguments: in each case, French governments have sought to protect and promote their assets in equal measure, and their motives have been commercial as much as political. We then, second, survey the cultural practices and behaviours that define contemporary France, and surmise here that notions of lifestyle are as much part of the image that France projects as its claims to 'exceptional' creativity and heritage; and that the French amuse themselves in broadly similar

Table 6.1   But is it culture?

Ranking	Site	Number of visitors (million)
1	Disneyland Paris	14.5
2	Louvre Museum, Paris	8.3
3	Eiffel Tower, Paris	6.8
4	Georges Pompidou Centre, Paris	5.5
5	Chateau de Versailles	5.3
6	Musée d'Orsay, Paris	3.2
7	Cité des Sciences et de l'Industrie	3.0
8	Parc Astérix, Paris region	1.6
9	Parc Futuroscope, Poitiers	1.6
10	Arc de Triomphe, Paris	1.5

Source: Data from INSEE (2010a: 24), figures for 2007.

ways to their counterparts in the UK, the USA and beyond. In our conclusions, we emphasize the complexity that lies behind the dominant, stereotypical images of French culture: virtually all aspects of French cultural life have a market and often international dimension, for example; and tales of 'decline' are apocryphal. In France, the past – 'History' – has commercial value, as does the 'heritage' business in many countries; but it also constitutes what Sonntag (2008) has aptly called a 'prison wall' that is perceived by policy-makers as risky and costly to cross. Culture– its practice, its value, its significance – is closely linked to the evolution of society at large.

The Politics of French Culture

State and Nation

Culture may well have intrinsic value, but for centuries in France it has also served a variety of political purposes. All presidents of the Fifth Republic, drawing on their considerable powers, have sought to make their mark on the cultural face of France, and to bequeath to the nation their very own cultural legacy. Dating from the very beginning of the Fifth Republic in 1958, the principal cultural agendas pursued by French presidents have been threefold. First, is the promotion of France's *heritage* (*le patrimoine*). Heritage has intrinsic value – in commemorating (and glorifying) the past which, in turn, is designed to unify French society, and commercial value – in terms of tourist receipts. André Malraux, friend of de Gaulle and first Minister of Culture of the Fifth Republic, referred to this agenda as 'making accessible the key works of humanity, and especially those of France, to the greatest possible number of French people'.

A second agenda is to foster creativity and cultural production – '*la création*' – by encouraging and supporting creativity in its own right, and as an 'industry', such as the cinema. This, Malraux defined as 'giving preferential treatment to the creation of works of art and of the spirit which enriches our cultural heritage' (thus defining culture rather narrowly). The third broad policy goal – favoured notably by Presidents Charles de Gaulle, François Mitterrand and, most recently, President Sarkozy – and closely linked to, but potentially in contradiction of, the two previous goals is the more nebulous notion of 'democratization': making more culture more accessible to more

Box 6.1   Access to culture: it's a right

The Preamble to the Constitution of 27 October 1946, which has force of constitutional law in contemporary France, states that:

'The Nation guarantees equal access for children and adults to instruction, vocational training and culture.'

Source: Elysée (2010b).

(types of) people. Indeed, equal access to culture has been a constitutional right for the French since 1946.

In reality, these three agendas overlap, and they have each also evolved with time to reflect changing habits, practices and technologies. Thus, in 2009, the French Ministry of Culture and Communication presented its priorities as heritage, creation, the cultural industries and the media. In Sarkozy's France, entry to France's national museums' permanent collections has become free for those aged under 26 from France and other EU countries – and their teachers. Tax breaks have been devised to encourage the private funding of cultural creation, and to attract foreign production companies to make films in France, hence showcasing France's natural assets. More funding has been earmarked for the Ministry of Culture. The teaching of art history is to be expanded in schools; public television and radio broadcasting is the subject of significant reforms. Additionally, in 2009, President Sarkozy expressed his desire for no less than the creation of a 'Museum of the History of France' – an idea met with considerable scepticism by historians and cultural figures alike.

President Sarkozy is by no means the first French President to presidentialize the cultural agenda. The city of Paris itself offers an exemplary chronology of presidential cultural politics in the form of eye-catching architectural projects, in some cases housing cultural treasures, known as *les grands projets*. Georges Pompidou's cultural centre in the heart of Paris (known as *le centre Pompidou* or *Beaubourg*) is one of the top five most visited 'cultural sites' in France (Table 6.1). François Mitterrand (President, 1981–95) was the most ambitious of all: the Pyramide du Louvre; la grande Arche de la Défense; the Opéra Bastille and the Bibliothèque française (the national library building in the 13th *arrondissement* in Paris) all symbolize this aspect of Mitterrand's presidential agenda for culture, and were celebrated in style on the occasion of the 1989 bicentenary celebrations of the French Republic – itself a conspicuous cultural event. For Looseley (1995: 139) Mitterrand's *grands projets* were a cornerstone of the President's ambition to 'reassert but redefine a national culture' and of 'enhancing France's international prestige and Paris' tarnished image as a cultural capital of the world'.

Critics, indeed, deride Paris as a 'museum city' that reeks of national nostalgia for the past. Many of its monuments, such as the Arc de Triomphe, are testaments to past victories, but the city has moved with the times. The Pyramide du Louvre and the Pompidou Centre in particular were deemed, in their time, shockingly modern and transgressive of traditional norms of taste to those opposed to the dramatic developments, and the grande Arche de la Défense could not be more different from the Arc de Triomphe. The Louvre, for its part, has projected itself into the future with plans for a sister Louvre in Lens, northern France (to open in 2012) and, more daringly, the Louvre-Abu Dhabi. The Pompidou Centre has its own sister museum in Metz, Lorraine.

Alongside his *grands projets*, François Mitterrand supported a policy of *le tout culturel* (translatable as 'everything is cultural' or, to its critics, perhaps, 'anything goes'). This was the 'democratization' plank of cultural policy under Mitterrand and it was, by and large, the work of the Minister for Culture appointed by Mitterrand to his first government in 1981, Jack Lang. It was also part of a policy to encourage *la création* and, thereby, to boost the economic and business receipts of cultural activity, demonstrating not only how closely these different aspect of the politics of culture are intertwined, but how tightly connected culture can be with broader political agendas. Looseley has pointed out, for example, how these 1980s attempts to get 'beyond high culture' (1995: 113) were part of a much broader Socialist Party manifesto of social reform that prioritized the recognition of the 'right to difference', working with those marginalized by society, and the fight against racism. The decentralization agenda of this decade (see Chapter 4) was also reflected in cultural policy.

In today's France, the annual *fête de la musique* – launched by Lang in the mid-1980s – takes over the streets throughout France in June and has proved popular, as has the *fête du cinéma* of September each year, when cinema tickets are available at bargain prices, and the joys of cinema-going are advertised using state funds. Just as popular are the *Paris Plage* summer event, when a stretch of the Seine in Paris is turned into a summer resort with sand and palm trees; the *nuits blanches* or 'all night' openings in cities across France every October; and, more formally perhaps, the September *journées du patrimoine*, when the state opens its buildings to the public at large. It is estimated that 12 million visitors queued to see inside the Elysée Palace – the official residence and office of the President – in September 2008 on the occasion of the 25th 'Heritage Day' in Paris. Overall, however, those on the margins of society, targeted by Mitterrand and Lang, remain excluded from the cultural life of the nation; and increases in state spending on culture invariably benefit those already used to accessing culture of all kinds.

Language Policy

Thus, the French state has a history of aiming to steer the image, production and consumption of French culture, both in France and internationally. Its legislation on the use of the French language exemplifies these efforts and their limitations. For centuries, language policy has been used as a tool to attempt to unify the French around a common language by means, at different times, of repression or regulation seeking to protect and/or promote the use of French within France's boundaries. Even today, the status of France's regional languages is contentious: only since 2008 have regional languages been identified in the French Constitution as part of France's 'heritage', but not in the Preamble of the Constitution itself, as supporters would have wished (see Box 6.2).

The move in 1539 (the Villers-Cotterêts ordinance) from Latin to French for official purposes was an early example of the use of language as a tool of cultural policy; and the 1992 amendment to the constitution of the Fifth Republic to add to Article 2 the declaration that 'The Language of the Republic shall be French' is a more recent example of French governments turning to the law – here, the highest law in the land – to control the pace and impact of social change and, just as significant, to shore up the usage of French at home and abroad. The *Académie française* to this day continues a centuries-old tradition of codifying and standardizing the language, particularly in its written form, and acting as watchdog over its 'purity'. This amounts to proposals for amending, or stiffening, rules of grammar and vocabulary in line with social developments such as feminism, and the openness of French society to foreign terms. In practice, language regulates itself and respects the law far less than it subjects itself to fashion and trends. Language, in France as elsewhere, is a source of creativity, too, and this is reflected in contemporary French literature, cinema and especially music – reflecting ethnic origins, for example, and youth culture.

Indeed, the laws of the mid-1990s in France – which placed quotas on the amount of French-language music to be broadcast in prime time on France's music radio stations, and which imposed the use of French in any number of professional and public settings (see Box 6.2) – were justified in terms of the importance of the French

---

Box 6.2   It's the law: regulating the use of the French language

The Constitution of 4 October 1958:

- Article 2: 'The Language of the Republic shall be French'
- Article 75-1: 'Regional languages are part of France's heritage'
- Article 87: 'The Republic shall participate in the development of solidarity and cooperation between states and peoples having the French language in common.'
- Article 88: 'The Republic may enter into agreements with states which wish to associate with it in order to develop their civilisations.'

The Toubon Law 94-665, 4 August 1994 'relative to the use of the French language':

- Article 1: 'Established by the Constitution as the language of the French Republic, the French language is a key element in the personality and the heritage of France. French shall be the language of instruction, work, trade and exchanges and of the public services. It shall be the bond between the States comprising the community of French-speaking countries.'

Quotas for radio playtime of French music:

- A complex set of legislative provisions ensures that private radio stations that play pop music air a minimum of French language songs. Since 1996, and on the basis of a law passed in 1994, at least 40% of the playlist broadcast between 6.30 pm and 10.30 pm must be French language songs, and at least 50% of this music must be 'new talent' or 'new productions' sung in French or in a regional French language. In practice, and since 2000, the regulatory body, the CSA (*Conseil supérieur de l'audiovisuel* – the Superior Audiovisual Council) can authorize derogations to the rule, where radio stations specialize either in traditional (French) music or in young talent *per se* (not exclusively French; see CSA: 2010). These provisions, overall, have encouraged home-grown musical talent that is inspired as much by world music influences as by traditional French song.

language as a source of cultural creativity (artists must not be stifled by being forced to write/sing in English in order to sell records). French-language music has flourished and been exported, especially rap, as has non-lyrical electronic music known as the 'French Touch', 'world music', especially African and *raï*; and French music sung in English. By virtue of the law, in addition, French (speaking) citizens have the right not to be forced to struggle with other languages just to go about their business. By way of example, all adverts featuring foreign-language slogans used the world over (McDonald's *I'm Lovin It*, by way of example) must carry a French-language translation (*C'est tout ce que j'aime* – It's got everything I like/love). Such legislation can be seen as a means of promoting citizens' right to expect their native language to be sufficient to carry them through their daily lives.

But the agenda of language policy is complex: it promotes uniformity (all must speak French) at the same time as acknowledging the value of diversity (there is more than one language – English – in the world. There is French). Thus, plurilingualism has, for several years, been part of language policy in France; namely, the obligation in the school curriculum for children to learn at least one foreign language from a relatively early age. At the international level, the corollary of the policy of plurilingualism is a sustained campaign of support for cultural and linguistic diversity on a global level.

International Cultural Diplomacy

French language policy is a top priority of France's cultural diplomacy, where it serves the same twin objectives as domestically; namely, to *protect* the French language (as a means of preserving a key aspect of French national identity), and to *promote* its use – in this case, in other countries worldwide, as well as in key international organizations such as the EU, the World Trade Organization (WTO), and the United Nations (UN). Politically, these objectives are designed to bolster French global influence, but they are limited in their effects. Indeed, in the case of the EU's institutions, French efforts to force greater use of French as a working language are typically read by observers as evidence of declining *influence*: France's EU partners, especially those newest to the EU, and predominantly English-speaking, are less and less inclined to make an exception for the French language. Rhetorically-speaking, the purpose of spreading French on a global scale is to preserve the cultural diversity of the world, which is a condition of our humanity and civilization; here, French governments have a better record of agenda-setting and policy influence.

La Francophonie *and the Promotion of 'Cultural Diversity' Worldwide*

When French Foreign Minister Bernard Kouchner declared that France must 'reconquer the world narrative' (2007), he was couching a political objective (to restructure France's overseas broadcasting apparatus) in familiar rhetorical terms: 'If we can't make ourselves heard', he argued, 'we will become invisible and inaudible, run the risk of losing our language, our culture, our creativity, our capacity to offer the world an original message. In short, if we can't be heard, we will count for less, and we cannot resign ourselves to this second class destiny.' The challenge, as outlined by Kouchner, was to improve the reach and ratings of French-content broadcast news across the world. The difficulty of this challenge for France is to strike a balance between its *voice* being heard – its ideas and perspectives – and the use of its *language* in order to do so.

Broadcasting in English is, inevitably, part of the answer, and in 2007, former President Chirac launched a heavily state-sponsored CNN à la française, *France 24*, which broadcasts in English and Arabic, as well as French. This was to complement the all-French language television channel *TV5 Monde*, created in 1984, which is supposed to be the voice of the entire French-speaking world, but which is heavily financed by France. The Franco-German television station *Arte*, created in 1992, broadcasts Franco-German content, mainly arts and documentaries, in French and German; and *RFI* (*Radio France Internationale*) is France's flagship radio broadcaster, in French, throughout the world. President Sarkozy has made clear his support for an 'offensive' approach to these matters and, in particular, his preference for an umbrella broadcasting organization, *France Monde*, to air exclusively French-language content. The battle to be heard, in French, is far from won.

Making France heard is a goal that drives French cultural diplomacy overall, which itself is an important dimension of contemporary French foreign policy alongside the country's military strategy and resources. This marriage of cultural diplomacy and foreign policy is nothing new, but has gained in significance since the second half of the twentieth century saw France lose its military and colonial influence in the world. This pursuit of this influence by cultural means revolves around a combination of instruments that include a strong French state presence across the world in the form of an extensive network of embassies, consulates and cultural institutes; a broader system of 'outreach', where cultural activities are part of a range of means by which France assists other countries and populations; and the support and promotion of prized aspects of French culture, such as its gastronomy, its international sporting presence, and its cinema. By way of example, the French Ministry for Foreign and European Affairs in 2006 created a body called *CulturesFrance* with the mission to 'make known, abroad, French heritage, creativity and creative industries' (cited in Vaïsse, 2009: 551.

French cultural diplomacy also relies heavily on the weight of France in the institutions of *la Francophonie* – the organization of countries 'having French in common', and whose mission is to promote cultural diversity, democratization, human rights, sustainable development and conflict resolution across the world. *La Francophonie*, established in 1970, was not originally initiated by France but, rather, by certain of its former colonies seeking mutually beneficial relations with France. *La Francophonie* has institutions (it is properly known as the OIF – *l'Organisation internationale de la Francophonie* (the International Francophone Organization), headquartered in Paris, and very heavily subsidized by France); it has a Charter; it organizes summits; and it has around 70 members and associate observers. It puts the number of people speaking French worldwide at around 200 million. In contrast, Vaïsse (2009: 545) gives a figure of 175 million French-speakers worldwide, making French the 10th most spoken language in the world. Compagnon (in Morrison and Compagnon, 2010: 99) breaks this down into 80 million mother-tongue speakers of French, and around 128 million second- or third-language speakers of *le français*. Vaïsse (2009) also points to the decline in number of French language learners across the world; and there has been a steady drop in use of French in international organizations, including the EU and the UN. Significantly for France, the OIF's mission also embraces the worldwide promotion of linguistic and cultural diversity, and France relies on its Francophone allies in other international bodies, such as the UN, for support in this quest. The 2001 UNESCO Universal Declaration on Cultural Diversity, and its October 2005 Convention on the Protection and Promotion of the Diversity of Cultural Expressions, are typically presented in Paris as success stories of French cultural diplomacy.

Box 6.3 *La Francophonie* **and UNESCO: spreading 'humanism' and 'cultural diversity' throughout the world**

- **La Francophonie:**

   'The International Organisation of La Francophonie represents one of the biggest linguistic zones in the world. Its members share more than just a common language. They also share the humanist values promoted by the French language. The French language and its humanist values represent the two cornerstones on which the International Organisation of La Francophonie is based.' (Francophonie, 2010)

- **The 2005 UNESCO Convention on the Protection and Promotion of the Diversity of Cultural Expressions (UNESCO, 2010):**

   Article 4:

   '"Cultural diversity" refers to the manifold ways in which the cultures of groups and societies find expression. These expressions are passed on within and among groups and societies. Cultural diversity is made manifest not only through the varied ways in which the cultural heritage of humanity is expressed, augmented and transmitted through the variety of cultural expressions, but also through diverse modes of artistic creation, production, dissemination, distribution and enjoyment, whatever the means and technologies used.'

   Article 6:

   The Convention invites its signatory states to 'adopt measures aimed at protecting and promoting the diversity of cultural expressions within its territory'.

Trading in the 'Cultural Exception': French Cinema

French support for international cultural diversity, however, is best understood in the context of the so-called 'exceptionalism' of culture, French and otherwise, when it comes to international trade. An important aspect of French cultural diplomacy is the French pressure brought to bear within key international organizations, especially the European Union (and through the EU, the World Trade Organization – WTO) and the United Nations, to exempt from market liberalization what have become known as 'cultural products' in the audio-visual field; namely, film and cinema. (Foodstuffs specific to given *terroirs* – such as Camembert cheese, quality French wines or Champagne – benefit from a similarly regulated trade regime by virtue of the labels of and designations of quality; these restrictions are not limited to French produce.) The rationale behind such rules is that, without them, such 'products' – which in France are deemed to have intrinsic cultural or artistic value – would be crushed by mass-produced competitors. They are, therefore, exceptions to the rules of international trade, different to commodities of other kinds.

In an environment marked by English-speaking global forces and 'Anglo-American' norms of entertainment, the right to protect and promote cultural 'industries' and 'products' (such as film) with subsidies and quotas is strongly supported across the political spectrum in France, with notable success. This situation has become loosely known as the French 'cultural exception', although the specific term 'cultural exception' has, for some years, been dropped from official French discourse for its undiplomatic and insensitive connotations (implying that French culture is superior to all other). Instead, French cultural diplomacy is couched in terms of a quest for 'cultural *diversity*' – linguistic, artistic, and so on – across the globe. In support of this goal, France has successfully turned to international organizations such as the EU, the WTO and UNESCO for support – as seen in Box 6.3. The case of French cinema demonstrates French support for the regulation of culture both as a traded commodity, and as a vector of the diversity that should, ideally, characterize global humanity.

During the Fourth French Republic in the 1940s, French politicians made themselves unpopular at home by agreeing to restrict the number of French films shown *in France*, let alone the numbers exported to the USA. This was in order to free up screening time and space for Hollywood imports that had been halted during the War years; these were the Blum-Brynes agreements of 1944, and they remind us that the regulation of cinematic trade does not necessarily operate exclusively in France's favour, as common mythology might suggest. We also recall how closely culture and commerce are intertwined in the Franco-American relationship, historically and to this day, and how much they shape the fortunes and health of the relationship, precisely because they relate to French national identity. The USA was in the ascendant in Europe following World War II, and was physically present in France in the shape of military personnel and cultural programmes (in the context of the Marshall Plan or the

European Recovery programme) and also via the import of material comforts designed for the mass market – and to which French baby-boom teenagers were receptive. American cinema and Coca-Cola not only became symbols of real commercial threats to the nascent post-agricultural markets of Fourth Republic France, but also represented a potentially more insidious reminder of the power of the market to win hearts and minds, and of the ease with which the USA was dominating both these market and cultural forces. A form of cultural rivalry continues to characterize the Franco-US relationship, and this mingling of trade, culture and identity is its context.

In France, cinema is referred to as the 'seventh art', and there is little disagreement at political level that cinema is, indeed, an art form in its own right. Former President Jacques Chirac called it a 'national treasure' that underpinned the French nation's 'vitality'; and the term *la cinéphélie* – cinephilia – is commonplace in discussion of French cinema and cinema-going. The French *nouvelle vague* or new wave that characterized French cinema of the 1950s, and the equally familiar notion of *cinéma d'auteur* – authors' or directors' (as opposed to producers') movies – are just as symbolic of the emphasis in France on the artist as a creator, with the freedom (from market pressures) to create. At the same time, cinema in France, as elsewhere, is a 'cultural industry' embedded in market structures that, left to their own devices, would ignore this intrinsic – exceptional, we have said – aspect of the value of cinema.

On the basis of international agreements and conventions permitting state intervention in the market for film, the French state has therefore, over the years, developed a complex system of support for home grown and European cinematic production. Significant mechanisms regulating the market in France today were created in the Vichy period; in particular, the state-run CNC (the National Centre for Cinema and the Animated Image – *le Centre national du cinéma et de l'image animée*). This agency still oversees the mechanisms for collecting and redistributing revenue, and it plays a role in selecting candidates for support. A similarly entrenched device to support French cinema is the 'ticket tax': revenue levied on cinema box office takings that are channelled back into film production. Some of this aid is automatic, meaning that it is calculated 'irrespective of any judgement of quality' and made 'available to all *French* producers planning to reinvest' (Looseley, 1995: 197, my emphasis). Some is selective, rewarding aesthetic quality and innovation rather than previous commercial success (Looseley, 197–8). Further sources of

Box 6.4   Making an exception for French cinema?

The 'cultural exception'

In the early 1990s, France was successful at the GATT Uruguay Round trade talks in rallying EU support around the principle that an *exception* should be made for international trade in audio-visual services because of their 'cultural specificity'. This was in the face of US opposition and calls for open access to the EU's national audio-visual markets (for films and television, principally). The final text did not make an exception for these products; neither did the USA gain free access to EU markets. EU countries were left free to impose their own measures to protect their cultural treasures and industries.

The European Union

Since then, the EU has kept such national measures under strict observation as part of its market liberalization agenda, with a review of state aid provisions due by the end of 2012. At the same time, Article 3 of the EU's 2009 Lisbon Treaty states that: 'It [the EU] shall respect its rich cultural and linguistic diversity, and shall ensure that Europe's cultural heritage is safeguarded and enhanced.'

revenue have been constructed over the years, including the co-funding of film and television productions by the subscription, cable TV channel *Canal Plus*, created in 1984; and the EU's own MEDIA programme of support to cinema. In addition, the EU's 1989 '*TV sans frontières*' directive permits the imposition of quotas by national governments.

French cinema has undoubtedly benefited from these mechanisms: around 30–40% of all European films are produced in France. This equates to around two hundred films per year, most of which are entirely French-produced. Cinema-going is still popular in France, which is home to over five thousand screens, the most in Europe; and there is room in the French market for cinema both as art and as entertainment, both of which are popular. French government support has been extended to foreign producers seeking to make their films in France. Notoriously, the rules on what constitutes a 'French' film are tortuous and controversial. Tax-breaks are given for private investors in film; and Unifrance, a state body, plays the role of promoter and distributor of French cinema abroad. Cinema in France remains an important cultural and commercial asset for national identity and the national economy, but the regulation of trade in this 'commodity' continues to divide France not only from its US trading partner, but also from EU partners and the EU's market liberalization regimes (see Box 6.4). French people, today, show themselves to be as open to US-style influences in cinema and other aspects of popular culture as was the case over half a century ago. French cinema and French culture at large are certainly not dead (Morrison, 2007; Morrison and Compagnon, 2010), but it is open to challenge from the world at large, and from the evolutions of French society itself.

Contemporary Culture and Cultural Identities

The spread of leisure was a defining feature of twentieth-century France, and the twenty-first century is not set to change this, despite the 'value of work' ethic championed by President Sarkozy. As far back as 1936, the Popular Front government famously introduced a limited working week (40 hours) and the principle of paid holidays (known as *les congés payés*: then limited to 12 days; now a matter of five weeks). Subsequently, the practices of sport for pleasure and holidays away from the home took root. In the late 1990s, just as famously, the Socialist government of Prime Minister Lionel Jospin introduced legislation to bring about the 'reduction of working time' (known as *la réduction du temps de travail* – RTT) by capping the working week at 35 hours. Since President Sarkozy came to power in 2007, these provisions have been eroded (see Chapter 7), but they have meant that a new generation of workers, especially in white-collar and professional occupations, have developed new leisure habits (such as taking a mini-break, already growing in popularity thanks to the dramatic growth of cheap air travel from the 1990s). The young retired (aged between 55 and 64 years) in contemporary France are particularly hungry for art and culture, from the television to visiting museums. The spread of the television into people's homes in the second half of the twentieth century for its part further 'sensitized' people (Looseley 1995: 35) to the notion of leisure and pleasure, and the social uprising of May 1968 (see Chapter 1) raised expectations regarding an individual's right to self-expression and pleasure, irrespective of the state and its strictures. As schooling and literacy spread, moreover, so did the taste for and consumption of culture; and we saw earlier (Box 6.1) that the 1946 Constitution referred to culture as a right for all.

Accordingly, successive governments of the Fifth Republic, best symbolized by Jack Lang in the early 1980s, have sought to 'democratize' culture through the encouragement of diverse modes of cultural expression and creation. The decentralization agendas of the early 1980s and late 1990s, moreover, (see Chapter 4), included provisions for greater powers at local and regional levels over cultural matters. In any case, as Dubois points out (2008: 25), watching television 'is immune from official cultural action'. People's cultural practices, in other words, have a habit of escaping the state, and new technologies are an important aspect of this. Nevertheless, the state remains vigilant, especially where technology is perceived to encroach upon core cultural values or goals.

Thus, the liberalization and privatization of the television and radio airwaves that occurred in the 1980s and 1990s in France was accompanied by the language laws, and by a stiffening of the powers of the regulator to oversee the activities of both state and market regarding the media, in the name of pluralism and freedom. As recently as 2008, President Sarkozy announced a bold move to ban commercial advertising from France's public television channels; and 2009 saw the proposal of highly controversial legislation, and a new administrative authority, with the remit of cracking down on Internet piracy, especially illegal downloads. Certain of these measures were subsequently deemed contrary to civil liberties by the country's Constitutional Council. Similarly, in 2010, the French government aired proposals to tax the advertising revenue of Google and other Internet search engines to help fund France's creative industries.

From a different perspective, one of Jack Lang's most memorable legacies is the 'single book price', which forbids retailers from discounting the cost of books to the customer, thereby forcing retailers to compete on quality and choice rather than price. This applies to Amazon.fr, as well as to bookshops and other stores. The consequences for the reading public are positive; a visitor who may only be passing through France en route to elsewhere will find that airport and train station outlets are well-stocked with a wide range of books, including many foreign titles in French translation. Those with longer to stay will discover rich pickings in independent book shops as well as the large FNAC stores in big towns, and even in the out-of-town hypermarkets and budget stores. Books *are* expensive in France, but many publishers produce good value paperback editions of popular fiction and non-fiction titles. If the content matters more than the cover, then book-buying – and so, perhaps, reading – is an entirely affordable exercise.

To buy books – and *bandes dessinées* ('drawn strips' – akin to comics, but extensively read by adults) – and to read is also to be part of a national passion for literature: the annual *rentrée littéraire* in September, with its array of new titles and prizes, is a cultural phenomenon in France. Critics, however, argue that non-establishment figures, such as self-styled 'bad boy' Michel Houllebecq, or writers from France's ethnic minorities are frozen out of this scene, which rather rings true (but see p. 173).

In this context, what are the 'cultural practices' of the French? The French Ministry of Culture and Communication periodically commissions surveys to discover how the French spend their time and money. The latest (Donnat, 2009), was published in late 2009, with specific reference to how the French entertain and cultivate themselves in the 'digital age'. Donnat's findings confirm the growth in home entertainment (television, DVD and Internet use); moreover, it is the French government's intention that 100% of French households will be viewing digital television by 2011 and, by 2012, have access to the Internet (Donnat puts the figure in 2008 at 83%). We recall in passing that the adoption of the Internet in France was delayed by virtue of the state's decision in the 1980s to develop and 'market' (by giving away free hardware to French households) an early alternative. This was the Minitel, much loved for its messaging (*messagerie*) functions, especially the telephone directory and dating services. It was cheap, practical and accessible to all, but has been overtaken by digital technologies. These have not, at least for the time being, deterred French people from going out: to the cinema (with 186 million cinema entries in 2007 compared to 120 million in 1990), to the restaurant with friends, or to participate in a local *association*. Some of the biggest Internet users, particularly amongst baby-boomers, go out the most. However, fewer people of all ages are buying books, and fewer younger people are buying and reading newspapers. According to *le Monde*, in its editorial of 14 October 2009 on the subject of Donnat's study (2009), the sharp rise in 'non-readers', particularly amongst manual labourers, was symptomatic of the failure of the French state's decades-long attempts to 'democratize' culture in the face of powerful technological and social trends, particularly given what critics see as the Ministry's in-built bias towards the *beaux-arts*: the fine arts of painting, sculpture, architecture, dance (ballet), classical music, literature and theatre.

The Media, New and Old

Thus, French society is not immune from the tendency of technology to tempt people into fundamentally individual and passive pursuits, and French people do spend rising proportions of their budget for entertainment and culture on audio-visual equipment for the home; and spend more time watching DVDs, playing video games, and making their own digital entertainment. Habits related to watching television and listening to the radio have been indirectly shaped by the decades of state-regulated public broadcasting, which held back home-grown TV quality productions. In the present day, the historical PBS bias to French TV lives on in the form of ubiquitous and lengthy talk show formats for the mainly serious discussion of literature and politics in particular; although television news itself is rather cursory and as sensationalist as elsewhere. Furthermore, the French now have the choice of (for terrestrial television) five public, national channels, and three private channels (*TF1*, M6 and the subscription channel *Canal Plus*, whose proceeds are one source of support for France's cinematic film production industry). The viewing of full-length films on television is being pushed out by the popularity of television series – some French but predominantly US imports, but the Franco-German channel *Arte* offers predominantly high-brow and serious programming.

The print media, for its part, continues to decline in popularity in France: only around one quarter of the population reads a daily newspaper on a daily basis. The difficulties of the national daily titles *Libération* and *le Monde* (which is losing money and readers on a dramatic scale) have demonstrated the slowing demand for highbrow content and, in 2009, prompted President Sarkozy to announce a showy measure for 'emergency aid' for the press, including a free subscription to a French newspaper for every 18-year-old. The origins of the print media in France are in literature and politics, functioned as the mouthpiece for public intellectuals, and these titles still make considerable space for opinion and tribunes. This decline is particularly notable when compared with the investigative journalism of, for example, the weekly (and illustrated) Paris Match. The political weeklies such as *le Nouvel observateur* and *l'Express*, by contrast, are popular, as is the regional press, with over 100 titles; and the satirical, national, weekly titles *le Canard enchaîné* and *Charlie Hebdo*. France's leading national daily remains the sports paper *l'Équipe* (with a circulation of around 300,000). As elsewhere in

Europe, the print media is under pressure from free newspapers, distributed in large cities, as well as from online media offering free content. In addition, France has a history of tight union and state control over the printing and distribution of its newspapers, and vested interests here have hampered reform; journalists, for their part, are relatively pampered professionals.

Despite all this, reading, listening to music, and going to the cinema remain the top three cultural activities of the French today. More and more people of all ages listen to music in France, and it is integral to the daily life of the young. Music, moreover, is a clear marker of identity in relation to age, and social origin in particular; not unlike the role of music for some young people in UK and US societies in defining the 'tribe' to which they belong. But it is the cinema that is the most democratic of the 'arts'; for Donnat, it is the 'king' of culture across all ages and social classes.

A Taste for America?

What do the French go and see at the cinema, and how does state-supported French cinema fare? Its fortunes vary from year to year, as do those of independent, art-house cinema *per se*. French companies produce their own blockbuster-type movies (such as the comedy *Bienvenue chez les Ch'tis – Welcome to the Sticks*, which was a huge box office hit in 2008) alongside its more traditional *cinéma d'auteur* and historical epics, and France certainly has its own international movie stars, such as Gérard Dépardieu, Catherine Deneuve and, more recently, Audrey Tatou (of *Amélie* fame) or Vincent Cassel, who move comfortably between French and 'Anglo-American' cultural contexts. French multiplex screens in France's big cities have sustained cinema-going as a cultural 'practice' amongst the French, particularly in *la banlieue*; as have state-sponsored initiatives such as the annual Cinema festival (*la fête du cinéma*) which encourages cinema-going by means of bargain tickets. French film has a long tradition of international popularity, moreover, from the postwar New Wave to *Amélie* itself. By way of example, 2008 was a particularly good year for French film. Box office takings for French productions exceeded those for US alternatives; the French film, Laurent Cantet's docu-drama *The Class* (*Entre les Murs*) won the Palme d'Or award at the Cannes film festival; and Marion Cotillard, a French actress, won the Oscar Best Actress Award for her part as Edith Piaf, herself a French cultural icon, in the French film, *La Vie en Rose (la Môme)*.

Cinema-going in France is characterized just as much by the demand for this American-style experience as it is by the art house-type productions for which France is known.

Illustration 6.1   A multiplex cinema in the Bercy Village district of Paris

But US films are popular in France, particularly amongst the young (as are US television series). In 2007, nearly 50% of all box office entries in France were for US-made films, as against 37% for French films. The top US films that year, ranked by box office takings, were *Ratatouille* and *Spider-Man 3*, outranking the most popular French (co-produced) films *la Môme* and *French Taxi 4* (Ministère de la Culture, 2009: 137).

In matters of food and music, as well as film and television, there is a taste for America in France. To quote Philippe Roger (2005: 451), himself relating an anecdote, 'Wearing Nikes doesn't stop you from wanting to screw America'. Indeed, anti-American attitudes in France relate far more frequently to political issues than to matters of cultural and popular tastes – and this has been the case for over half a century. France is McDonald's largest European market in revenue terms, serving what its critics call *la malbouffe* – junk food – to growing numbers of French customers, as well as the thriving tourist trade. In 2008, McDonald's profits in France rose by over 11%, the highest rise in the company's European markets, and its turnover was €3.3 billion (McDonald's, 2010). The company is also a very significant private sector employer (see Steinberger, 2009), offering job opportunities (derided by critics as 'McJobs' – temporary and poorly-paid) to ethnic minorities who have been shown to experience discrimination elsewhere in the labour market. The popularity of fast food is only one part, moreover, of a broader picture in which French women *do* get fat, and obesity is a significant health problem in France as elsewhere, as 'family values' lose their grip on the structure of the working day, with home-cooked food a casualty in France as elsewhere. At the same time, French *haute cuisine* itself has been forced to move with the times. Michelin stars are now awarded to restaurants outside of Paris (in New York, London and Tokyo, for example) and, in 2008, Tokyo had more Michelin stars in total than did Paris.

Taking Part: Grass Roots, Gastronomy, Sport and 'The Street'

Culture is not only passively consumed in France: sport, and *la vie associative* at the local level (see Chapter 4), are amongst the most popular ways of participating in the cultural opportunities on offer in France. The smallest village in rural France habitually runs a full range of cultural activities through its associations, with only minimal support from state bodies such as the mayor (see Box 6.5). Similarly, France's peasant traditions (see Chapter 2) live on in the form of enthusiasm for predominantly rural traditions such as markets and festivals, and in support for *artisan* products of all kinds. Gastronomy, for its part, remains popular in France in the form of dining out, and as a more intellectual interest in the whole subject of food, eating and cooking. This interest, moreover, links France's agricultural tradition with the international prowess of its chefs and food-writers, past and present.

'Street' activity is not confined to rural areas: the annual, national, grass-roots music festival occurs in June in towns and cities across France; and Paris leads the way with its summer 'beach' and 'white nights'. Paris is also the site for France's annual Agricultural Salon, a showcase for French agricultural produce – and business; and May 2010 saw the country come to Paris in an initiative aptly named 'Nature Capital'. For several days, the iconic Avenue des Champs

---

Box 6.5   Culture by association in Barro, Charentes

We saw in Chapter 4 that associations were an important part of local life and government in France, and the example of Barro demonstrates this perfectly. In this village of fewer than four hundred inhabitants in the west of France, the local *comité des fêtes* (events committee) organizes and oversees cultural events such as an annual photography competition, ski weekends, twinning trips and themed dinners. Residents can also enjoy specialist activities, each organized by its own association. *La Coulée douce* (living is easy) is for art and music activities; *Les Z'Abeilles* (the busy bees) for handicraft; *les Arfonies* for the choir; *Gym ton corps* for keep-fit and, for senior citizens' bingo, *les Tamalous* (a pun on the French for 'where does it hurt?'). In 2008, each registered Barro association was entitled to €93 of public money each, and was allowed to use village property and facilities for their meetings and activities.

Elysées was covered in miniature plots of plants and crops, and flanked by farm animals in a heavily subsided effort to remind the French of their rural roots – and of the importance of agriculture to the French economy (see Chapter 7).

Just as French agriculture and gastronomy bridge the worlds of popular culture and cultural diplomacy, so is sport an important dimension of France's international presence, and also a popular pastime amongst the French population. Around 16 million French people are members of sports federations: amateur sport clubs whose membership is regulated by the state. The democratization of sport during the twentieth century was also very much the doing of the state, including during the Vichy years, when some of today's structures were established by means of the 1940 Sports Charter. Sporting activity is embedded in school life through 'discovery' classes, including physical activity, that take children at subsidized rates to the sea, snow and countryside; skiing in France, moreover, is very much a staple winter activity of the middle classes. State employees are amongst the personnel that coach and train amateur sportsmen and women, and local communities are generally well-equipped in sports infrastructure.

Participation in sport also extends to enthusiastic support for France's flagship annual sporting event, the *Tour de France*. This extraordinary event is about far more than professional, elite cyclists enduring extremes of suffering as they speed through France on an epic three-week journey averaging over 150 miles per day at speeds of up to 50 miles per hour. Originating from the early twentieth century, the *Tour* showcases the country in its glorious diversity, revealing it to the French themselves as well as to the world at large, thanks to commercial sponsorship and worldwide media coverage. The *Tour* is anything but a spectator sport: fans line the route, often perilously close to the riders, sometimes with tragic consequences for rider, spectator (or stray pet). The point is to be part of the drama, and the event is supposed to be conducted very much in the public eye in a country where cycling is seen as an indigenous sport and is a top amateur sport amongst the French population, along with rugby, tennis and football (soccer). The daily sports newspaper *l'Équipe*, we remember, is France's best selling title.

France also lays claim to having launched the modern Olympic movement in the late nineteenth century and, during the Fifth Republic, strenuous efforts and resources have been put into training athletes for such prestigious, international championships. In the 2000 Athens Summer Olympics, France was seventh in the medal table. France also sees itself as a choice host for such events; has hosted the Winter Olympics on three occasions (1924, 1968 and 1992); and has bid for the games again in 2018, having lost out to China (2008) and the UK (2012) in its bids to host the Summer Games. France did host and win the 1998 football World Cup, and much was made of the success of its rainbow team, which included famous players from France's ethnic minorities, such as striker Zinédine Zidane. This team, it was suggested, was repainting the French flag: no longer blue, white and red (*bleu*, *blanc*, *rouge*), but *noir*, *blanc et beur* (white, black and *beur* – the word used to denote the children, born in France, of France's North African, post-colonial population).

This notion of the team positively representing an evolving French national identity was shattered a decade later when the French team failed to move beyond the first stage of the 2010 World Cup hosted by South Africa. This was disgrace enough, but was compounded by sex scandals concerning certain players; rifts between players, manager and coach; and unfavourable – doubtless unjust – comment (including from politicians) on the presence in the team of players from the suburbs who were said to have imported unpatriotic values and behaviours into the squad, with disastrous consequences for the team's performance. Predictably, President Sarkozy ordered an official enquiry into the *débâcle*. The ignominy of South Africa 2010 served to demonstrate both the fragile connection between French sporting and national identities, and the importance that is attached in France, as in many other countries, to the role of sport in consolidating state, society and the national soul.

Cultural Canons and Debates

France's many cultural achievements and practices – spanning traditional arts, popular culture and everyday icons of French taste, design and aesthetics – have been integral to the process of 'inventing the nation', to use Baycroft's term (2008). Being French, the argument goes, implies buying into myths about what does and does not represent the 'Frenchness' of the French nation; conversely, challenging those myths is to contest the nation and one's place in it. Subsequently, and to a considerable extent, we can speak of a 'Franco-French' canon (Keaton, 2006) of cultural references that young people are assumed to acquire at school, and which they then must convert into cultural capital if they are to progress in society – and the market economy (see Chapter 5). These references span French history and geography, as well as culture *per se*, and include a very proper mastery of the French language in its written and spoken forms, where form itself is of paramount importance: arguments must have a recognizable shape, however well-informed their content. But these are norms that may well be at odds with young people's reality, and one aspect of cultural life in contemporary France is the co-existence of competing claims to represent the 'real' France in any number of art forms, including, for example, music, film and urban street culture, as well as specifically youth and suburban vernaculars and varieties of the French language.

It would be surprising if this were not the case in a country as diverse and culturally creative as France. Indeed, the French intellectual tradition itself has a history of resistance and opposition to the norms of the day, especially political and religious. From the centuries-old café culture, still in evidence in France today, to France's world-renowned thinkers, writers, philosophers, psychoanalysts and sociologists, the tradition prizes spirited argument and public expressions of (exquisitely-formed) opinion. In today's televised age, intellectuals engage in public spectacle as much as anything else, and the contemporary philosopher Bernard-Henri Lévy is the living embodiment of the celebrity intellectual, derided by his critics as all looks and no substance. Emile Zola, Jean-Paul Sartre and Simone de Beauvoir were the celebrity minds of their day, typically politically 'engaged': for or against anti-Semitism, Marxism (famously, in the Cold War years), the USA, globalization, neo-liberalism and so on. The intellectual realm today remains largely the preserve of a mainly white, elitist establishment still enthralled by the *Académie Française* itself, whose members – all leading minds in their field – are dubbed 'the Immortals'. More prosaically, nevertheless, the argument as a form of communication and the potential robustness of verbal exchanges between 'ordinary' French people today remain a noticeable and characteristic dimension of the French psyche, inculcated from a very early age, and perpetuated thereafter by education and experience. To be French, perhaps, is to argue.

Conclusions

Culture in France, we have seen, links into a number of political agendas, principally in the matters of foreign policy, education, sport, health and, crucially, the economy. The state finds it impossible not to intervene, given the critical links between culture, on the one hand, and national identity, on the other; we have also seen how embedded culture is into France's economic fortunes. Governments habitually fight hard to maintain the budget of the Ministry, and 2010 was no exception. Culture as a vector of French identity is vulnerable to critics of change, who experience loss and nostalgia (for imagined past traditions; for dominant norms); and to critics of stasis, for the repressive dimensions of a respect for traditional forms. In today's France, it is less acceptable than in the past to believe in an elite cultural establishment, although France's would-be cultural dissidents, such as novelist Michel Houellebecq, insist that it exists; in November 2010, Houllebecq nevertheless won France's prestigious literary prize, the Prix Goncourt. French culture, moreover, is not immune to the reform of the state – and, in particular, to ongoing processes of cost-cutting, and the elimination of duplication and waste. In the domestic sphere, as in the global market place, French culture, increasingly, must make itself heard, pay its way, and compete.

7

Economy and Business

Introduction

France has a diverse, open and internationalized economy which, in 2007, was ranked as the eighth largest in the world. With a GDP of US$2.8 trillion, and a GDP per capita of US$46,000, the French economy sits comfortably above the EU27 and OECD averages (OECD, 2009). Since 1 January 2002, France uses the Euro single currency, and is second in size only to Germany in the 16-country Euro zone. France is home to multinational companies and prestigious products of worldwide renown, is the fourth world destination for foreign direct investment (FDI), and invests heavily abroad, in turn. It boasts an agricultural sector that makes France the second largest exporter of food stuffs and food products in the world after the USA, and is equally renowned for its industrial heritage. In particular, the French economy generates much high-tech activity and scientific know-how in the fields of transport (infrastructure and equipment), defence, aeronautics, aerospace, automotives, pharmaceuticals and nuclear energy. France's industrial history is a matter of national pride, and the ongoing de-industrialization of the French economy is a political headache of the first order.

Indeed, France today is, by any definition, predominantly a service economy, with world class provision in tourism and travel (tourism alone accounting for easily 5% of French GDP), a financial market with ambitions to rival the city of London, a banking sector of increasingly acquisitive and global dimensions, and a quarter of the workforce employed in the service sector. Furthermore, France is located centrally and accessibly in Europe, and invests heavily in its transportation and telecommunications infrastructures; its population is healthy, educated, productive, and long-lived and, seen from outside, appears to enjoy an enviable quality of life. These are key business strengths, by any international standard (see World Economic Forum, 2010a).

At the same time, the French economy is marked by persistently high unemployment (10.2% in 2009, above the Eurozone average, equating to around three million people without work), punitive levels of public debt (well over 60% of GDP in 2009), and a sorry record of public deficits since the early 1980s (with an expected deficit of at least 8% of GDP in 2010). Government spending routinely amounts to over 50% of GDP, around one quarter of the country's work force is employed by the state and, in the first decade of the twenty-first century, France experienced sluggish GDP growth – something that incoming President Sarkozy swore he would address in 2007, shortly before a serious and global financial crisis triggered an economic recession in the Eurozone that thwarted these ambitions. Moreover, France entered the second decade of the twenty-first century acutely aware of the acceleration of the rate at which its industrial base has been shrinking since the year 2000.

Traditionally characterized by state intervention in the market – broadly known as *dirigisme*; a tightly-regulated labour market, including a maximum working week and a national minimum wage; conflictual industrial relations, especially in France's large and costly public sector; and an apparently pervasive scepticism towards capitalism, big business, entrepreneurship, the profit motive *and* globalization, the French economy has typically defied classification, styling itself as a 'model' in its own right. 'France', states Culpepper, 'is emphatically not a liberal market economy' (2006: 46).

In this chapter, we begin with an overview of what is deemed to make France so exceptional in economic terms – namely, the 'egalitarian ethos' (*Economist*, 2009) of its republicanism, and we review the numerous challenges that the global economy poses (or is believed to pose) to this socio-economic model. This leads us to look more closely at the role of the state in today's French economy and this, in turn, requires us to consider the costs, constraints and opportunities for the French economy of France's EU membership. This particular balancing act has contributed to a transformation of France's economy – and, accordingly, of the relations in France between state, labour and capital – and we examine these matters in some detail. Finally, we highlight a number of key issues that dominate today's French economic and business agendas, such as the competitiveness of the French economy, attitudes to work, and the

Table 7.1 France in the global economy: facts and figures

Service or industrial economy?
- Industry counts for less than one-quarter of French GDP
- France is the world's 4th largest exporter of services and the world's 5th largest exporter of goods
- France is the world's 5th largest financial market
- France's pharmaceutical industry is 1st in Europe and 3rd in the world
- France leads the world in highly-transformed products (such as yoghurts, chocolate, biscuits)
- French wines and spirits provide France's biggest agri-food surplus.

(Invest in France Agency, 2009)

Openness
- Ranked 4th as a world destination for foreign direct investment (FDI)
- High foreign ownership of share capital of top 40 publicly-quoted companies (approximately 50%)
- High foreign ownership of government bonds (over 50%).

Competitiveness
- France slipped from 8th place to 18th in the world in the 25 years preceding 2007 (*Financial Times*, 2007a)
- France's ranking in the 'global competitiveness' index compiled by the World Economic Forum was 16th in 2009–10
- The World Economic Forum lists France's weaknesses as the 'low flexibility' of its labour market, and the 'poor labor-employer relations in the country' (World Economic Forum, 2010b).

---

ongoing liberalization and de-industrialization of the French economy. We finish by asking ourselves how distinctive the French economic socio-economic 'model' really is, and how resistant or adaptable to apparently unstoppable economic forces it is in the present day.

The French Republic in the Global Economy

High levels of commitment to the delivery of public services still characterize today's French political economy, but the state's overall role in the French economy has been radically transformed. Over the last thirty years or so, governments have learned to make way for markets, entrepreneurship, domestic regulatory authorities and the international rules of the economic game. Nevertheless, and as in other fields of policy-making, expectations of the state are still high, and French governments often allow themselves to sound as though they are in control of business and the economy when, in reality, they often are not, or not entirely.

In particular, a Republican rhetoric of equality and welfare still pervades the discourse of economic policy-making in France. In his New Year's Eve address to the French people on 31 December 2009, President Sarkozy, accordingly, claimed that France had been 'less hard-hit' by the economic crisis than other countries. He said that 'We owe this to our social model which cushioned the impact and the tough measures which were taken to support economic activity and above all ensure that no one was left behind' (Sarkozy, 2009c). In practice, there are serious and entrenched structural inequalities in the French economy, with social consequences including episodic and large-scale unrest (as seen in Chapter 3). These eruptions are, indeed, often decisive in influencing the course of public policy.

Structural problems include France's high unemployment rate (over 8% for decades) – which is especially marked amongst those aged under 24 (over 20%) – and equally notoriously conflictual relations between labour and capital, particularly in France's large public sector. Here, many workers typically have significant vested interests to protect (known as social *acquis*, such as jobs for life, and generous pensions provisions), unlike many of their counterparts in the private sector, where workers may justifiably feel their position on the labour market is 'precarious'.

In both the private and public sectors, costs are being trimmed, and there is real evidence, especially in the private sector, of 'the working poor' juggling more than one job to make ends meet, undermining any real quality of life. This includes France's leading industries, such as the agri-food business, where working conditions can be harsh, and where foreign labour and unqualified personnel can be seen as business assets. A succession of suicides in 2008–09 in one of France's leading private sector companies, France Telecom (mobile phone operator and broadband provider), was linked to working conditions not untypical of big business in a grindingly competitive environment, particularly following the recession that hit France, as it did several other EU countries, in 2009. These come as shocks in a country that has prided itself on the social gains made for its industrial workers over the course of the twentieth century (see Chapter 1). Paid holidays now stretch to five weeks per year; labour law is highly regulated in protection of the employee, and is a characteristic identified in international comparisons as a structural rigidity of the French labour market; and the class consciousness that once typified French labour has, inevitably, ebbed away.

Unsurprisingly, *la précarité* (discussed in Chapter 5) has thus become a byword in France – as in the UK and the USA, by way of comparison – that crystallizes people's fears about their economic future. They observe that their spending power has diminished, and this was a specific problem that President Sarkozy vowed to address as a matter of priority on coming to power in May 2007. In recent years, the street protests for which France is known – and which belie very low levels of trade union membership (around 8% in the public sector, and lower still around 5% in the private) – have begun to draw in workers from the private sector fearful for their jobs, together with those in the public sector fighting to maintain their often privileged working conditions.

Underlying battles for jobs is a sense, in France, that there is – or used to be, more to the point – a uniquely French 'model' of political economy that is somehow less ruthless, and more moral and humane than the neo-liberal norms castigated by successive French presidents as 'Anglo-Saxon'-style, *laissez-faire* capitalism. At the level of corporate governance, especially regarding France's big employers, this translates into an expectation that bosses will refer to the 'social interest' as well as the profit motive when taking strategic decisions, where social interest refers to a firm's duty of care to its workers and, beyond them, to the social fabric of France as a whole. This is part and parcel of the republican ideal of social cohesion (Chapter 5). Increasingly, however, the drive for international competitive advantage has 'forced French companies to provide value for shareholders' (Maclean, 2008: 157). Such perspectives are behind recent and high-profile cases in France of 'boss-napping' and lock-ins (albeit not new phenomena in France), and other forms of protest against strategic decisions made by companies to close or downsize factories, lay off workers, and/or move production overseas.

Political language about the French model has, indeed, come to centre on the pros and cons of globalization, with reference to specific consequences – such as the 'outsourcing' of labour, known in French as *la délocalisation* – whereby French employers are seen as tempted to offload their labour (and, especially, manufacturing) costs abroad at the expense of the local workforce (as broadly seen in the examples above). It is, indeed, notable how many more goods made in China and elsewhere are available on the French high street (in textiles and clothing, for example) than was the case in the latter half of the 1990s. Moreover, there are high levels of support in France for increased and tighter regulation of global flows of capital, and the so-called 'alter-globalization' ('other' globalization) movement (see Chapter 3) shapes the political agenda at home in France by circumscribing what can be said in economic policy-making. Indeed, Culpepper notes the 'discursive illegitimacy' of the free market (2006: 45–6) and, as recently as 1981, the French President – François Mitterrand – was elected on an explicit manifesto to 'break with capitalism', an experiment that lasted barely two years.

But an open economy needs markets that are both regulated *and* liberalized, and consumers want a choice of products. France is a member of the key global institutions charged with overseeing the global economy – namely, the World Trade Organization (WTO), the G8 group of highly industrialized nations and the G20 (both of which France was to chair in 2011) and, above all, the European Union; and France regularly seeks to influence global agendas via such institutions. Indeed, the EU's single market and single currency provide the framework for French competitiveness, and for the bulk of its trade flows with EU partners and with the rest of the world. The EU also functions as a platform from which France seeks to influence the rules of international trade – especially, but by no means exclusively, with regard to the protection from trade liberalization of agriculture and 'cultural products' (see Chapter 6).

On balance, a liberalized global economy is inevitably in the French economic interest, but, equally inevitably, at some social cost, and has been a key driver in France's postwar socio-economic transformation. It has created in its wake global winners such as the large, French, multinational companies Danone (foodstuffs) and Accor (hotel and restaurants), to name but two of France's global players (see Table 7.2). In Sarkozy's France, moreover, big business is not a dirty word, and the President himself is no stranger to ostentatious displays of wealth (earning him the pejorative nickname of the 'bling-bling' President in his early months of office). But, like other Presidents before him, he has maintained a political language that underlines the need to restrain capitalist forces at home and abroad,

Table 7.2   Big French business at home and abroad

French global companies, many of which are majority foreign-owned or in foreign partnerships, include the following household names:

Company name/sector	*Activity*
Financial services	
Axa	Financial services (insurance)
Crédit agricole	Financial services (retail banking)
BNP-Paribas	Financial services
Société Générale	Financial services
Manufacturing	
Renault-Nissan	Automobiles
PSA Peugeot-Citroën	Automobiles
Saint Gobain	Construction materials
J.C. Decaux	Urban furniture
Alstom	Transport and energy infrastructure and equipment (e.g. TGV rolling stock; nuclear power)
Utilities	
EDF	Energy
Total Fina Elf	Energy
France Télécom	Telecommunications
GDF-Suez	Energy
Areva	Nuclear energy
Veolia	Water and waste
Suez environment	Water
Retail	
Carrefour	Hypermarket (second only in the world to Wal'mart)
Defence, aerospace and aeronautics	
Thales	Defence, aeronautics, security
EADS (includes Airbus)	Defence, aeronautics
Other	
Danone	Agri-food (dairy)
Pernod Ricard	Wine and spirits
Accor	Hotels (includes the Novotel, Sofitel, Mercure and Ibis chains)
Publicis	Advertising and communications
Lagardère	Media and communications
L'Oréal	Beauty and cosmetics (world leader)
PPR Group	Luxury goods and clothing retail; owns FNAC (high street cultural and electronic goods)
LVMH	Fashion clothing and travel goods, wines and spirits, perfumes and cosmetics (over 60 brands including Moët & Chandon champagne, *Benefit* cosmetics)
Sanofi-Aventis	Pharmaceuticals and health

for fear of shattering the French republican ethos and fomenting social disquiet. These contradictions have long typified the French 'model' of business and the economy.

Dirigisme, the State and the Market

France's reputation as a state-centric, public service-oriented economy must therefore be weighed against these realities of its global economic performance, where state action is limited by market forces and international regulation. However, systematic, intensive and widespread state intervention was characteristic of the Fourth Republic (1946–58), when the rebuilding of the French economy after World War II was of paramount importance. During these years, the state became best-known for its system of 'indicative planning' of the economy. This denoted a set of rolling plans for production and output, especially that relating to agriculture and industry (see Chapter 2).

State intervention was also a hallmark of Charles de Gaulle's presidency (1959–69) where economic interventionism was designed to boost national independence and greatness, or at least give the impression that it was. This recent past has meant that the 'tradition' of state interventionism in the French economy has become entrenched, mythologized and embedded in contemporary norms of political discourse and policy-making. It even harks back to the days of the *ancien régime* in the seveenth century under King Louis XIV, when ministers such as Jean-Baptiste Colbert invested in large-scale, industrial infrastructure projects (including the building of roads and towns) in order to shape modern France and its destiny, and from whom the doctrine of *colbertisme* – the notion of state interventionism in the economy that is virtually synonymous with the more commonplace term *dirigisme* – is derived. The French state may, in the current day, be in retreat from the market in the face of powerful global forces that defy or escape state control – such as the globalization of technology, and European Union rules – but it still maintains a robust language of activism, in some cases backed up by action, and especially in industrial policy. The forms taken by state intervention in the French economy, and the limitations on these, boil down to the roles of strategic planning on the one hand, and regulation on the other (*Economist*, 2009).

Strategy

From Public Ownership to (Part-)Privatization
State ownership of industrial and other enterprises, such as utilities, was long the preferred means of providing the public service that is deemed essential for delivering 'social cohesion' in France; ensuring the security of energy supply (such as in the nuclear industry); and providing employment for both top civil servants, and the working classes. Since the symbolic nationalizations of the postwar years, and a full-scale nationalization programme undertaken by Socialist governments in the early 1980s, the French state has subsequently sold off many of its assets as a means of reducing public debt, providing firms with more competitive autonomy on the global market, and complying with EU and international regulations for a liberalized global economy. Telecommunications and energy are key examples here. The GDF–Suez 2006 merger in energy, by way of illustration, reduced the state's presence down to approximately 36% from what was more than an 80% holding in GDF (Gaz de France).

Political Patronage
Linked to public ownership is political patronage. This refers to the network of elites running public enterprises on the one hand, and the close links between private sector and state corporations via their elites, on the other. These relationships have long 'operated as a coor-dinating mechanism of French capitalism' (Clift, 2009: 158), giving rise to a 'system of cross-shareholdings and overlapping board memberships of large French firms' known as *noyaux durs* or 'hard cores' (*ibid.*). These *noyaux durs* have been weakened by the foreign ownership of big companies although, according to *le Monde* (2010), the majority of those running France's top forty publicly-quoted companies (on the exchange known as the CAC-40), come from the French senior public service – *les grands corps*, as seen in Chapter 4 – or from ministerial cabinets, where they pursued a political career. All graduated from France's most elite *grandes écoles*. All 95 bosses are also men, with an average age of 57, and count only 15 foreign nationals (including the EADS boss).

State Aid
Broadly defined, state aid can take various forms. It is very often constrained by the EU's competition policy, and can be more or less

direct. It is usually controversial, but not always illegal. Examples include:

- In the 2008–09 financial crisis, the nearly €6 billion package to French car manufacturers. President Sarkozy gave the impression at the time that this was conditional on companies such as Renault (in part state-owned) moving production units back to France from Eastern Europe. Such strings are not allowed under EU law.
- In 2007, France Telecom was required by the EU's highest court (the European Court of Justice – ECJ) to pay back €928 million of state aid (in the form of tax breaks) paid by French government in the 1990s, which the European Commission, in 2004, had judged illegal. France did not cooperate with the Commission, hence the referral to the ECJ.
- In 2009, France was required to pay back agricultural subsidies in the form of 'handouts to fruit and vegetable farmers over 10 years' (see the *Financial Times*, 2009a), amounting to over €330.
- Government interference in mergers and acquisitions, especially cross-border, in pursuit of national champions – particularly, but not exclusively, in industry and not always successful. Successes include BNP-Paribas in banking; Sanofi-Aventis in pharmaceuticals; Danone (food business) protected from a hostile Pepsi-Co bid. High-profile failures include Mittal's takeover of Arcelor (steel); and some 'national champions' such as Alstom survived only following state rescue plans (*The Times*, 24 October 2008: 63).

Regulation

'Social Charges'
These are the notorious charges imposed on companies to help finance the welfare state. These are on top of VAT and other taxes, and are well above the EU average as a percentage of GDP, edging towards 20% of GDP in 2007. Government policy periodically offers to offset part of these charges as incentives; for example, in compensation for the 35-hour week introduced in the early 2000s.

Rules
Rules are embedded in the numerous legal codes governing or touching the economic sphere, such as labour law (the *code du travail*) and business law (the *code du commerce*). These codes provide governments with scope for the tight regulation of many

aspects of the market economy, not uncommon in other countries. Examples include, significantly, the length of the working week, the nature of employment contracts, and industrial relations practices. Also covered are matters such as rules on Sunday trading and other retail practices, and restrictions on the total number of practitioners allowed to exercise certain professions – such as taxi drivers or pharmacists.

Overall, the extent of state involvement in the French economy has, in the present day and without doubt, diminished in real terms, with state powers over the economy increasingly transferred to local authorities and independent agencies, as in other policy domains, as seen in previous chapters. Following President Sarkozy's election in 2007, moreover, France saw some loosening of labour market regulations, in particular to circumvent the 35-hour week (but without scrapping the legislation itself altogether). But the picture thus far demonstrates how open and international the French economy has become, and this aspect of French economic life is sustained as well as constrained by France's *voluntary* membership of the European Union since its very beginnings in the 1950s, when French minds were behind the creation of the first community for the pooling of production and markets in coal and steel. The EU provides France with its key markets, and is the source of the most stringent constraints on the freedom of the state to shape the French economic and business environments.

France in the European (EU) Economy

The EU provides France with a market of approximately 450 million people, and this accounts for easily half of all French export trade, and for three quarters of its agricultural exports. France's immediate neighbour, Germany, is France's number one trading partner, and the two countries have established a bilateral relationship within the EU to foster cooperation and agreement across a wide range of policy areas. Nowhere is this more important to the smooth running of the EU and to the bilateral partnership itself than in economic matters; here, the two countries have long shared an interest in overcoming differences for the sake of peaceful and productive relations. The two countries were the key architects of the early European Communities of the 1950s and, in the 1990s, of the foundations of today's European Union (see Chapter 8). Since German reunification in

1990, France has had to work harder to preserve its influence over Germany, and the two countries frequently clash over macro-economic policy at the EU level, including the Common Agricultural Policy (CAP), responses to the 2008–09 global financial crisis, and the EU's financial priorities in general.

The Costs and Benefits of European Economic Integration

For nearly thirty years, European economic integration was largely limited to the highly expensive CAP, the common market in coal and steel, and the Common External Tariff, which established a 'Community preference' in virtually all trading with the rest of the world. When France acquiesced, in the late 1950s, to the extension of the 1951 Coal and Steel Community to a broad spectrum of economic sectors, it negotiated important conditions and limitations. These constituted, principally, preferential agreements with its former colonial markets, and a good deal for its agriculture in the form of the CAP, which subsequently became part and parcel of the modernization and mechanization of rural France seen in Chapters 1 and 2.

De Gaulle himself played a large part in bringing to life the CAP which, to this day, is still the most costly of the EU's common policies, and in which the supranational and independent Commission plays the pivotal role. The policy has, for five decades, cushioned France from the blows of an increasingly competitive global market for agriculture and its products, and turned its biggest farmers into an important political lobby, making change so costly for successive French politicians that none have been prepared to address it with real conviction. What is at stake, the farmers argue, is good food at reasonable prices produced locally in a countryside protected from undue urban development. As ever, in reality, the picture is more complicated, since the beneficiaries in France of the CAP include more farmers responsible for vast tracts of arable land (making France the second largest exporter of wheat in the world after the USA) than small farmers protecting land, tradition, and wildlife.

France has, over time, received the most in CAP farm subsidies of all member states, which helps to balance out the fact that it is also a large contributor to the EU's funds (to the tune of nearly one fifth of the overall budget). In 2006, for example, France received approximately one fifth of the total CAP funds, worth €10 billion. Germany, in contrast, has long been relied upon as the EU's 'paymaster'.

France, therefore, has a vested interest to the current day in controlling the pace and scope of reform of the EU's budget and, in particular, of its benefits for France's farmers. However, the potential for national state action is limited in the face of competition from foreign producers (for example, in the wine industry), particularly from newly-emerging countries; and given the looming CAP reform that plans to reduce the overall EU budget to agriculture on the one hand and, on the other, to shift aid away altogether from individual producers towards rural and environmental development and protection.

France, Germany and the Single Currency

Furthermore, and following the economic downturn of the 1970s and then the failure in France, in the early 1980s, of President Mitterrand's counter-cyclical, *dirigiste* re-launch of the French economy (see Chapters 2 and 3), the European Community has become an ever more important policy framework for French economic policy. In 1983 the French President lent his support to EC-wide plans to 'complete' European economic integration by, principally, working to remove existing barriers to trade *between* the EU member states as a way of boosting opportunities for French trade, and economic growth in general. This agenda led to the gradual liberalization of the (now) EU's *single, internal* market, which is still ongoing, and in time to a slackening of the 'community preference' principle in the EU's trade (including in agriculture) with the rest of the world.

Former German Chancellor Helmut Kohl threw his weight behind the 1980s 'Single Market Programme' such that by the early 1990s, and in the throes of German reunification, plans for Economic and Monetary Union were set, and by 1 January 2000 France had adopted the single currency, the Euro. To French President Mitterrand, this dramatic development was considered a more than acceptable trade-off with national sovereignty than had been the case of the previous decade, when French governments had pursued a policy of pegging the French franc closely to the German Deutsch Mark, despite lagging behind German levels of competitiveness. This approach, accordingly, hurt French exports, and contributed to the steadily rising levels of unemployment in France.

Indeed, since the mid-1990s, the popularity of the European Union has declined in France, culminating in May 2005 with a 'no' vote by referendum to a reform of the EU's treaties (the

'Constitutional Treaty') in which French negotiators had secured a good deal for France (see Chapters 3 and 8). European economic integration had by now, for the 'no' voters, become indissociable from the economic pain associated with the opening up of the French economy to the harsh global forces deemed threatening to the French socio-economic model. These take the form of the 'delocalization' of production, with the resultant loss in local jobs; the import into France of 'Anglo-Saxon' shareholder values; an undermining of the social gains made for workers in France over the course of the previous century, and the unpicking of the state's autonomy to deliver high-quality, high-cost public services. In the Single European Market, *dirigisme* of the sort associated with France's recent economic history is systematically curtailed by the strict rules of competition policy, and more broadly by what is frequently derided in France as a 'neo-liberal' approach to the deregulation of the market in general.

France in an Enlarged EU

In President Sarkozy's France – and, specifically, following the 'no' vote of May 2005, and the enlargements of the EU in 2004 and 2007 to include 10 former Soviet bloc countries of East and Central Europe – the language of EU economics in France has significantly hardened, and EU rules have been flouted, softened or both. It has long been customary for French governments to criticize the European Commission for over-reaching its authority in matters of competition policy and world trade talks – where it has a mandate to speak on behalf of the EU intergovernmental consensus – and Sarkozy's governments have been no exception in this respect. Shortly after coming to power, Sarkozy authorized his government to announce that the date by which the French economy was expected to reduce its deficit in line with EU rules was to be postponed by two, and then four years. Furthermore, President Sarkozy himself has carried on a French tradition of finding fault with the governance arrangements for the Eurozone. In particular, he has criticized the independence of the European Central Bank (situated in Frankfurt in Germany) from political direction, or any form of 'economic government', as French leaders usually refer to this idea. The principle of the Bank's independence was a German condition for agreeing to the Single Currency, and France has yet to formulate an acceptable alternative to this system.

In the matter of the gradual liberalization of the EU's services sector, French opposition has been even more vocal. It was this aspect of EU integration that contributed to the 'no' vote in the 2005 referendum in France, partly because opponents to government policy depicted a future France in which foreign service providers (the 'Polish plumber' was the figure invoked) would, in a mass migration of workers from the poorer and newer member states, undermine local work and wage conditions for the sake of 'competition' alone. France was not alone in expressing such concerns, and the EU's infamous 2006 'Services Directive' was subsequently watered down. Labour migration itself, in the French case, has been little more than a trickle. In a similar vein, President Sarkozy personally saw to it that, in the renegotiation of the failed 'Constitutional Treaty' (following the 2005 'no' vote), the expression 'fair and free (undistorted) competition' was excised from the Preamble of the revised Treaty, although it was confirmed in the form of a protocol to the revised Treaty, to the effect that the internal market system ensures that 'competition is not distorted'. 'Competition', claimed Sarkozy, should not be treated as 'dogma', even though it is a founding principle of European economic integration.

Crisis, What Crisis?

French calls, at domestic and EU levels, for a more balanced political economy in which *dirigisme* has some part to play, found an opening in the world financial crisis that erupted in autumn 2008, at precisely the time when France was holding the chair of the Council of Ministers of the EU, and could thus exert some control over the EU's agenda. This was an opportunity, at EU level, for France to rehabilitate the language of the strong state in the service of a *European* social model, even though the crisis had the effect of illuminating important differences between the EU's biggest economies – France, Germany and the UK – in precisely these matters. From the French chair, President Sarkozy called for an EU-wide plan for bailing out ailing banks, and for EU sovereign wealth funds to protect EU-based companies from hostile takeover bids. The mood was also favourable to the argument that salaries and bonuses in the financial services industries should be capped and taxed, and the sector itself far more heavily regulated. The crisis, from this perspective, popular in France, was in no small part a failure of the excesses of Anglo-Saxon, *laissez-faire* economics and their admiration of untrammelled wealth.

The situation provided opportunities for debate on such matters, allowing the French argument to be heard. But, in real terms and by and large, the EU member states each took unilateral action to safeguard their domestic economic interests. Thus, former British Prime Minister Gordon Brown implemented a VAT tax cut in the UK designed to boost consumption. This was criticized by President Sarkozy who, in France, authorized a reflationary programme of infrastructure spending worth €26 billion, amounting to 1.3% of GDP. This was shortly followed in Paris by a €6 billion package specifically for the car industry in the form of preferential loans, and a bank bail out scheme of €360 billion. These were all measures that increased France's public spending deficit. Nevertheless, France and Germany managed to agree on how to curb bank bonuses (in the form of taxation); the 2008 French EU Council presidency succeeded in negotiating a Euro zone 'toolbox' (the *Financial Times*, 2009) of crisis measures; and President Sarkozy's tone throughout was combative, claiming a 'triumph' of French ideas over, in particular, the UK-style capitalism that was seen to have driven the EU's single market agenda for over two decades.

Labour, Capital and the State

In a political context in France whereby economic transformations of the sorts discussed above are deemed by their opponents to threaten the very fabric of the French republican model of society, relations between the state and the 'social partners' – labour and capital – and between the partners themselves are notoriously conflictual, and typically held responsible for 'blocked' reform; but they are also changing in pace with economic change itself.

In France, regulation and legislation are as much part of the business environment as dialogue and negotiation; and the 'social partners' in France have traditionally been co-opted by the state as part of the policy-making process. They also, crucially, share responsibility with the state for administering much of France's social security system – specifically, unemployment and other social benefits, and pensions. This system is known as tripartism, and has been a keystone of the postwar quest in France for a cohesive society, as seen in previous chapters. As with other dimensions of the French socio-economic model, the system is finding itself transformed by changes in the economic and business climate, including the fading

of class consciousness which, for decades, sustained conflictual relations between the partners, and fragmented the labour movement
from within.

French Industrial Relations and the Social Partners

Trades unionism in France, for its part, emerged in the late nineteenth
century from a history of banned associations and, over the past
hundred years, the movement has reflected the many political, ideological and religious divisions in French society, and has been shaped
in particular by the strong forces of postwar Communism and
Socialism. It taps into strong emotions relating to the 'social gains' –
improvements to working conditions – made by labour, and by the
political left, over the course of nearly a century. Unions have, as a
rule, proved themselves more effective at disruption, and at getting
their voice heard by government, than at building their membership,
or at representing the diversity of employees in the workplace; or
even, at times, at negotiating good conditions for 'outsiders' or new
entrants to the labour force such as women or immigrant labour.
Recent developments have included the employers – capital –
seeking greater autonomy from the state, particularly in the early
2000s after employers' organizations failed to prevent legislation
introducing a 35-hour week; new unions seeking independence from
the old organizations and their rules; and old unions changing their
spots. The state itself has begun to legislate to force unions to earn
their right to speak and disrupt in the name of workers by insisting
that unions are more representative – and, therefore, legitimate – at
the level of the firm; and firm-level negotiations are spreading, taking
their place alongside the national and industry-wide bargains that
have long been the norm in France.

Thus, the old rulebook – whereby the state authorized a small
number of unions to sign agreements on behalf of the entire workforce, irrespective of how representative they were, or how low their
membership levels were – are being ripped up. 'Minimum service'
agreements, moreover, have been imposed upon public service
providers (in transport, for example) as a way of preventing France
from grinding to a complete halt when public transport workers take
to the street; and on the key issues for state, labour and capital in the
twenty-first century – unemployment, *la précarité*, pensions reform
and the updating of working practices such as the 35-hour working
week – the state in Sarkozy's France has initiated a new round of

tripartite talks intended to diffuse traditional power relations, by a combination of communication, and the force of legislation and regulation.

The first decade of the twentieth century saw significant reforms to French industrial relations, and to the business environment in general. These were accelerated following the election of President Nicolas Sarkozy in May 2007. Sarkozy had campaigned on an explicit platform of shaking up French working practices, and rehabilitating the work ethic *per se*, and had openly lauded the UK's flexible labour market as a source of inspiration for French reforms. Where critics saw an ideologically-driven intent to concentrate power into the hands of capital, especially big business – by loosening regulations, for example, on hiring and firing – the picture is more nuanced. Many of the structural rigidities of the French labour market, upheld by powerful unions to uphold hard-won workers' rights, have contributed to high levels of unemployed, particularly amongst the inexperienced young, and especially when they are poorly-qualified. Symbolically, so-called 'McJobs' in France divide opinion – do they offer employment to people who otherwise would be out of work (McDonald's itself provides jobs in many of France's run-down suburbs), or do they seek to undermine reasonable working conditions?

By the time Sarkozy came to power, for example, the 35-hour working week was fully part of the business environment for the largest and the smallest of firms, but was still controversial, and he set about loosening its impact on the French economy. France had seen a gradual reduction in the length of the working week since the 1960s, using legislation as a key tool to implement the reductions; and the most (in)famous of these laws were the bills passed between 1997 and 2002 by governments of the left, named after the minister in charge, Martine Aubry. Sarkozy's government stopped short of repealing the legislation itself, but his intention remains to erode the edifice, and change the habits of those who have become accustomed to one of its benefits; namely, more leisure time in the form of RTT (*Réduction du temps de travail* – reduced working hours). Similarly, President Sarkozy inherited and accelerated an ongoing process of reform with respect to pensions provision (raising the length of pensionable service in the private and public sectors; and, in general, attempting to defuse the time bomb of the combination of a growing deficit in the public pensions sector of France's social security system, and the coming-to-retirement age, in the present decade, of

France's postwar 'baby-boom' generation); and the loosening of the rules surrounding job contracts.

One such reform in 2005–06, to introduce more flexibility for employers when hiring a young person in their first job, was so badly handled by the government of the day that mass protests were held on the streets, and the government bill was effectively withdrawn. This episode neither improved job prospects for young people as intended (by encouraging employers to open more positions, on the condition that they had more control over the hiring and firing), nor satisfied employers themselves. In the matter of pensions, reform by 2010 was underway to extend pensionable service in both the private and public sectors, but sticking points remained, particularly concerning the raising of the retirement age from 60 to 62 years. On both pension reform and work contracts, President Sarkozy acted fast to consult the key players amongst the social partners, with some success in reforming the law. Social unrest around this issue, however, remains a political headache.

Illustration 7.1   Paris street demonstration

The French Business Environment in the Twenty-First Century

Other reforms were introduced in the first three years of Sarkozy's presidency with the explicit intent to 'modernize' the French economy, principally by relaxing the business environment with relation to regulation, codification and taxation. The over-riding aims of the programme, other than the broad objective of exhorting the work ethic, were to facilitate entrepreneurship; encourage the growth of France's dense network of medium-sized enterprises (which account for over four fifths of employment in France), who would then be more active on the export market; and to concentrate resources in 'centres of excellence' (*pôles de competitivité*) clustered around France's most dynamic regions (including the richest of France's regions, the Paris-centred Île de France; and the country's second largest economic centre, focused on Lyon and the Rhône Valley in the southeast of France).

These reforms and initiatives include in particular:

- The August 2007 'Tepa' law to promote work (*le travail*), employment (*l'emploi*) and purchasing power (*le pouvoir d'achat*). It included controversial tax cuts, on inheritance, for example.
- The 2008 law to 'Modernize the Economy' in order to 'liberalize competition' within the domestic market, and make the French economy more competitive. It was based on the findings of a committee that reported in January 2008 and which was headed by a writer, intellectual and former political advisor to President Mitterrand, Jacques Attali. The report recommended at least three hundred measures to free up the economy, only a small number of which were adopted. Amongst the more eye-catching were a relaxing of the laws on Sunday retail opening hours in large towns and villages of 'tourist interest' (*The Guardian*, 2007: 23), and those on price controls imposed on large retailers (limiting discounts to consumers). Amongst the measures rejected were the opening up of professions, such as taxis, where supply is restricted by law (hence the virtual impossibility of hailing a taxi on Paris streets).
- Growth in the number of the *pôles de competitivité* established in 2005; and the consolidation of the attractiveness of France's biggest and richest region, the Île de France which, according to the Invest in France Agency (2009), is the top economic and most

highly populated region in Europe, ahead of London, with a GDP in 2007 of €534 billion accounting for nearly one-third of France's national output.

- The abolition from 2010 of the *taxe professionnelle*, a tax raised on businesses at the local level for the purposes of funding training and education.
- In 2009, help worth €2 billion to small businesses to counter the recession.
- The launching by President Sarkozy, on New Year's Eve 2008, of a debate on the 'politics of civilization', leading to the commissioning of a report into how the quality of life might be factored into measurements of the health of a national economy, alongside existing statistics recording economic growth. The job was given to two Nobel prize-winners, Amartya Sen and Joseph Stiglitz, whose report proposed new economic indicators 'such as environmental protection and work/life balance as well as economic output to rate a country's ability to maintain the "sustainable" happiness of its inhabitants' (*The Guardian*, 2009a: 27).

Conclusions

As fanciful as the happiness agenda might sound, it did solicit serious responses, at precisely the time when the French 'model' of political economy appeared to have allowed France to survive the global crisis and recession reasonably well – as President Sarkozy himself claimed (p. 177). In late 2009, the French government finalized its plans for a *grand emprunt* or 'big loan' of €35 billion targeted at spending on higher education, research, green technology (sustainable development) and the digitalization of 'France's national treasures' (see *The Guardian*, 2009b; *le Monde*, 2009). Did this signify the rebirth of *dirigisme* in the form of reflationary, state-guided spending?

The concept of the French socio-economic model is certainly still relevant to understanding French economic policy, its limitations and its frustrations. The state is still expected to play its part in regulating, planning and balancing the economy. It is still blamed when individuals – as workers, consumers, voters, public servants, managers, directors, entrepreneurs, shareholders, investors – feel the pain of living in an open economy; and it is critiqued for its difficulties in carrying out structural reforms that many economists deem necessary for France to flourish in the twenty-first-century global economy. Yet, the French state is manifestly only one of the many actors and forces shaping France's economic fortunes, a fact not lost on the French people who voted against the EU's Constitutional Treaty in May 2005. The importance for national economic survival of France's links to the global economy go beyond the EU, to include its trading partners in the USA, in Asia, and in the fast-developing markets of countries such as Brazil, India and China. In particular, the interests of big French business – in defence procurement, in nuclear energy and so on – are part of a bigger picture in which France seeks to project its influence across the wider world, using commercial, diplomatic, cultural and military means. In the economy, as in foreign policy, France likes to shape the debate, if not change the course of events.

8

France in the World

Introduction

For centuries, France has maintained an international presence of global dimensions, and the twenty-first century is no exception: France is still a major world player culturally, commercially, militarily and politically. As recently as the 1960s, Paris directly ruled countries as large as Algeria, and as distant as New Caledonia. Today, France possesses only fragments of its former Empire, but France as a physical entity still extends far beyond the *métropole* (mainland France) to the Atlantic, Pacific and Indian oceans, where two million French citizens live in France's remaining overseas departments and territories (as seen in Chapter 2). France has an independent nuclear deterrent, (known as its *force de frappe*) and, on this basis alone, qualifies as one of the world's most influential powers.

France increasingly operates in the world multilaterally – together with other countries – through international organizations such as the European Union (EU), of which it is a founder member; the United Nations (UN) where, as a nuclear power, it holds one of the five permanent seats on the Security Council, and so the right of veto; and *la Francophonie* – the French-speaking 'Commonwealth' of 68 members and associate members, many but not all French former colonies, having 'in common' the use of the French language.

Membership of such organizations offers France opportunities to make its voice heard on the global stage in matters of vital national interest such as security, defence, culture and trade. At the same time, the inclination to act in concert with other countries, and under the umbrella of joint organizations, constrains the freedom of manoeuvre of French policy-makers, and contrasts with a sense of the past where France projected itself as an independent, sovereign, so-called 'exceptional' actor in the world. French foreign policy is still marked by a strong self-image that lends itself to stereotype and even carica-ture, especially in its relations with the USA, another 'exceptional' world player.

This chapter evaluates France's international influence in the contemporary era, and assesses the role of French foreign policy in defining the national identity of contemporary France. It does so by means, first, of an overview of the changes forced upon French strategic thinking about defence and security by the environment of the post-Cold War world; second, by exploring France's most impor-tant relationships – with Germany, Britain, the EU and its other member states, the USA, and France's former colonies, especially in Africa; and third, by briefly examining the process by which contem-porary France chooses to remember certain events in its past activi-ties abroad, and the impact of these tussles with the past on current domestic life in France.

The Weight of the Past

France has a history (as seen in Chapter 1) marked as much by mili-tary failure as victory. Inevitably, it is the stories of victory that stiffen the backbone of France's sense of identity as a world player. The present day is nourished by France's seventeenth-century domi-nation of Europe, often at the expense of the UK; by the revolution-ary spirit of 1789, when France saw itself as a pioneer of democracy in modern Europe; and by the nineteenth-century Napoleonic wars that earned France the label of the *grande nation* of Europe. Cogan (2003) argues that a sense of these historical achievements (added to colonial conquests, however controversial from a present day perspective) underpins contemporary quests for an influential French voice in international affairs, where History, with a capital 'H', is an ever-present force. But we saw in previous chapters how reverence for the past tends to act as a brake on change in the present day, and this is very true of French foreign policy. This sense of a glorious history is reflected physically in the home of the French Ministry for Foreign and European Affairs, situated on the banks of the Seine in Paris, and known as the *Quai d'Orsay*. In the splendour of its envi-ronment, and in its once powerful status within the French core exec-utive, the *Quai* symbolizes France's long past as a world-class diplomatic player, and strongly suggests its appetite for global power.

Underpinning the *Quai*'s memories of France's glorious past is the specific organizational culture that still dominates the French foreign policy-making elite, and which has lent it an image of an arrogant country, prepared to act unilaterally to secure its national interests. This is a world characterized by close-knit networks of diplomats and officials predominantly trained in the National School of Administration (*l'ENA* – see Chapter 4). These individuals are imbued with a strong sense of hierarchy, and encouraged to emphasize certain characteristics of French intellectual thinking such as the importance of powerful rhetoric, and abstract, intellectual rationales for action. These are all qualities that have lent both strengths and weaknesses to contemporary French diplomacy, particularly with respect to how it is perceived by its partners abroad in a policy domain heavily marked by protocol and routine. Sonntag (2008) has described the situation as a 'prison wall' behind which France is trapped by its quest for prestige, rather than any more modest purpose in today's world. Indeed, in France today, the President increasingly squares up to the *Quai*, appointing his own foreign policy advisors at the *Elysée* palace, outranking the Foreign Minister in important diplomatic decisions, and puncturing the myth of an all-powerful foreign policy elite immune from change. Neither has the *Quai* been immune from cost-cutting: its budget for 2010, at €4.9 billion, represented only a fraction of an increase on the previous year's (€4.6 billion). Significantly, savings were to be made from rationalizing and reforming the functioning of the *Quai* itself, both in its premises in Paris, and in its embassies and consulates across the world.

Contemporary France also remembers its nineteenth- and twentieth-century mortal combats with Germany; its earlier, repeated losses of territory and pride to the British; its Cold War struggle with Communism; and its many experiences as Europe's 'underdog' (Cogan, 2003). These events and relationships all revealed the limitations of French power, and, latterly, the virtues of collective security. Reconciling these historical experiences of aggressive and defensive diplomacy is key to understanding France's voice in contemporary global matters.

The Gaullist Legacy

Indeed, global greatness and rank (known respectively as *la grandeur* and *le rang*) were key objectives pursued by President Charles de

Gaulle when in power between 1958 and 1969. De Gaulle sought to restore France – as he saw it – as a sovereign, high-ranking world player independent from both of the two Cold War superpowers, the USA and the USSR; and to link France with its past glories after the *débâcle* of the experience of World War II (as seen in Chapter 1), in part by declaring such dark periods to be aberrations in an otherwise glorious past. Such goals were to be reached by developing an independent nuclear capacity, establishing friendships with countries of the 'Third World' and other non-aligned powers, courting Germany as a means to building an independent Europe, holding the UK at bay, and reinvigorating the long-held idea that France had a unique 'civilizing mission' in the world. At the same time, France's loyalty to the 'West' during the Cold War was never seriously in doubt, neither was its dependence on the USA and the transatlantic alliance for its security; nor its friendship, however troubled, with the UK.

De Gaulle, in his day, became the voice and face of French foreign policy, and the presidential powers and precedent that he created to this purpose are part of his legacy today, as are the guiding ideals of French foreign policy – independence; autonomy – that were outdated even in de Gaulle's own days in power. Nevertheless, these ideals still enjoy rhetorical support from across the political spectrum in France, and are as uncontroversial as they are ambiguous and ambitious. But, says Sonntag (2008), they are another of the barriers between French diplomacy and the real world; and President Sarkozy set out to breach this particular obstacle, as we see. The 1958 Constitution gave the President far greater powers in foreign policy-making than under previous republics and, as first President of the Fifth Republic, de Gaulle implemented these powers as he saw fit. Treacher (2003) notes how 'malleable' the 1958 constitution is in this respect (see Box 8.1), to the point where de Gaulle was seen as carving out a 'reserved domain' for presidential foreign policy-making, leaving little room for consultation with Parliament, or even within government itself. In the present day, the President still has more power to set foreign policy objectives than most of his counterparts in the EU, and he can be a very vocal and sometimes powerful figure on the world stage. In his victory speech, delivered on the evening on Sunday 6 May 2007, President Sarkozy emphasized the importance of French foreign policy in shaping the 'old' and 'great' nation of France; and he subsequently indicated his commitment to ending the *domaine reservé* by involving more bodies in decision-making in foreign and defence policy, notably the Parliament. In

---

Box 8.1   Is it in the Constitution? The (im)balance of powers in French foreign policy-making

Article 5: '[The President] shall be the guarantor of national independence, territorial integrity and due respect for Treaties.'

Article 13: '[The President] shall make appointments to the civil and military posts of the State.'

Article 14: 'The President of the Republic shall accredit ambassadors and envoys extraordinary to foreign powers.'

Article 15: 'The President of the Republic shall be Commander-in-Chief of the Armed Forces. He shall preside over the higher national defence councils and committees.'

Article 20: 'The Government shall determine and conduct the policy of the Nation. It shall have at its disposal the civil service and the armed forces.'

Article 21: 'The Prime Minister shall direct the actions of the Government. He shall be responsible for national defence.'

Article 52: 'The President of the Republic shall negotiate and ratify treaties. He shall be informed of any negotiations for the conclusion of an international agreement not subject to ratification.'

Article 53: 'Peace Treaties, trade agreements, treaties or agreements relating to international organization .... may be ratified or approved only by an Act of Parliament.'

Source: National Assembly (2010).

---

practice, however, the President still leads the way in matters of foreign policy, including European Union affairs, and is relatively untroubled by the other institutions of French government. Public opinion is another matter, especially if the President chooses to call a referendum, as has been the case on three occasions in the matter of European policy (in 1972, 1992 and 2005). It is, however, a distinctive feature of the Fifth French Republic that foreign policy is, by and large, a matter of public and political consensus, and the Gaullist legacy, for good or for bad, is part of this picture.

The Challenge of the Future: Post-Cold War Review

French foreign policy during the Fifth Republic has, indeed, been characterized by continuity, despite changes of political leaders. The Cold War, in particular, provided a strangely stable climate in which the French authorities could strive to realize their ambitions of independence, and the global spread of democracy, liberty and peace. But the contemporary global era has, in many respects, brought about an acute loss of 'Cold War comfort' (Keiger, 2005: 140) for France and, with it, an explicit challenge to de Gaulle's foreign policy legacy. The collapse of the Soviet Union, German unification, the unilateralism of US foreign policy for nearly a decade after 9/11, the enlargement of the European Union, and the growing reach and pace of globalization: all of these developments have challenged France's global positioning, and complicated its quest for influence in Europe and further afield. In this context, the early years of the twenty-first century were characterized in France, in some circles, by a pessimistic sense of the decline of French influence in Europe and in the world at large, while strategy, policy and diplomatic instruments and tactics were simultaneously undergoing significant review.

French Military Capacity and Doctrine

The conflicts of the 1990s and early twenty-first century began to make France's military capability look irrelevant and unfit for purpose – in particular, its nuclear deterrent. The conflicts of the present and future were unlikely to be resolved or won by military hardware designed for a different age, and called for improved coordination and cooperation between France and her allies, within Europe and further afield. French defence policy needed a rationale and doctrine to fit the post-Cold War era, and this revolved around the long-standing French notion of Europe taking responsibility for its own defence and security. Thus, former President Jacques Chirac marked his first term of office (1995–2002) by taking a number of key, strategic decisions. French policy since 1995 has been to modernize its troops and weapons to the point where they are more compatible both with the types of demands that the twenty-first century seems to place on the 'West' in the form of counter-terrorism and peacekeeping, and with the forces and weapons of its principal allies, especially the UK and the USA.

Some of these changes took 'exceptional' French forms, such as Chirac's surprise announcement in June 1995 that France would resume nuclear testing following his predecessor Mitterrand's moratorium on testing. This decision that took France's partners by surprise, and created a furore of negative public opinion, particularly in those countries neighbouring the test site, of which Australia and

New Zealand, but also in France itself. However Gaullist in style this gesture, it nevertheless spelt the beginning of the definitive end of such testing, the subsequent signing by France of the Test Ban Treaty, and the downgrading over the following decade of the French nuclear deterrent.

Chirac also decreed the end of national service and conscription in a key move towards the professionalization of the French army, making it more compatible with other European armies. He began a lengthy and rocky process of *rapprochement* with NATO's decision-making bodies (de Gaulle having removed France from NATO's military structures in 1966) which Chirac's successor, Nicolas Sarkozy, completed in 2009. This French policy of working towards the strengthening of the EU's own military capabilities has met with only limited support from France's EU partners, wary of wastefully reproducing NATO capability. Nevertheless, newly-elected President Sarkozy's decision to invite military detachments from all of the 26 other EU member states to join French regiments in the 2007 traditional Bastille Day parade was symbolic of France's firm belief in ongoing attention to Europe's potential as a military force.

'Le Rayonnement': Culture, Commerce and Cash

The bolstering of the EU's capacity to play a role as an international actor in its own right falls squarely within a longer-lived French worldview in which the spread of French values is a valid ambition. Thus, French foreign policy continues to emphasize, in its rhetoric and spending plans, the role that France can play in spreading democracy; for example, by assisting the economic development of peoples and nations abroad, or fostering a respect for international law (which is seen a legitimate vehicle for conveying such French ambitions). From this perspective, 'Europe' is another scene on which to showcase and promote such ideas. The term *rayonnement* is applicable here, its literal meaning of 'radiating' in this context value-laden with what the French *Quai d'Orsay* typically refers to as '*outreach*'; namely, a vehicle for conveying France's vision of the international community across the globe. In historical terms, the concept of *rayonnement* shaped France's colonial policy and, in the present day, underpins French support for humanitarian missions abroad, both governmental and non-governmental (such as the world-renowned *Médecins sans Frontières* – or 'French Doctors'). It also relates to the ongoing mission of promoting French language and culture overseas, as well as the tools of 'soft' diplomacy of commercial trade and development assistance.

Influencing International Society

Alongside its military capabilities and presence throughout the world, and its diplomatic network of embassies and consulates that the *Quai d'Orsay* describes as the second most extensive in the world (after the USA), contemporary France gives high priority to its ability to influence decisions and policy of global significance by means of a weighty presence in the world's most prestigious international institutions, especially the UN and the EU. Together with its permanent seat on the United Nations Security Council, French senior administrators account for approximately 6% of the top personnel in this organization. In the EU, this figure approximates to roughly 13%, taking all the EU's institutions into account. France also has a strong record of success in placing its men and women (predominantly men) at the very top of other powerful international bodies (see Table 8.1) By its presence in such organizations, and also by a decades-old

Table 8.1   The French in high places

Name	Institution and role	Dates and notes
Jean-Claude Trichet	President European Central Bank (ECB)	2003–present; *énarque**
Pascal Lamy	Director World Trade Organization (WTO)	2005–present; *énarque**
Dominique Strauss-Kahn	President International Monetary Fund (IMF)	2007–present; EU nominee
Marc de Brichambaut	Secretary-General Organization for Security and Cooperation in Europe (OSCE)	2005–present; *énarque**
Jacques Delors	President European Commission	1985–1995; French Minister of Economics and Finance, 1981–1984

Note: *A graduate of the École nationale d'administration.

quest to maintain the use of French as a working language in these organizations, and to support the use of French in the French-speaking world (as well as at home), France attempts to wield influence across the globe. Above all, it seeks to shape the rules produced by international organizations for regulating world trade, building solidarity with poorer nations, and ensuring collective security. It has experienced both success and failure in these respects; France failed at the UN, for example, to prevent the US-led invasion of Iraq in 2003. Its fight to preserve the French language as a lingua franca is also largely a rearguard battle that brings little influence in its own right, but it does ensure a cultural presence on all continents of the world. In world trade talks, notably, France has succeeded on significant occasions in shaping regulations designed to preserve what its leaders call the 'cultural diversity' of the world by means of exemptions from liberalization accorded to, for example, French and European cinema in the global market (see Chapter 6).

In what follows, we offer concrete examples of the trends outlined by means of a focus on the key contexts and priorities of contemporary French foreign policy, beginning with France's role in the EU. This – a European France – is the face that France was most determined to project in the second half of the twentieth century, and is the primary context for its policy-making in the present day. It is the focus of the dilemma facing contemporary French policy-makers as they seek to balance traditions of independence and pride in national sovereignty, on the one hand with, on the other, the need for concessions and coordination with partners in order to exert global influence of any kind at all.

The European Union

France's unique role in the early 1950s in the founding of what is now the European Union formed a critical turning point in French diplomatic history. This was a postwar solution to a century-old problem, that of stabilizing relations with Germany for mutual security, and it is impossible to underestimate its novelty or significance. The new European institutions of the 1950s provided the framework for a constructive partnership and, by the 1960s, the Franco-German relationship was the backbone of the European Economic Communities. With the backing of the USA, without a viable alternative from the UK, and thanks to the ingenuity of its author Jean

Box 8.2   The Schuman Declaration, 9 May 1950

French Foreign Minister Robert Schuman took virtually everyone by surprise when, on 9 May 1950, he made a short speech outlining a novel way of keeping the peace in Europe. The second paragraph of the speech is the most famous:

'World peace cannot be safeguarded without the making of creative efforts proportionate to the dangers which threaten it. The contribution which an organised and living Europe can bring to civilisation is indispensable to the maintenance of peaceful relations. In taking upon herself for more than 20 years the role of champion of a united Europe, France has always had as her essential aim the service of peace. A united Europe was not achieved and we had war.

Europe will not be made all at once, or according to a single plan. It will be built through concrete achievements which first create a de facto solidarity. The coming together of the nations of Europe requires the elimination of the age-old opposition of France and Germany. Any action must in the first place concern these two countries. With this aim in view, the French Government proposes that action be taken immediately on one limited but decisive point.

It proposes that Franco-German production of coal and steel as a whole be placed under a common High Authority, within the framework of an organisation open to the participation of the other countries of Europe. The pooling of coal and steel production should immediately provide for the setting up of common foundations for economic development as a first step in the federation of Europe ... The solidarity in production thus established will make it plain that any war between France and Germany becomes not merely unthinkable, but materially impossible ... [and] will lay a true foundation for their economic unification.'

Source: Europa (2010).

Monnet, the declaration endorsed by French Foreign Minister Robert Schuman on 9 May 1950 took France into an unprecedented experiment in the voluntary sharing of decision-making power in the key economic sectors of coal and steel, under the authority of new, European-level institutions.

The Franco-German Relationship

Over time, the Franco-German partnership developed into a highly-structured, special, bilateral relationship, subsequently framed by the

Elysée Treaty of 1963, which formally enshrined the bilateral friendship, signalled a common intent to build a united Europe, and established joint working procedures. In 2003, the fortieth anniversary of
the Treaty was celebrated with great formality; by then, joint Franco-
German Councils of Ministers were held twice-yearly, and political
cooperation in the specific fields of defence, security, the economy,
finance and the environment had taken root. Moreover, genuine –
sometimes unlikely – personal friendships were established between
several pairs of French and German leaders, most significantly
Charles de Gaulle and Konrad Adenauer in the 1960s, and François
Mitterrand and Helmut Kohl in the 1980s and 1990s.

An end to the division of Germany in 1990 spelled the beginning
of a new phase in the Franco-German relationship. By 2000,
Germany had won additional representation in the institutions of the
EU by virtue of its population size, now one fifth larger than that of
France (France lost nine of its European Parliament seats as a result,
along with Italy, Spain and the UK, while Germany gained another
12); this was a difficult moment for French relations with its neighbour, but it did not derail the relationship. Henceforth, it was harder
for France to dictate terms to its larger partner, although the habit of
cooperation was by then entrenched, and policy agreements were still
possible on matters of critical importance to the EU, of which agricultural funding, institutional reform and the introduction of the
single European currency – the Euro. In the present day, the relationship is based, as ever, on a shared determination to overcome significant differences, in order to preserve the peace and prosperity that
the partnership, inside the European Communities, had established.
Symbolic acts of reconciliation between the two countries remain an
important facet of the relationship to this day.

French Leadership of a 'Political Europe'

From a strategic perspective, France's friendship with Germany was
intended to allow France to exert influence in the form of leadership
on the European continent and, in turn, to enable Europe to exert
influence as an autonomous bloc, known in French as 'power
Europe', or *l'Europe puissance*. De Gaulle himself spoke of the day
when Europe would reunite from the 'Atlantic to the Urals', making
the East–West division of the Cold War a thing of the past, and
bolstering Europe's strength; this was a vision that, by 2007, had
become a genuine but tantalisingly elusive possibility. Germany was

key to de Gaulle's notion of building Europe as a third source of regional power in the world at a time of extreme tension between the USA and the USSR superpowers. Had Britain been willing to join de Gaulle in this venture on French terms, then France would undoubtedly have looked across the Channel as well as the Rhine for a three-way 'triumvirate'. But de Gaulle drew lessons from the UK's exclusive commitment to its US partner in matters of nuclear and conventional defence, and, on two occasions in the 1960s, rejected the UK's bid to join the European Economic Community. On these occasions, de Gaulle memorably caricatured the UK as the 'Trojan Horse' for US influence inside the Community, an image that still shapes contemporary French thinking about the USA.

De Gaulle, in his day, argued for a strong Europe in the form of common European policies on matters of culture, education, the economy and defence. But he disparaged the European Communities' common institutions, favouring instead cooperation between sovereign governments that would form a 'Union of States'. In the matter of European defence, for example, and when still out of power in 1954, de Gaulle had already incited his supporters in the French National Assembly to scupper a plan – hatched in the mid-1950s by the French government itself – for a European Defence Community and a European Political Community. De Gaulle's argument was that these organizations would have left France exposed to binding decisions by a majority of which it was not part, in matters of national interest as vital as defence and national security. The Union of States idea was intended as a direct alternative to this, but it foundered in the face of opposition from all five of the other member states of the ECSC, including Germany. This defeat, at the height of de Gaulle's domestic powers, gave an early indication of both the limitations of France's commitment to European integration via common institutions, and of the willingness of other member states to concede to French interests.

Subsequent French attempts to build a European 'pole' of defence and security, both during and after the Cold War, have met with similarly limited success. In the 1960s, de Gaulle was unable to persuade his German counterparts to diminish their commitment to the USA as the sole provider of security for the West. He was similarly unsuccessful in attempts to persuade the UK to see de Gaulle's France as an equal match for the USA when it came to nuclear weapons and technology. By 1966, de Gaulle's isolation in these respects was such that he ordered the departure of tens of thousands of NATO troops from French soil, with serious economic consequences for the local economies around the NATO bases, quite apart from the damage the decision inflicted on French prestige at large. At the same time, he withdrew French staff from the organization's joint command committees, and pushed ahead with the development of an independent nuclear deterrent that was of questionable value in either the Cold War or post-Cold War contexts other than as an icon of French identity, and a statement of power.

Today, still, French preferences for Europe's 'political' existence favour a European common foreign, security and defence that for its key partners, Germany and the UK, still demands unrealistic levels of autonomy from NATO, and runs the risk of replicating capacity, at great expense. Thus, French reintegration into NATO has been tricky, with Jacques Chirac's attempt in the late 1990s faltering on French demands for a greater (French) role in NATO's command and control, thus far denied by the USA. Sarkozy, since, has compromised on these conditions, to some considerable discomfort in Paris. Franco-British cooperation on the EU's military role and identity, and on matters of defence procurement, has been substantial, but still, in practice, insufficient to overcome the differences across the Channel regarding the degree of decisional autonomy to accord the EU's nascent forces. France, the UK and Germany all agreed on the foreign policy provisions of the EU's Lisbon Treaty which give the EU a figurehead, and some shared resources. Finally, the allied invasion of Iraq in 2003 was undertaken in the face of the explicit opposition of France and Germany; the precise extent, therefore, to which Europe can take shared responsibility for its own security and defence is an ongoing and unresolved dilemma for French diplomacy. President Nicolas Sarkozy, nevertheless, declared in his first major foreign-policy speech after his election in 2007, that the European Union was the only regional power with the legitimacy and resources to tackle global challenges and prevent global-scale conflict; this was both a reaffirmation of his predecessors' vision of *l'Europe puissance* (albeit couched in slightly more diplomatic language), and a bid to lay out a plan and timescale for French global influence during his mandate.

French Attitudes towards the European Union: From Referendum to Referendum, 1992–2005

European affairs in France have become a permanent political balancing act that has itself become an integral part of contemporary

Frenchness. France and Europe have, indeed, become entangled in terms of the policy-making process, to the extent of having a significant and increasingly negative impact on French public opinion, to a degree that has damaged contemporary France's reputation and influence amongst the EU's member states.

The first indication of these high stakes came in 1992, when President Mitterrand put to referendum the ratification of the Maastricht Treaty, thus giving the French electorate the opportunity to express itself on over a decade of Mitterrand's European policy. The referendum was not obligatory, but its result would be binding. Following the momentous international changes of 1989–91, which saw the reunification of Germany and the collapse of the Soviet system, Germany's Chancellor Helmut Kohl steered his ally and friend, French President François Mitterrand, into devising a new treaty for the new times. Signed at Maastricht in December 1991, the Treaty on European Union (TEU) represented a considerable step towards just the 'political' Europe that French leaders had consistently called for. It provided for a single European currency – the Euro; a common European defence and security policy (the CFSP); and a provision for European 'citizenship', including the right of the nationals of EU member states to stand and vote in local and European (EP) elections in another EU member state.

President Mitterrand called on the French population to ratify this treaty in a referendum held on 20 September 1992 and, in a surprise result, won by only a very narrow margin (51.04%). Opponents of the Treaty based their Euroscepticism on intellectual arguments about France's history and identity as a sovereign power, supposedly under attack from the Maastricht Treaty. These arguments illustrate perfectly the contradictions inherent in French policy towards the EU, and represent a parallel with French political responses to the proposed European Defence Community in 1954. As in 1992, French leaders in 1954 had played a substantial role in proposing developments at the European level that would offer bold new solutions to new challenges (in 1954, a common European army in the face of the escalating Cold War; in 1992, institutions to generate a stable and strong Europe in a very unstable post-bipolar world order). In both 1954 and 1992, there was a backlash in France itself against the French-led proposals. Political opposition in both cases was central, not marginal, to the political system, and demonstrated in each case that the French pioneers of *la construction européenne* of the early 1950s had started a process

that struck at the heart of traditional French identity as an independent, sovereign nation.

Over a decade later, when President Chirac put the EU's 2004
Constitutional Treaty to the test of a referendum in May 2005, he was
far less fortunate than his predecessor, losing the vote by a resounding margin (54% against the Treaty). What had changed? Chirac, like
Mitterrand, had been in power for over a decade, and opinion polls
suggested that he too was deeply unpopular. But the European Union
itself had changed, almost doubling its membership from 15 to 25
member states overnight on 1 May 2004. French public opinion was
consistently amongst the least favourable to enlargement in poll after
poll at this time; political opinion was also sceptical, especially
amongst traditional pro-Europeans who feared that the French vision
of a 'political Europe' was now definitively scuppered. There was,
thus, little support in France for a Europe whose borders were not
fixed and which, in particular, might embrace Turkey in the future.

The No campaign in 2005 capitalized on these fears, and linked
them to another key factor behind the rejection of the treaty; namely,
its supposed preference for an 'Anglo-Saxon'-type vision of world
affairs – supposedly favoured by the new Central and East European
EU member states – characterized by fierce and unfettered economic
competition in a vast, open market. President Chirac himself
explained the result with reference to the Treaty's 'Anglo-Saxon'
market liberalism. These were messages that tapped into long-lived
French prejudices regarding, notably, the 'Americanization' of
global politics, culture and economics (see Chapter 6), and were
sufficient to convince a majority of French voters that the EU was
perhaps now even irrelevant as an independent force capable of
shaping world rules and, crucially, of protecting their jobs, way of
life and livelihood.

Thus, by 2005, France had reached a decisive point in its postwar
identity as a nation built on the premise of European unity and
distinctiveness. In 2007, newly elected President Sarkozy responded
directly to this development with his promises to ensure that the EU
would henceforth 'protect' its citizens from negative global forces,
as he described them. One immediate proposal from Sarkozy's office
was for a 'Mediterranean Union' composed of those EU member
states bordering the Mediterranean, along with their counterparts in
Africa and the Middle East. The plan was significantly watered
down by France's EU partners, especially Germany; but, from the
French perspective, the Mediterranean Union would have provided

an additional framework for the resolution of seemingly intractable problems of global significance, such as the Middle East crisis, and illegal immigration into Europe. The other key framework for the management of such global forces is the transatlantic relationship between France, the EU, and the 'Anglo-Saxons' across the Atlantic (and the Channel).

France and the 'Anglo-Saxons'

France's relationships with the UK and the USA are marked by centuries of contradictory forces, including rivalry, jealousy, antagonism, incomprehension, friendship, fascination, mutual attraction and support. Language, food, agriculture, film, wine, music and foreign policy are all topics that episodically divide and enrage the governments of the USA and France, but not necessarily their populations. Relations between the peoples of France and the UK, for their part, have reached a peak of familiarity since the construction of the 'fixed link' Channel Tunnel in 1996, and the advent of cheap air travel between the UK and the continent. Indeed, Cogan (2003: 15) argues that Franco-British relations have been definitively tamed, and that the USA has supplanted Britain as 'France's greatest rival and philosophical antithesis'.

Yet, these relationships are characterized by their flexibility and firm foundations: France and the 'Anglo-Saxons' operate far more frequently as global allies than as opponents, and certainly not enemies, and, while not rivalling France's 'special relationship' with Germany, these relations have firm institutional and traditional foundations, despite periodic crises, or the appearance thereof. Contemporary France defines itself as the USA's 'critical friend'; and one hundred years ago established an *entente cordiale* with the British, based then, as now, on both mutual self-interest (in 1904, regarding their respective colonial spheres of influence), and the attraction for both peoples of the other's country and culture.

In many respects, the Franco-British relationship has been subsumed into the European Union, where the two countries maintain a relationship characterized precisely by the ambiguities suggested above. On the one hand, the two countries are natural allies, since their governments share a suspicion of strong, supranational European institutions; they are also the biggest military powers in the EU; and, on this basis alone, they periodically cooperate to thrust forward Europe's own military capacity, despite strategic disagreements. On the other hand, they routinely oppose each other on key European issues, principally the funding of the CAP, and the extent to which national markets need be regulated by means of the EU legislative framework (see Chapter 7). Furthermore, their governments differ over the EU's borders, with the UK typically favouring a large, inclusive EU as a powerful trading bloc; where French governments into the twenty-first century see EU enlargement as a threat to their project of a 'political Europe' and to the French 'social model'.

France, Globalization and the USA

How France relates to Europe has direct consequences for its transatlantic relations. Together with its belief in *l'Europe puissance*, France also supports a set of recurrent arguments relating to the identity of Europe (minus the UK) as culturally distinct from the English-speaking world. Culture, here, is taken in both its narrow sense (of taste), and the wider meaning of civilization: France's many discourses of anti-Americanism are all based fundamentally on the premise that the European way of life is superior in the broadest sense.

Placed within this context, the vexed question of globalization in the French setting makes sense. Globalization denotes a world both concrete (the flows of people, capital, goods, and so on) and virtual (the erosion by technology of state capacity to retain its citizens' loyalty, particularly regarding communications and access to the worldwide web of knowledge and opinion). France has managed to develop a reputation as home for vocal anti-globalization protesters who effectively enjoy political backing in the form of French politicians' strident criticism of 'untamed' international capitalism. What gives this political discourse an edge in France is that it is married to a spirited defence of French national culture as expressed through particular cultural 'products' such as film and music, and the French language itself (see Chapter 6). The specific problem here is not so much globalization itself, but the fact that 'Globalisation has an American face in France' (Kuisel, 2001: 5).

Indeed, the man who at the turn of the twenty-first century best symbolized French resistance to globalization, José Bové, denies any Canute-like dreams of stemming global flows. His central argument is that globalization must be *altered* (hence the term '*alter-globalization*' to describe the movement associated with him) in order to balance out, precisely, its overly American influences. Bové's principal concern in this respect is what he calls *la malbouffe* (junk food), around which he has built passionate arguments relating to agricultural production and trade (and which led him, in 1999, to dismantle the building site of a new McDonald's restaurant in Millau, central France, for which he was jailed).

Bové has been unsuccessful in mobilizing direct electoral support (as a presidential candidate in 2007, he scored barely more than 1% of the votes); in any case, this is not his preferred mode of action. His significance lies in the legitimacy that his various campaigns, waged across the entire world, give to what Meunier (2003) has called the 'double talk' that characterizes French politics regarding globalization. This refers to the fact that successive governments and presidents in France have talked up the perceived dangers of globalization, particularly its threat of cultural uniformity, and talked down its benefits. Renault, Michelin, Axa, Danone, l'Oréal, LVHM and so on are, after all, global brands with which we are all familiar (see Chapter 7).

This 'double-talk' has created political opportunities for the French far right in the shape of the National Front, whose policy of 'national preference' taps into the fear, distrust and false expectations generated by an official discourse of distrust of global forces. More significantly, it has encouraged the rise of Euroscepticism, as demonstrated in 2005 by the rejection of the EU's Constitutional Treaty. Successive French politicians, including Jacques Chirac, have portrayed the EU as insufficiently equipped to 'protect' its member states from unbridled global flows. President Sarkozy, in his victory speech on the night of 6 May 2007, stated his intent to bolster the EU's role in 'protecting' its citizens from undue global influence. In policy terms, this subsequently involved a sustained critique of what he called the 'dogma' of free competition that characterized the EU's external and internal policy, a stance that set him at odds with most of France's EU partners, including Germany (see Chapter 7).

Yet, it is precisely at the EU level that France has the most room for manoeuvre in shaping the rules of global governance. The more influence France can wield within the European Union, the more it can hope to spread its ideas and preferences regarding global affairs. This fact of French life has come, increasingly, to characterize French relations with the wider world in the twenty-first century.

France in the Wider World

France's traditional sphere of influence extends far beyond the 'West' or the 'North' to reach into Africa (both North and sub-Saharan), Asia and the Pacific. France's bloodiest experiences of decolonization in the 1950s and 1960s were in these regions, particularly in what is now Vietnam, and Algeria. French colonization operated on the principle of cultural assimilation, and its decolonization occurred through strife, bloodshed and resistance, on both sides.

From la Françafrique *to* la Francophonie

Decolonization *à la française* has led to different sets of relationships between France and the regimes and peoples formerly under French rule, involving France in over thirty military missions in as many years. Some of these, such as France's role in failing to prevent or halt the Rwandan genocide of 1994, have brought Paris international opprobrium; others, such as its intervention in the Ivory Coast in 2004, have led to a review of policy and redistribution of resources, particularly in the context of the post-Cold War doctrinal renewal discussed earlier. Thus, the early twenty-first century saw France scaling back military bases and operations in Africa, and increasing its contributions to UN and EU-led peace-keeping operations instead, and to the collective attempts of the western powers to combat international terrorism and nuclear proliferation. The UN is of particular significance to France's global role, in that, for French policy-makers, it offers an alternative source of legitimation for foreign operations other than US-led 'coalitions of the willing'; this was the context to the unsuccessful French opposition at the UN in 2003 to any non-UN action in Iraq. Simultaneously, France's growing recognition of its limitations as solo peacekeeper, let alone peace-maker, in its former 'backyard' (known as its *pré carré*) has led it to support and foster local solutions in the form of regional peace-keeping forces such as Africa's RECAMP, launched in 1997. By 2006, France had approximately 14,000 men and women directly committed to military operations throughout the world, principally in Africa and central Europe; by 2009, the number of operational staff was closer to 10,000. Roughly half of these missions were multilateral (predominantly UN or EU), and included both military and civilian peace-keeping operations. Amongst these, by way of example, were UN missions in the Ivory Coast, the Democratic Republic of Congo, Darfur and Lebanon; and EU operations in Bosnia and Somalia. France, moreover, is a major contributor to the NATO-led operations in both Afghanistan (with around 3700 troops stationed there by 2010, one third as many as the UK, and one quarter fewer than Germany); and Kosovo.

France's relations with, in particular, its former colonies in sub-Saharan Africa have been dubbed by its critics as a family affair known colloquially as *la françafrique*; the term has connotations of dubious diplomatic and commercial favours based on material interests and a determination to maintain French presence across the globe. During the superpower conflict of the Cold War, to this end, France positioned itself as 'champion' of the non-aligned countries, and the 'third world' (not to mention the Soviet satellite states), and President de Gaulle made a number of high-profile – often controversial – foreign visits in the 1960s to underscore this particular margin for manoeuvre from the western 'camp'.

The years of de Gaulle's presidency were equally notorious for the tightness of Franco-African networks and the corruption and familiarity that these bred; but his successors in the twentieth century did very little to reform matters. Thus, President Giscard d'Estaing became notorious for gifts of diamonds from a shady central African dictator; and François Mitterrand's family and close advisors were accused of having been implicated in arms and trade scandals (see Chapter 3). France's keen commercial interest in the manufacture and trade of arms, including to dictatorial regimes, is also well-known, as are the close personal relationships that have at times existed between Presidents of the Fifth Republic and their opposite numbers in countries such as Gabon, Libya and Syria.

Other relationships – not exclusively with former colonies – have evolved into predominantly cultural links in the framework of the *Francophonie* organization based on the 'use of the French language in common'. The organization does also operate a more political agenda that goes beyond the promotion of 'cultural diversity' across the world, with a recent focus on development politics and the alleviation of world poverty (see Chapter 6). This aspect of the French-speaking world – *la Francophonie* with a capital F, denoting the organization that structures its activities – is both more and less than the British Commonwealth; less, in that its common thread is the French language, and not allegiance to a head of state; more, given its claim to a voice in cultural and development politics.

Beyond its nominal role as the head of *la Francophonie*, present day France explicitly pursues its policy of *le rayonnement culturel* – 'outreach', we have said – through the tools of development aid, and French government support for French-language schools, cultural centres and research throughout the world. *TV5*, the French satellite television channel, and more recently *France 24*, the heavily-state subsidized French alternative to *CNN*, broadcasting in French, English and Arabic, are the new instruments promoting the same ends as for decades; namely, the right of France to be present across the globe, and for its perspective on global affairs to be seen and heard.

Beyond the Comfort Zone?

But twenty-first century France, especially since President Sarkozy came to power in 2007, has had to confront harsh truths and difficult realities regarding virtually all of its foreign policy ambitions. Most notable is the stark fact that defence and diplomacy have not escaped the budget cuts and state-trimming that we have seen elsewhere in this volume – far from it. The 2008 White Paper on Defence and National Security commissioned by President Sarkozy was drafted in precisely this context, and proposed a radical overview of both strategy and spending (see Box 8.3). Already, French troop numbers on operation throughout the world have been cut by at least one quarter since 2006, especially in Africa, where President Sarkozy explicitly set about renegotiating all military agreements.

Elsewhere in the world, France not infrequently finds itself out of step with its partners in the EU and beyond – in its friendship with Putin's Russia, for example; in 2007, in new ties forged around defence contracts between France and Libya; or in seeking to lift embargos on arms sales, for example to China, a big and important commercial customer for France. At the same time, France has sought to act in concert with its EU allies over attempts to prevent Iran from developing nuclear weapons capabilities, for example. The opening in 2009 of a French military base in Abu Dhabi in the United Arab Emirates is also part of France's enhanced emphasis on shaping affairs in that part of the world.

Box 8.3   Scaling back? The 2008 White Paper on Defence and National Security

In 2007, President Sarkozy commissioned a White Paper on Defence and National Security, intended to define French strategy and spending in this field for the coming 15 years. He did so in the following terms:

- To 'establish the credibility of our defence, whilst respecting the country's financial constraints'.
- To outline the 'choices we shall have to face in order to adapt our defence capability, strengthen the link between the nation and its armed forces, and organise the transformation of the defence industry and research in a national and European framework. It will be part of a process designed to maintain and bolster a defence effort of around 2% of GDP.'

Source: Sarkozy (2007).

The White Paper itself, published in June 2008, contained the following recommendations, amongst others. It specifically emphasized the importance of concentrating France's efforts around building EU capacity in the military and diplomatic fields. The White Paper proposed:

- The reorganization of decision-making, centred on a Defence and National Security Council chaired by President Sarkozy.
- A commitment to substantial contributions to multilateral military operations in a zone incorporating the Atlantic and Indian oceans.
- Defence spending to rise by 1% above inflation per year after 2012. In 2009, defence spending amounted to 2.3% of French GDP, or around €30 billion.
- The reduction of armed forces by one fifth, with a loss of approximately 54,000 jobs in total, the closure of many military bases across France, and the cutting of jobs in the Defence Ministry itself.

Sources: *Financial Times* (2008b; 2008c).

Remembering the Past, Shaping the Future

Despite these shifting priorities, it is the French experience of Empire and decolonization that continues to have serious repercussions on French domestic policy. France has traditionally turned to its colonies for soldiers and workers, and the twentieth century was no exception in this respect. The manner in which certain former colonies – above all, Algeria – won their independence meant that

France was subsequently home to both European settlers who fled the newly-independent Algeria in 1962, and to indigenous Algerian individuals and families who had either fought alongside the French in the battle to keep Algeria French (known as *les harkis*), or who subsequently came to France for work and a better life. The manner in which France has chosen to integrate such individuals and their families into the fabric of secular, Republican, French life is still a matter of much controversy (see Chapter 2).

The *harkis* and their families, in particular, have been subjected to institutionalized discrimination, which in recent years has come under scrutiny. Indeed, one specific aspect of the relations between today's France and its former colonies arises from discussions in France regarding how best to remember and commemorate these aspects of French history. An important part of Jacques Chirac's legacy will undoubtedly be his part in a series of official apologies for France's past actions, especially in relation to French collaboration in the Holocaust (see Chapter 1). But this climate has bred a backlash, particularly regarding France's fight against Algerian independence; former French Army generals have unapologetically 'confessed' to their use of torture in Algeria (already an established fact). Before becoming President, Nicolas Sarkozy had lent his support to a controversial clause in a 2005 bill regarding financial compensation for *les harkis*. The clause required French schools and universities to emphasize the 'positive role' played by France in its former colonies – meaning, principally, the benefits of *le rayonnement culturel*. Such was the opposition to the clause that Chirac subsequently withdrew it. It was then revived in other terms by Sarkozy who, on the very night of his election victory, proclaimed that the time for 'repentance' for the past was over since, however misguided past actions might have been, it equated to self-hatred, was divisive and beneath the dignity of France. He, instead, would restore the 'honour' of the nation, and of French identity. Accordingly, President Sarkozy embarked upon a series of foreign visits intended to 'normalize' relations with, to begin with, Algeria and Rwanda; he was assisted in this by his Foreign Minister Bernard Kouchner. This was a clever appointment, given Kouchner's international credibility as the founder of the 'French Doctors' and since, as a man of the French left, he also represented the decades-old political consensus at home, supporting France's action in the world. In the power balance between *Quai* and *Elysée*, moreover, Sarkozy has won the upper hand.

Conclusions

French fears of a loss of influence in the twenty-first century, it would appear, have both subjective and objective foundations. These fears have been addressed in practical ways by contemporary French political leaders, who have gradually toned down the Gaullist rhetoric of *la grandeur* in favour of the language of bilateralism, multilateralism and global partnership. Sarkozy's break with the Gaullist past in foreign affairs has been sharper and more distinct than that of his predecessors, in line with his personality, and his many promises of '*rupture*' with the past. He has encountered parliamentary opposition as a result, including a vote of no confidence in April 2008, over his decision to send more French troops to Afghanistan, and to rejoin NATO's integrated military command. Nevertheless, the President continues to set the tone of French foreign policy; and the EU – and, within the EU, Germany – remain the primary vehicles for the projection of French influence – and, by extension, identity – onto the world stage. The singular characteristic of French diplomacy, still today, is the conviction that the world benefits from France's universal presence.

Conclusions

It is impossible to take a neutral stance on France, such is the strength of the images it projects outwards to the world. In this volume, we set out to identify, enjoy, and then move beyond the stereotypes associated with such pictures (Brouard *et al.*: 2009). But scholars have their own battles with the study of France, and especially with the concept of the 'French exception'. Brouard *et al.* see 'French exceptionalism' as a perspective that can blind us to the fact that 'France [...] lies no further outside the spectrum of advanced industrial economies than any other' (2009: xiv). Chafer and Godin are less categorical, but still conclude that 'the French exception' is probably more parody than politics (2010: 239). Accordingly, we asked not, 'is France exceptional?' but, rather, 'is France still France?' (Kuisel, 1995: 31), especially given the extent of change undergone since the very beginning of World War II. This is the theme that has run through these pages, and a matter that has already preoccupied French governments at the start of the twenty-first century, leading in 2009–10 to an awkward, unpopular and inconclusive public 'debate' on the matter.

This concern with national identity chimes with the nostalgia experienced in contemporary France, as indeed elsewhere, that things are not what they used to be – as if, somehow, a golden age had once existed. By way of example, best-sellers on the 'decline' of France proliferated in French bookshops throughout the 1990s; and the publication in *Time* magazine in November 2007 of Donald Morrison's long article on 'The Death of French Culture' (2007) unleashed a storm of protest in France, goading Morrison into expanding on his ideas in a subsequent, even longer publication (Morrison and Compagnon, 2010). Yet, in our chapters, we saw that France is still very much France, at least in the sense that it is still highly attractive to the outside world, still speaking up for itself on the world stage, still resisting change for change's own sake, still exhibiting the impressive array of unique characteristics we would expect from such an long-established nation state; and still very much conditioned by developments occurring outside its own borders. Indeed, we have discovered that the most incontrovertible dimension of French contemporary identity is the country's openness to forces and factors of all kinds, as well as the challenges and opportunities that living in such an open society has created – not just for policy-makers, but for the French as a whole.

France is even the hexagonal shape it is because its geographical location in Europe has historically made it extremely vulnerable to its neighbours on all sides, including across the Channel, but especially Germany, and it has had to fight over the centuries to secure and stabilize its external borders. Since World War II, military struggles have been supplanted by tussles over power-sharing arrangements with its neighbours, slugged out in the framework of the European Union. Choosing this route to postwar reconstruction has taken France on an unpredictable journey that has taken some explaining by its political leaders. French membership of the European Union potentially manages French exposure to all sorts of flows and forces, especially markets and migrants, and has amplified its voice internationally. It has also added a layer to French identity, a sense of belonging to a bigger entity with distinct values and visions of the world in the shape of a 'Franco-Saxon' European Union, in opposition to an 'Anglo-American counter-identity' (Hayward, 2007: 1–38 and 335).

Or, at least, these have been the most compelling accounts of France's commitment to *la construction européenne* over the last sixty years. In reality, the price of managing the outside world by means of common European rules has been high, necessitating substantial change to constitutional and political tradition. And, when the EU itself is seen to fall short of French ambitions, the potential for social conflict is also high. This was the lesson of the 2005 referendum in France. President Sarkozy has since attempted to build EU capacity – to fight climate change, to manage immigration, to lead Europe's economies out of the financial crisis that erupted in 2008 whilst France was in the EU Council chair – while giving the appearance of being in control of a process that Hayward has aptly described as 'leaderless' (*ibid.*: 342).

This is a precarious and ambitious balancing act, yet is only one aspect of the ongoing challenge for French leaders of securing the integrity of French territory and, by extension, of the French nation itself. Boundaries within France itself have proved to be as permeable and fragile as its external frontiers. France's overseas territories

are themselves restless, and far from united regarding the relationships they wish to have with Paris and the *métropole*. Further afield,
the French-speaking world in the shape of *la Francophonie* cannot be
relied upon to relay France's influence throughout the world, let
alone its language. Some members defect (as is the case of Rwanda,
for example); all are courted by the world's rising powers, especially
China. Even Corsica, counted as part of mainland France, periodically expresses a desire for greater autonomy from the actual mainland, with some success. These are not necessarily separatist claims
per se, but remind French decision-makers of the traditionally
diverse nature of the population and territory in a country as big as
France. In keeping with modern trends, moreover, and with an eye on
mounting costs, French governments have gradually decentralized
important aspects of central administration. But open economies and
virtual technologies, at the same time, comprise serious difficulties
for the French state – as for any state – in its attempts to control flows
of information, knowledge, trends, fashions, opportunities and funds
within and outside its territory.

All these developments have not been without problems for a
country where the state has been so important for nation-building and
where, as we have seen, expectations remain high. Yet, the French
state struggles to balance the three core principles of French republicanism – liberty, equality and fraternity – in the face of France's own
diversity, let alone the impact of outside influences. There is simply
no one single mix that can satisfy all demands. One result has been
continuous and often controversial constitutional change to fine-tune
the 200-plus-year-old revolutionary triptych. For example, the state
at least now acknowledges that it is pluralistic in its policy-making;
it recognizes that discrimination – regarding women, for example –
has actually been structured into the Republic, and that these cases
require special treatment; and it preaches tolerant attitudes towards
difference.

But this process of what often gets called 'banalization' is incomplete. France experiences extraordinary and ongoing difficulties in
catering for individuals – and more significantly their communities –
who are the product of France's colonial past. So, we have witnessed
cultural battles over the notion of Frenchness – epitomized by the ban
in 2010 on 'clothing designed to conceal the face –in particular, the
"integral veil"'. We have seen the tightening up of immigration policies; and witnessed the links made between immigration on the one
hand, and a nervous national identity on the other.

In these respects, France is not entirely unlike other countries in Europe (such as the UK, Belgium and the Netherlands), which all face broadly similar challenges to established national identities. But France has to contend with a highly specific set of political parameters within which solutions must be found. For all its 'consolidation' (Brouard *et al.*, 2009: xv), French political culture does still harbour some practices that tend to undermine its democracy, even allowing for the fact that all democracies are work-in-progress and incomplete. These characteristics include an unhealthy ideal of the individual-cum-saviour; a general fixation with the personalization of politics and the cult of the celebrity, even in politics (to the point of coining a new term, 'pipolization'); and a lingering but persistent elitism. This mix translates into hopelessly high expectations of the President and of the office of the presidency, and the 2012 elections are unlikely to be an exception to this rule. Since the days of President Charles de Gaulle, France expects something special, almost otherworldly, from its Presidents, and Presidents do not come much worldlier than Nicolas Sarkozy. Accordingly, he has experienced virulent opposition from within the political class as well as from the electorate, despite his decisive victory in May 2007. But again, France is not really alone in these respects: the Obama phenomenon in the USA in 2008–09 amply demonstrated a contemporary weakness for charismatic figures that perhaps can change lives. Furthermore, France's democratic institutions have, without doubt, evolved since de Gaulle's day, and they are certainly more balanced, particularly with regard to the rule of law emanating from within France's own institutions, and from outside bodies such as the EU; and the growing sense of exposure to the media, French and global.

All these trends amount to a picture where France is no more 'fragmented' now than it was 'one and indivisible' in 1979; and Hayward himself admits that he was exaggerating for effect when he coined these notions (Hayward, 1973, 2007). Neither has President Sarkozy brought about radical, transformative change, despite his intentions. The Fifth Republic is too resilient, and it has outlasted almost all of its predecessors. France still holds others – scholars included – in its thrall. It has moved with the times, and its current problems are less a matter of mourning the past, than they are a battle for future survival, a challenge shared with many countries. French identity and France's problems in this twenty-first-century context are matters of neither black nor white. They will certainly never be any shade of grey.

Bibliography

Baycroft, T. (2008) *Inventing the Nation. France* (London: Hodder).

Bayley, S. (2002) 'Am I getting a little Brazilian woman?', *The Observer, Escape* supplement, 17 February: 2.

BBC (2001) 'Vichy. Listening to Silence' (Radio 4, 11 and 18 June).

Brame, G. (2006) *Chez vous en France. Mille et une clés pour faciliter la vie* (Paris: Documentation française).

Brayfield, C. (2004) *Deep France* (London: Pan).

Brouard, S., A. Appleton and A. Mazur (eds) (2009) *The French Republic at Fifty. Beyond Stereotype* (Basingstoke: Palgrave Macmillan).

Chafer, T. and E. Godin (eds) (2010) *The End of the French Exception? Decline and Renewal of the 'French Model'* (Basingstoke: Palgrave Macmillan).

Clift, B. (2009) 'Economic Interventionism in the Fifth Republic', in S. Brouard *et al.*, *The Fifth French Republic at Fifty* (Basingstoke: Palgrave Macmillan): 153–73.

Cogan, C. (2003) *French Negotiating Behaviour: Dealing with la Grande Nation* (Washington, DC: United States Institute of Peace Press).

Crook, M. (2002) *Revolutionary France* (Oxford and New York: Oxford University Press).

CSA (Conseil supérieur de l'audiovisuel, 2010) 'An Independent Authority to Protect Audiovisual Communication Freedom'. Available at http://www.csa.fr/multi/index.php?l=uk, accessed 9 July 2010.

Culpepper, P.D. (2006) 'Capitalism, Coordination and Economic Change: The French Political Economy since 1985', in P. D. Culpepper, P. A. Hall and B. Palier (eds), *Changing France: The Politics that Markets Make* (Basingstoke, Palgrave Macmillan), pp.29–49.

Davidson, M.B. (1971) *A Concise History of France* (London: Cassell).

Dickens, C. (2000 [1859]) *A Tale of Two Cities* (London: Penguin Classics).

Donnat, O. (2009) *Les Pratiques culturelles des français à l'ère numérique* (Paris: La Découverte).

Dubois, F. (2008) 'Cultural Policy in France – Genesis of a Public Policy Category', GPSE Working Papers (University of Strasbourg), http://workingpapersgspe.eu 28 October (accessed 6 July 2010).

Economist, The (2009) 'Vive la différence', 7 May.

Elysée (2010a) 'The Declaration of the Human Rights' (1789) [*sic*] Available at http://www.elysee.fr/elysee/elysee.fr/anglais/the_institutions/founding_texts/the_declaration_of_the_human_rights/the_declaration_of_the_human_rights.20240.html, accessed 3 August 2010.

Elysée (2010b) 'Preamble to the 27th of October 1946 Constitution'. Available at http://www.elysee.fr/elysee/anglais/the_institutions/founding_texts/preambule_ to_the_27th_of_october_1946_constitution/preambule_to_the_27th_of_october_ 1946_constitution.20243.html, accessed 8 July 2010.

Europa (2010) Available at http://europa.eu/abc/symbols/9-may/decl_en.htm, accessed 8 July 2010.

Evans, M. and E. Godin (2004) *France 1815–2003* (London: Arnold).

Financial Times (2007a) 16 April.

Financial Times (2007b) 3 October.

Financial Times (2008a) 15 October.

Financial Times (2008b) 19 June.

Financial Times (2008c) 17 June.

Financial Times (2009a) 4 August.

Financial Times (2009b) 26 September.

Flynn, G. (ed.) (1995) *Remaking the Hexagon. The New France in the New Europe* (Boulder, CO: Westview Press).

Francophonie (2010) 'Welcome to the International Organisation of La Francophonie's Official Website'. Available http://www.francophonie.org/ English.html, accessed 9 July 2010.

Guardian, The (2007) 16 July.

Guardian, The (2009a) 15 September.

Guardian, The (2009b) 'Sarkozy unveils €35bn "big loan" for universities and museums', 15 December.

Hargreaves, A. (2007) *Multi-Ethnic France. Immigration, Politics, Culture and Society*, 2nd edn (London: Routledge).

Hayward, J. (1973) *The One and Indivisible French Republic* (London: Weidenfeld & Nicolson).

Hayward, J. (2007) *Fragmented France. Two Centuries of Disputed Identity* (New York: Oxford University Press).

INSEE (2005) *Fiches Thématiques. Les Immigrés en France*. Available at http://www.insee.fr/fr/ppp/sommaire/IMMFRA05.PDF, accessed 10 August 2010.

INSEE (2010a) 'La France en Bref/France in Figures'. Available at http://www.insee.fr/fr/pdf/intfrcbref.pdf, accessed on 6 July 2010.

INSEE (2010b) 'Être né en France d'un parent immigré'. Available at www.insee.fr.fr/themes/document.asp?ref_id=ip1287, accessed 2 April.

INSEE (2010c) 'Acquisitions de la nationalité française'. Available at http://www.insee.fr/fr/themes/tableau.asp?reg_id=NATTEF02161, accessed 4 April.

Invest in France Agency (2009) Available at www.investinfrance.org/uk/en, accessed 11 January 2009.

Keaton, T.D. (2006) *Muslim Girls and the Other France. Race, Identity Politics and Social Exclusion* (Bloomington: Indiana University Press).

Keiger, J.F.V. (2005) 'Foreign and Defence Policy: Constraints and Continuity', in A.Cole *et al.* (eds) *Developments in French Politics 3* (Basingstoke: Palgrave Macmillan): 138–53.

Kelly, M. (ed.) (2001) *French Culture and Society. The Essentials* (London and New York: Arnold).

Kouchner, B. (2007) 'La narration du monde', *Le Monde*, 3 December.

Kuisel, R. (1995) 'The France We Have Lost: Social, Economic, and Cultural Discontinuities', in G. Flynn (ed.), *Remaking the Hexagon. The New France in the New Europe* (Boulder,CO: Westview Press): 31–48.

Kuisel, R. (2001) 'The Gallic Rooster Crows Again. The Paradox of French Anti-Americanism', *French Politics,Culture and Society*, 19(3): 1–16.

Ledésert, D.M. (1976) *Introducing France* (London: Harrap).

Le Monde (2009) 14 December.

Le Monde (2010) 11 January.

Looseley, D. (1995) *The Politics of Fun. Cultural Policy and Debate in Contemporary France* (Oxford: Berg).

Madeley, J. (2006) 'The State and Religion', in P. Heywood *et al.*, *Developments in European Politics* (Basingstoke: Palgrave Macmillan).

Maclean, M. (2008) 'French Corporate Governance in a Globalised World: A Changing Business Model?', in M. Maclean and J. Szarka (eds), *France on the World Stage. Nation State Strategies in the Global Era* (Basingstoke: Palgrave Macmillan): 144–61.

McDonald's (2010) Available at http://www.mcdonalds.fr/graphics/pdf/whoweare/les-chiffres.pdf, accessed 4 April.

Mendras, H. and A. Cole (1991) *Social Change in Modern France. Towards a Cultural Anthropology of the Fifth Republic* (Cambridge: Cambridge University Press).

Meunier, S. (2003) 'France's double-talk on globalisation', *French Politics, Culture and Society*, 21(1): 20–34.

Milward, A. (2000) *The European Rescue of the Nation State*, 2nd edn (Abingdon: Routledge).

Ministère de la Culture et de la Communication (2009) *Chiffres Clés 2009* (Paris).

Morrison, D. (2007) 'In Search of Lost Time (The Death of French Culture)', *Time*, 21 November.

Morrison, D. and A. Compagnon (2010) *The Death of French Culture* (Cambridge: Polity).

National Assembly (2010) *The French Constitution*. Available at www.assemblee-nationale.fr, accessed 6 July 2010.

Observatoire de la Parité, L' (2010) Available at http://www.observatoire-parite.gouv.fr/portail/reperes_statistiques.htm, accessed 10 August.

OECD Factbook (2009) *Economic, Environmental and Social Statistics* (accessed at http://stats.oecd.org/viewhtml.aspx?queryname=18152&querytype=view&lang=en [4 April 2010]).

Robb, G. (2007) *The Discovery of France* (Picador).

Roger, P. (2005) *The American Enemy. The History of French Anti-Americanism*, S. Bowman (trans.) (Chicago and London: University of Chicago Press).

Sarkozy, N. (2007) 'White Paper on Defence and National Security – Letter of Engagement from M. Nicolas Sarkozy, President of the Republic, to M. Jean-Claude Mallet, Member of the Conseil d'État. Available at http://www.ambafrance-uk.org/Preparation-of-new-White-Paper.html, accessed 10 August 2010.

Sarkozy, N. (2008) Press conference, 8 January.

Sarkozy, N. (2009a) 'Un nouvel avenir pour notre agriculture', Speech delivered in Poligny, France, on 27 October. Available at http://www.elysee.fr/president/les-dossiers/agriculture-peche-et-ruralite/agriculture-et-ruralite/poligny-27-10-2009/un-nouvel-elan-pour-notre-agriculture.6193.html

Sarkozy, N. (2009b) 'Discours de M. le Président de la République française' (La Chapelle-en-Vercors, 12 November). Accessed at http://www.elysee.fr/president/les-actualites/discours/2009/discours-de-m-le-president-de-la-republique.1678.html

Sarkozy, N. (2009c) New Year's Address. Accessed at http://www.ambafrance-uk.org/President-Sarkozy-s-New-Year-s-Eve,16606.html.

Scott, J.W. (2007) *The Politics of the Veil* (Princeton, NJ: Princeton University Press).

Shields, J.G. (2007) *The Extreme Right in France. From Pétain to le Pen* (London: Routledge).

Sonntag, A. (2008) 'The Burdensome Heritage of Prestige Politics', in M. Maclean and J. Szarka (eds), *France on the World Stage. Nation State Strategies in the Global Era* (Basingstoke: Palgrave Macmillan).

Steinberger, M. (2009) *Au Revoir To All That. The Rise and Fall of French Cuisine* (London: Bloomsbury).

Treacher, A. (2003) *French Interventionism. Europe's Last Global Player?* (Aldershot: Ashgate).

UNESCO (2010) 'World Heritage Sites'. Available at http://whc.unesco.org/en/statesparties/fr, accessed 2 April 2010. http://unesdoc.unesco.org/images/0014/001429/142919e.pdf

Vaïsse, M. (2009) *La puissance ou l'influence? La France dans le monde depuis 1958* (Paris: Fayard).

Village d'Etape (2010) http://www.village-etape.com/index.php3?lang=en (accessed 6 July 2010).

Wadham, L. (2009) *The Secret Life of France* (London: Faber & Faber).

Weber, E. (1976) *Peasants into Frenchmen: The Modernization of Rural France, 1870–1914* (Stanford, CA: Stanford University Press).

World Economic Forum (2010a) *The Global Competitiveness Report 2009–2010*. Available at http://www.weforum.org/en/initiatives/gcp/Global%20competitiveness%20Report/index.htm, accessed 4 April 2010.

World Economic Forum (2010b) *Country Highlights*. Available at http://www.weforum.org/pdf/GCR09/GCR20092010CountryHighlights.pdf, accessed 4 April 2010.

Wylie, L. (1964) *A Village in the Vaucluse* (Cambridge, MA and London: Harvard University Press).

Yost, D.S. (2006) 'France's New Nuclear Doctrine', *International Affairs*, 82(4): 701–21.

Index